ERNST TROELTSCH:
WRITINGS ON THEOLOGY AND RELIGION

ERNST TROELTSCH

Writings on Theology and Religion

Translated and edited
by
Robert Morgan and Michael Pye

WESTMINSTER/JOHN KNOX PRESS
LOUISVILLE, KENTUCKY

First paperback edition 1990

Published by Westminster/John Knox Press
Louisville, Kentucky

PRINTED IN THE UNITED STATES OF AMERICA

2 4 6 8 9 7 5 3 1

Library of Congress Cataloging-in-Publication Data

Troeltsch, Ernst, 1865—1923.
    [Gesammelte Schriften. Selections. English]
    Writings on theology and religion / Ernst Troeltsch ; translated
and edited by Robert Morgan and Michael Pye.
       p.   cm.
    "The first three essays . . . translated . . . from Gesammelte
Schriften II, Tübingen, 1913 and 1922 . . . The fourth was published
separately, Tübingen, 1911."
    Includes bibliographical references.
    Contents: Half a century of theology—Religion and the science
of religion—What does "essence of Christianity" mean?—Note /
S.W. Sykes—The significance of the historical existence of Jesus
for faith—Troeltsch and Christian theology / Robert Morgan—
Troeltsch and the science of religion / Michael Pye.
    ISBN 0-664-25112-9

    1. Theology, Doctrinal—History—19th century. 2. Religion.
3. Christianity—Essence, genius, nature. 4. Jesus Christ—
Historicity. 5. Troeltsch, Ernst, 1865—1923. I. Morgan, Robert,
1940—   . II. Pye, Michael. III. Title.
BR85. T713   1990
230—dc20   89-70629
                                              CIP

Contents

Preface

The work of Ernst Troeltsch (1865-1923) is an important link between nineteenth- and twentieth-century religious thought. Troeltsch was perhaps the most sophisticated theorist among the liberal protestants who dominated German theology between 1870 and 1920. In particular he was associated with 'the history of religions school', a small group of scholars who rejected the compromise between historical consistency and ecclesiastical biblicism maintained by Albrecht Ritschl. This group looked to the great idealist thinkers of the early nineteenth century in their theological interpretation of history, but their fundamental importance lies in their unswerving recognition that the radically historical criticism of religious traditions cannot be evaded.

The neo-reformation theologians who came to prominence in Germany after the First World War branded Troeltsch as the last and most dangerous representative of an idealist theology which they wished to repudiate; and indeed Troeltsch saw himself as a trustee for the heritage of Schleiermacher. As a result Troeltsch's work was eclipsed by theologies which tended to bypass historical questions in taking the declaration of 'the Word' to man as their fundamental starting point. The last few years, by contrast, have seen a new shift of emphasis back towards an understanding of the world itself as the initial locus of theological statement, and it is in this context that a reconsideration of nineteenth-century theory has become necessary.

Troeltsch understood himself in the first place to be a theologian. But his strength lay not so much in an ability to proclaim and affirm, though in his own way he did that, as in his alignment with the main intellectual currents of his time. With his wholehearted acceptance of the modern historical consciousness, he joined in the nineteenth century's attempts to study religion historically, and above all to reflect upon its development and nature. In this connection his work is of interest not only to theologians but to everyone today who is concerned with a scientific and reflective enquiry into religion as a cultural phenomenon.

The rather lengthy introduction that follows gives some account of Troeltsch's work as a whole. This introduction was felt to be necessary in view of the relative lack of secondary literature in English on Troeltsch as theologian and theorist of religion. However, some readers may wish to turn first to the translations themselves and return later to the discussion of their context. The four essays which have been translated all stem from his heyday as a professor of theology at Heidelberg (1894-1914):

(1) *Half a Century of Theology: a Review* (first published in *Zeitschrift für wissenschaftliche Theologie*, LI, 1908). This is one of Troeltsch's masterly historical analyses of the development of theology in the nineteenth century. Apart from its permanent value for the history of ideas, it also illustrates the intellectual situation in which Troeltsch's own thought was conceived.

(2) *Religion and the Science of Religion* (first published in *Kultur der Gegenwart*, I, 4, 1906). This essay shows how Troeltsch tried to define an independent science of religion which would be relevant but not subservient to theology. His contribution here has been insufficiently considered in discussions of the origins of this discipline.

(3) *What Does 'Essence of Christianity' Mean?* (first published in *Die Christliche Welt*, 1903). In a piece of sustained methodological analysis Troeltsch here attempted to state what is involved in identifying the essential meaning of Christianity, recognising this as a historical, yet theological act. This essay should be read by every student of theology. It also sheds light in a most suggestive way on traditions other than the Christian one in which it was cast. It was a shared interest in this most important essay, and a shared respect for it, that first led the editors to collaborate in planning this volume.

(4) *The Significance of the Historical Existence of Jesus for Faith* (a lecture given at Aarau to a Swiss students' conference and published as a brochure in 1911). The provocative thesis of Drews that Jesus never existed was the immediate occasion of this essay, which has since proved to be one of Troeltsch's most widely read pieces. The central question is of course the more subtle one about the relationship of the historical Jesus to christology. Whatever the final verdict on Troeltsch's socio-psychological approach to this problem the fact remains that such observations arising out of the scientific study of religion are sure to be germane to theology.

Finally we have appended two essays of our own in order to indicate how we see the importance of Troeltsch today in the fields of theology and of the 'science of religion', respectively. The aim is not merely to encourage a wider appreciation in the English-speaking world of the historical importance of Troeltsch's work, but also to contribute to the continued development of thought about religious traditions of a kind which is at once clear in its categories, critical, and creative.

R.M. & M.P.

Sources and Acknowledgments

The first three essays of Troeltsch translated here are from the standard edition of his works, *Gesammelte Schriften* II, Tübingen, 1913 and 1922; reprint Aalen, 1962. The fourth was published separately, Tübingen, 1911 and 1929; reprint Munich and Hamburg, 1969. The editors thank Messrs J.C.B. Mohr (Paul Siebeck) of Tübingen who hold the copyright, for permission to translate all four. *Gesammelte Schriften* II contains some alterations made to the original form in which the essays were published, and a note on the changes made to 'What Does "Essence of Christianity" Mean?' is appended to the translation. Thanks are extended to Professor Stephen Sykes for contributing this. The editors are also grateful to Professor Brian Gerrish for some very helpful criticisms and suggestions concerning the translations and the introduction; also to Professors James Luther Adams and Walter Bense for access to unpublished translations and cooperation with the bibliography of English translations. Professor Clark Williamson kindly made available his draft translation of *Die Bedeutung der Geschichtlichkeit Jesu für den Glauben.*

Introduction

Ernst Troeltsch
on Theology and Religion

Robert Morgan

1

Ernst Peter Wilhelm Troeltsch was born on 17 February 1865, at Haunstetten, near Augsburg, Bavaria. His father, a medical doctor, encouraged him to take an interest in the natural sciences,[1] and a mildly free-thinking religious belief permeated the home.[2] After attending the humanistic *Gymnasium*, Troeltsch became a student at Erlangen in the winter semester, 1884-5,[3] hesitating before the choice of a subject and career. He was attracted by law, seeing here a key to the understanding of history which he already recognised to be conditioned by the character of its institutions. Classics was also a possibility, but he had concluded at school that the Hellenic ideal could not be realised in the modern world. Philosophy at the university was not at this time very attractive, and his interest in medicine was only theoretical. He therefore settled for theology, and never regretted his choice. 'Only here could one tackle both metaphysics and the exciting historical problems at one and the same time.'[4]

This was the classical period of the new historical theology, with Wellhausen, Kuenen and Reuss dominating Old Testament studies, and F.C. Baur's Tübingen school having revolutionised New Testament studies, and with Hase and the rising star of Harnack in

[1] See 'Meine Bücher', *Gesammelte Schriften* IV, Tübingen, 1925, pp. 3-18. This autobiographical sketch was first published in *Die Philosophie der Gegenwart in Selbstdarstellungen*, ed. R. Schmidt, Leipzig, 1922, vol.2.

[2] See 'Die "kleine Göttinger Fakultät" von 1890', *Die christliche Welt*, vol.18, 1920. Cols. 281-3. This obituary for Bousset contains also autobiographical information: ' ... während ich als Sohn einer alten Reichsstädter-Familie in einer milden religiösen Rationalismus aufgewachsen war und politisch einen Bismarckianer sans phrase vorstellte.' Col. 281.

[3] So. *G.S.* IV, p.4. A. Dietrich, *Deutsches Biographisches Jahrbuch V, Das Jahr 1923*. Stuttgart, Berlin, Leipzig, 1930, p.350, dates it a year earlier.

[4] *Ibid.*

Church history.[5] His philosophical interests were nourished upon the great tradition of German idealism from Kant to the late Schelling by his Erlangen teacher Gustav Class, who sought to establish the reality of the idea of God by combining Hegel's theory of objective spirit with elements from Schleiermacher and Kant. Troeltsch studied Kant, Fichte and Schleiermacher intensively, but 'the really determinative spirit' for him at that time was the neo-Kantian Lotze (1817-1881) whom he 'read again and again'.[6] This led to an interest in Dilthey, whose new psychological understanding also stressed the idea of the individual and psychic new creations.[7] Always an eclectic in his philosophical idealism, his focus was a few years later to shift from Lotze and Dilthey to Windelband and Rickert (see below, p.12).[8]

After a basic theological education in Erlangen, Troeltsch and his friend Wilhelm Bousset left for Göttingen to become two of the last pupils of Albrecht Ritschl (1822-1889). Troeltsch was greatly impressed by this powerful personality, and as late as 1894, in 'The Christian World-view and its Counter-currents'[9] shows signs of his influence. He was always prepared to call himself a pupil of Ritschl[10] from whom he learned to distinguish in Kantian fashion between knowledge and faith. But even as a student his disagreements with Ritschl were becoming important to him. These were concentrated on two fronts and have fundamental significance for Troeltsch's entire work. One concerns the rational basis of Christian belief and the other the impact of modern scientific history upon Christian theology.

At Göttingen both Bousset and Troeltsch were influenced also by the deeply religious but anti-ecclesiastical oriental philologist and father of modern Septuagint studies, Paul de Lagarde (1827-1891). Troeltsch later dedicated the second volume of his collected writings (1913) to his memory. Bousset and Troeltsch learned from de Lagarde and from B. Duhm, who taught the Old Testament in Göttingen until 1888, not to compromise their historical integrity for the sake of Christian doctrine. The problems posed for theology by radical historical criticism were made clear to both students.

[5] *Ibid.*, pp. 4f.

[6] *Ibid.*, p.5.

[7] *G.S.* II, p.227, n.11. The early intellectual influences on Troeltsch are discussed at length by E. Spiess, *Die Religionstheorie von E. Troeltsch*, Paderborn, 1927.

[8] *Ibid.*

[9] 'Die christliche Weltanschauung und ihre Gegenströmungen', *ZThK*, III & IV, 1893-4, and reprinted in *G.S.* II, p.227-327.

[10] *Das historische in Kants Religionsphilosophie*, Berlin, 1904, p.v. Troeltsch also discusses his relationship to Ritschl in the Foreword to *The Social Teachings of the Christian Churches* (Eng.tr.London, 1931), vol.1, pp.19-21. See also below pp.68f.

Troeltsch wrote at the end of his life of his 'deep and vivid realisation of the clash between historical reflection and the determination of standards of truth and value. The problem thus arising presented itself to me at a very early age ... I was inspired by ... the interest in reaching a vital and effective religious position, which could alone furnish my life with a centre of reference for all practical questions and could alone give meaning and purpose to reflection upon the things of this world. This need of mine led me to theology and philosophy, which I devoured with an equally passionate interest. I soon discovered, however, that the historical studies which had so largely formed me, and the theology and philosophy in which I was now immersed, stood in sharp opposition, indeed even in conflict, with one another. I was confronted, upon the one hand, with the perpetual flux of the historian's data, and the distrustful attitude of the historical critic towards conventional traditions, the real events of the past being, in his view, discoverable only as a reward of ceaseless toil, and then only with approximate accuracy. And, upon the other hand, I perceived the impulse in men towards a definite practical standpoint – the eagerness of the trusting soul to receive the divine revelation and to obey the divine commands. It was largely out of this conflict, which was no hypothetical one, but a fact of my own practical experience, that my entire theoretical standpoint took its rise.'[11]

Bousset also was a competent philosophical theologian, but his main effort was directed to pressing ahead with comparative historical work on early Christianity. Around 1890 Bousset himself, William Wrede, Herrmann Gunkel and especially the now little known Albert Eichhorn, formed the nucleus of what was called 'the little faculty' in Göttingen. This group of junior lecturers later achieved dominance in biblical studies as 'the history of religions school'.[12] They were influenced by Wellhausen on the Old Testament, Holtzmann on the New, and by the young Harnack whose *History of Dogma* appeared in 1886-90. But they criticised the too literary approach of these scholars from the standpoint of their better appreciation of how living religion developed and even more consistent application of historical method to the Bible and Christian tradition. They repudiated Ritschl's sharp distinction between canonical and non-canonical writings, traces of which remain in the works of Harnack[13] and Holtzmann,[14] and also

[11] *Christian Thought*, London, 1923, pp.4-6.
[12] In addition, J. Weiss had some contact with the group. W. Heitmüller and P. Wernle were associated with it a little later.
[13] See his treatment of the Fourth Gospel in his *History of Dogma* I.
[14] See Wrede's criticisms in *The Task and Methods of 'New Testament Theology'* (Eng. tr. London, 1973).

the isolation of Christianity, as a miraculous supernatural revelation, from its historical context in the surrounding world of religions, especially 'late' Judaism.

These scholars were interested in *religion* as such, which they thought could be known only from the study of its total *history*, not from the secondary conceptualisations contained in *theology* or church dogma.

Troeltsch was not a biblical scholar, and apart from his close friendship with Bousset had little contact with this group during his few years in Göttingen as student and lecturer. But he was being formed in the same mould of an uncompromising historical theology, and from 1895 onwards was the main systematics spokesman for the movement. It was his doctrinal articles in the greatest monument of the school, *Die Religion in Geschichte und Gegenwart* (1st ed. 1909-13) which earned him the title of its 'dogmatician'.[15] But his more characteristic work as theoretician of the movement is contained in 'Die Selbständigkeit der Religion' (1895-6), 'Geschichte und Metaphysik' (1898) 'Uber historische und dogmatische Methode in der Theologie' (1898) and *Die Absolutheit des Christentums und die Religionsgeschichte* (1902). Those extended essays provide something of the background to the essays translated in this volume to illuminate Troeltsch's contribution to Christian theology and the study of religion.

It was his commitments as a Christian theologian that led Troeltsch to try to establish by psychological and historical (including anthropological) and, a little later, philosophical reflexion upon religion and religions, first an empirical and rational basis for religion, and secondly, the supremacy or prime validity of Christianity. He saw himself heir to the authentic (and non-ecclesiastical) Schleiermacher who in his philosophical ethics had proceeded from a philosophy of history and of human consciousness 'and through his analysis of religion and its historical development pioneered the way first to the understanding and then to the justification of Christianity'.[16]

[15] See 'The Dogmatics of the "religionsgeschichtliche Schule" ', *American Journal of Theology*, XVII, 1913, pp.1-21. He meant by 'dogmatics' simply 'the exposition of a normative Christian religious system', (p.6) not, of course, acceptance of 'dogmatic method'. Some of the *RGG*[1] articles were first published in 1907.

[16] *ZThK* VIII, 1898, p.28. He continues: 'So I began like Schleiermacher by establishing the peculiar independence of religion by means of the psychology of religion, by showing that every attempt to derive religion from other basic activities (of the human consciousness) has failed. Only I did this on the basis of a psychology which is different from Schleiermacher's, and in the front against different opponents – not moralists and rationalists, but modern positivists and those who see religion as an illusion.' See also *The Absoluteness of Christianity*, Eng.tr. pp.40-1. 'Schleiermacher

But if he was heir to one side of Schleiermacher, Troeltsch was also heir to Hegel, whose concept of development had, when freed from an *a priori* and deductive scheme and associated with an inductively based historical research, provided an important stimulus to historical theology. He hoped by his 'idealism of historical development' to heal the damaging division between Schleiermacher and Hegel which had persisted throughout the nineteenth century and led to a deep gulf between 'scientific' or historical, and 'ecclesiastical' or dogmatic theology.[17]

It is important at the outset to see Troeltsch in connexion with the history of religions school, which represents the high point in the development of historical theology. His restless attempts to do theology on this historical critical foundation constitute his claim to the attention of succeeding generations who have still not fully mastered his problems. But Troeltsch's break with Ritschl's residual biblicism and ecclesiastical supernaturalism came less from the demands of a rigorously historical approach to the Bible than from his conclusions about the historical place of the Reformation and the theological place of natural theology.

This combination of historical and philosophical interests in his theological thinking is already apparent in the book with which after a few months as a curate in Munich (1890) he qualified as a lecturer in Göttingen: *Reason and Revelation in Johann Gerhard and Melanchthon.*[18]

This study in the history of doctrine investigates the beginnings of protestant orthodoxy and shows how the new protestant churches found it necessary to continue the apologetic task of relating Christian belief to the philosophical background of the time in constructing a Christian culture. The dogmaticians of the sixteenth and seventeenth centuries continued with modifications arising from the protestant scriptural principle and the humanism of the Renaissance, the synthesising task of the great medieval schoolmen who had combined specifically Christian elements with the classical stoic idea of natural

exhibits the attempt of German idealism to overcome this historical relativity by a way other than that of ahistorical rationalism, namely, by ontological speculation concerning history – speculation that, through reflection on the very multiplicity of history, leads to knowledge of the unitary ground of all life. It is by way of this path, I believe, that our work must ultimately proceed, even though Schleiermacher's position is definitely not the last word on the subject ... ' See also below, pp.79f.

[17] See below, pp.151f. This split was sharply discussed by C.A. Bernoulli, *Die wissenschaftliche und die kirchliche Methode in der Theologie*, Tübingen, 1897. Troeltsch's long review in *GGA* 1898 shows how seriously he considered this issue. See below pp.76f.

[18] *Vernunft und Offenbarung bei Johann Gerhard und Melanchthon. Untersuchungen zur Geschichte der altprotestantischen Theologie*, Göttingen, 1891.

law. Aristotle's logic and metaphysics were as influential in protestant as in catholic scholasticism.

One important consequence of this research was that Troeltsch introduced a new periodisation of Christian history in which not the Reformation but the Enlightenment of the eighteenth century was seen as the watershed between medieval and modern – between a European culture dominated and permeated by Christianity, and the autonomous, increasingly secularised modern world. In his later work he tended to emphasise the medieval elements in Luther and the Reformation, in conscious opposition to the modernising of Luther practised especially by Ritschl and Herrmann. The fact that the modernising and glorifying of Luther was continued by Troeltsch's German contemporaries and successors who had little else in common is one reason why Troeltsch has been less popular in Germany than in the English-speaking world.[19]

Equally important was the message for systematic theology which emerged from this dissertation in the history of doctrine. Christianity must always seek to relate itself positively to the rational knowledge of the day.[20] Theology is 'a kind of necessary evil',[21] tying the knots between faith and knowledge. This apologetic task must be continually attempted afresh, despite all its failures. Ritschl's (and later Herrmann's) hostility to apologetics, metaphysics and natural theology must be firmly repudiated. Actually, 'the attempt to prove that an apologetic is neither necessary nor grounded in the nature of the matter is itself an apologetic operation, albeit a very misguided one'.[22] Of course, the task will have to be undertaken in a completely different way now that the old dualism between human and divine truth has succumbed to modern rational criticism. We stand on very different ground – 'insofar as we have any ground under our feet at all'.[23] In this respect we lack the vantage-point occupied by our predecessors. Direct continuity with them is an impossibility for those

[19] See below, p.209f. W. Pauck claims that 'Today, Troeltsch's interpretation is generally regarded as correct because it is widely recognised that, in this age, the churches no longer determine the decisions which shape the character of civilisation and public life, and that Protestantism and Roman Catholicism, insofar as they are represented by ecclesiastical organisations, have more in common than they share together or singly with the men and powers that mould modern civilisation'. *Harnack and Troeltsch*, New York, 1968, pp.61f.

[20] *Vernunft und Offenbarung*, pp.1f.

[21] *Ibid.*, p.3. See also 'Die Selbständigkeit der Religion', *ZThK* V 1895, p.420, and VI, 1896, p.109.

[22] *Vernunft und Offenbarung*, p.2.

[23] *Ibid.*, p.213. This anticipates his famous 'everything is tottering' comment of 1896 (see W. Köhler, *Ernst Troeltsch*, Tübingen, 1941, p.1).

who have passed through the fires of the Enlightenment critique of religion and what has followed that. 'But we shall only be able to claim a share in their heritage if we make at least some progress towards solving this basic problem of dogmatics in a manner which corresponds to our modern needs.'[24]

The requirement modestly stated in these closing words of the monograph was to engage Troeltsch in Bonn (1892-4) as associate professor and Heidelberg (1894-1914) as full professor for systematic theology, and then indirectly in a personal chair of philosophy in Berlin from 1915 until his premature death on 1 February 1923. The aim 'to make at least some progress towards solving this basic problem of dogmatics in a manner which corresponds to our modern needs', stated at the outset of his career, provides a guideline to his subsequent literary productivity. The modern intellectual situation determines the form to be taken by theology. This is characterised by the intellectual revolution effected by modern science and critical history. Troeltsch's strenuous efforts to understand this modern intellectual and cultural situation led him into sustained work in the history of ideas, with special reference to the eighteenth and nineteenth centuries. Some of the results of these analyses are contained in his long essays on the Enlightenment (1897), Deism (1898) German Idealism (1900) and the English moralists of the seventeenth and eighteenth centuries (1903).[25] Troeltsch considered that the intellectual and cultural revolution of the eighteenth century requires that theology submit itself to a corresponding revolution in method. He was to characterise this as the transition from dogmatic to historical method.

What this meant was a break with the old supernaturalism which modern critical history had rendered impossible[26] and a purely historical approach to the Bible and Christian tradition combined with a rational defence of the metaphysical basis of religion. The result was to be a modern 'science of religion' the shape of which can be seen developing in Troeltsch's early theological writings.

---

[24] *Ibid.*

[25] Reprinted from the *Realencyclopädie für protestantische Theologie und Kirche* in *G.S.* IV.

[26] In 1898 Troeltsch wrote that his earlier essays 'confessed (his) allegiance to the fundamental anti-supranaturalism of the Enlightenment, far though (he) was from rationalism in other respects', 'Geschichte und Metaphysik', *ZThK* VIII, 1898, p.27. It is, of course, important that this 'specific and exclusive supernaturalism ... is by no means identical with theism, with recognition of the absolute goals of personal life, or with appreciation for the significance of the underivable and original revelations of human creativity in the great geniuses. To all these I too lay claim'. *Absoluteness*, Eng.tr. p.38.

In 'The Christian World-view and its Counter-currents' (1894)
Troeltsch summarised the orientation he was recommending as
'metaphysical idealism on an epistemological basis, an idealist ethic
which takes in imperative and goal in a unitary point of view, a theism
based on the total phenomenon of religion and its development, and
our German science of history with its basis in a cautious theory of
development'.[27] This long essay was consistently[28] followed in 1895-6
by an even longer one, 'The Independence of Religion'.[29]

Confronted with the problem of defending the authenticity and
validity of religious experience against those who like Feuerbach and
contemporary positivists denied the existence of its object, Troeltsch
followed Schleiermacher in developing a philosophy of religion which
was not philosophical treatment of the object of religion, but the
examination of religion itself as an area of human life.[30] Responding in
this way to the empirical and realist climate of the time, but without abandoning his idealist view of the world, he therefore took up
the new and blooming discipline of the psychology of religion. This
'enquires about the place, the origin and the significance of religion in
the human consciousness and so is alone in a position to say what can
be said about the truth of religion though we do not wish to ignore
speculative efforts concerned with the object of religion'.[31]

Troeltsch argued first that elements of a basically idealist outlook
could be defended experientially and would provide grounds for
accepting the validity of religion in general. The second task would
then be to examine the available religions historically, and to look for
laws of development, and for criteria by which the value of each might
be judged. These could only be found in history itself.[32] The result was
clear. 'The inner dialectic of the religious idea points in the direction
of the perfectly individual and therefore universal religion of
redemption. It can only be that, because it is perfectly spiritualised
and moralised ... the strictest, scientific objectivity shows Christianity
to be the most profound, the most powerful and the richest expression
of the religious idea ... In the personality of its founder and prophet it
has the most living and adaptable revelational basis. In this it
reverences the guarantee and model of its truth and yet depends not
on external and mechanical authority but on the purely religious and
moral significance of Jesus and his inner communion with God.'[33] The

[27] *G.S.* II, pp.240f.
[28] Cf. *Ibid.*, p.227, n.
[29] 'Die Selbständigkeit der Religion', *ZThK* V & VI, 1895-6.
[30] *ZThK* V, pp.367f. Cf. *ZThK* VIII, 1898, p.28, and below pp.87f.
[31] *ZThK* V, p.370.
[32] *Ibid.*, p.373.
[33] *ZThK* VI, p.200.

four fundamental concepts of religion, God, the world, the soul and redemption are most clearly and completely worked out in the Christian principle.[34] This does not prove that Christianity is the 'absolute' religion. Rational argument can only show it to be the relatively highest to date.[35] Nevertheless, Christian faith does make this claim to absoluteness, and in this early essay Troeltsch saw in this a distinguishing mark of Christianity.[36]

Troeltsch's hardest words in this essay were directed against the Ritschlian theologians. These had exploited the Kantian distinction between faith and knowledge to defend Christianity by a modified form of supernaturalism, while at the same time submitting other religions to a Feuerbachian or positivist criticism. Troeltsch argued that a positivist theory of knowledge had mortal consequences for any theology and must be resisted at all costs. He also considered that this isolation of Christianity was quite arbitrary; any religion could argue in the same way. 'To apply Feuerbach's theory to non-Christian religions and at the same time a supranaturalist theory of revelation to Christianity is an extremely dangerous experiment. Not many people will be able to find the truth of Christianity in any form secured by this. These are all attempts to except Christianity from the basic ideas of the philosophy of religion. One who has himself for a while made grateful use of this gambit for isolating Christianity as a way out of theological difficulties knows only too well how far the wish is father to the thought here.'[37]

A reply by Kaftan[38] gave Troeltsch opportunity to press this objection against the Ritschlians in another important essay, 'Geschichte und Metaphysik'.[39] His own alternative to the supranaturalist starting-point was to be through a metaphysics of history: 'One can even speak of a latent theology of *Historismus*' – which he considered it his task to make patent.[40]

It was further consideration of the history of religion which by 1895 had convinced Troeltsch that the Ritschlian escape route was inadmissable, and drove him to a science of religion in which Christianity would be treated psychologically and historically, in the

---

[34] *Ibid.*, pp.200-5.

[35] *Ibid.*, pp.206f.

[36] *Ibid.*, pp.212f.

[37] *ZThK*, V, p.375.

[38] 'Die Selbständigkeit des Christentums', *ZThK* VI, 1896.

[39] *ZThK* VIII, 1898, pp.1-69. See pp. 34, 51, 53. The subsequent history of protestant theology showed how well grounded Troeltsch's fears were. See below, pp.213f.

[40] *Ibid.*, p.69. He concludes the essay with an echo of Fichte's saying to the effect that only metaphysics, never mere history, has religious significance.

same way as other religions. It is a species of the genus religion, religion being 'a unitary phenomenon which moves according to its own laws in connection with the whole of spiritual and intellectual life. It asserts a relative independence against all other spheres of life. Its truth content must be looked for in itself. It only receives and reveals its full content in its historical movement and particularity'.[41]

The clearest statement by Troeltsch of the revolutionary effects of the new science of history upon theological method is found in his essay 'On Historical and Dogmatic Method in Theology' (1898).[42] The principles of criticism, analogy and correlation have proved themselves by their fruitfulness, and Christian theology cannot escape the transformation in our entire mode of thought – in particular our relation to tradition.[43] It was biblical studies that showed most clearly the methodological implications of historical study.[44] Troeltsch accepted as a Christian theologian, that 'in theology, the historical method must be applied with utter and uncompromising consistency. Thus there arises the challenge to construct a theology based on a historical method oriented to universal history; and since our concern is with Christianity as both religion and ethic, this means that the method will have to be that of the history of religion. This idea of a theology based upon the history of religion, which was envisaged from the very beginning of historical criticism (first by the Deists and then in various forms by Lessing, Kant, Herder, Schleiermacher, De Wette, and Hegel, and finally by Baur and Lagarde), I have sought to sketch in my previous works, attempting to give it the form required since the elimination of the rationalistic concept of religion in general and of the Hegelian dialectic of the Absolute'.[45]

Troeltsch admits some fluctuation in his earlier thought; he has 'tended to draw the consequences of the historical method ever more strictly, (and has) finally come to characterise the term "absoluteness" as only a rationalised and disguised vestige of the dogmatic method'.[46] But throughout these essays his aim is always theological and apologetic; while admitting that historical method 'relativises everything' he at once adds: ' – not in the sense that it eliminates every standard of judgment and necessarily ends in a

---

[41] *ZThK* V, pp.370f.

[42] *G.S.* II, pp.729-53. Troeltsch links this essay with the two discussed above in a footnote. On this subject see also his article 'Historiography' in Hastings *ERE* VI, pp.716-23, reprinted in J. Macquarrie (ed.), *Contemporary Religious Thinkers*, London, 1968, pp.76-97.

[43] See especially, *G.S.* II, pp.735-8, 753.

[44] *Ibid.*, p.737.

[45] *Ibid.*, p.738, following throughout an as yet unpublished translation of W. Bense.

[46] *Ibid.*, p.747.

nihilistic scepticism, but rather in the sense that every historical structure and moment can be understood only in relationship with others and ultimately with the total context, and that standards of values cannot be derived from isolated events but only from an overview of the historical totality.'[47] His view 'combats historical relativism, which is the consequence of the historical method only within an atheistic or a religiously skeptical framework. [It] seeks to overcome this relativism through the conception of history as a disclosure of the divine reason'.[48] He considers that 'for the deduction of such a scale of values it is indispensable to believe in reason as operative in history and as progressively revealing itself',[49] and sees here 'the undeniable merits of the Hegelian doctrine, which needs only to be freed of its metaphysics of the absolute, its dialectic of opposites, and its specifically logical conception of religion'.[50]

The same combination of 'drawing the consequences of the historical method ever more strictly' and 'the idea of a theology based upon the history of religion' is evident in *The Absoluteness of Christianity and the History of Religions*[51] which Troeltsch saw as following naturally from 'The Christian World-view and its Counter-currents' and 'The Independence of Religion',[52] and 'forming the conclusion of a series of earlier studies and the beginning of new investigations of a more comprehensive kind in the philosophy of history'.[53]

When religion is studied historically, the traditional isolation of Christianity (as miraculous divine revelation) from other religions (which are considered to be entirely false) is dissolved.[54] But not even the expedient by which Schleiermacher and Hegel had combined a developmental view of the history of religion with a conviction of the absoluteness of Christianity could be sustained in the light of subsequent historical research. According to Hegel Christianity is absolute religion because in and through Jesus the absolute principle of religion is realised. Troeltsch saw the impossibility of restricting the realisation of spirit to Christianity alone. At best one might acknowledge the 'supremacy' of Christianity, the religion of personalism, as 'the highest religious truth that has relevance for us', and on a basis of this acknowledgement organise an evaluative understanding rooted in religious faith and developed with reference

[47] *Ibid.*, p.737.
[48] *Ibid.*, p.747.
[49] *Ibid.*, p.746.
[50] *Ibid.*, p.747.
[51] 1902, rp. Siebenstern 1969. Eng.tr. by David Reid, Atlanta, 1971, London, 1972.
[52] *G.S.* II, p.227.
[53] *Christian Thought*, London, 1923, p.4.
[54] *Absoluteness*, Eng. tr., pp. 48, 52, 58-60, 132.

to the religions of the world.[55] Or 'faith may regard Christianity as a heightening of the religious standard in terms of which the inner life of man will continue to exist'.[56] Or Christianity may prove itself to be 'the convergence point of all developmental tendencies in religion and the elevation of the goal of religion to an essentially new level'.[57]

It is along these lines that Troeltsch wishes to provide Christian apologetics with a substitute for the old naive belief in absoluteness based on miracle, and the modification of this offered by classical German idealism. As a Christian theologian he is 'concerned not with the history of religion in general but *normative* knowledge acquired through the scientific study of religion'.[58] Here, as earlier, 'what is important is in the first place to derive the normativeness from the history of religion instead of from scholastic theories of revelation and apologetics against philosophical systems, and then secondly to give to the Christian world of ideas a form which corresponds to the present religious and intellectual situation'.[59] He considered it 'essential to place the scientifically oriented appraisals of religion on a broad foundation by demonstrating the truth of [his] ontological principle, and to answer the question as to the normative development of religion on the basis of a conceptual analysis of the higher types of religious life that appear in history'.[60]

This 'attempt to derive the normative from the study of history',[61] stands at the heart of Troeltsch's life work from his earliest lessons from German idealism that only the metaphysical, never the merely historical, brings true satisfaction, down to his latest efforts to 'overcome history with history'.[62] The 'beginning of new investigations of a more comprehensive kind in the philosophy of history' announced here in 1902, refers to an important shift in his thinking at about this time, resulting from his confrontation with the Baden school of neo-Kantianism represented by W. Windelband and H. Rickert. Troeltsch comments that 'the strongly Hegelian standpoint that appeared in 'Geschichte und Metaphysik' (1898) has here been transformed into a critical (i.e. Kantian) one, due to the influence of Rickert'.[63] Instead of trying to draw his norms from the

[55] *Ibid.*, p.107, modifying the translation.

[56] *Ibid.*, p.115.

[57] *Ibid.*, p.146.

[58] *Ibid.*, p.25, from the very important foreword to the first edition.

[59] *Ibid.*, p.26.

[60] *Ibid.*, p.32.

[61] *Ibid.*, p.31.

[62] *G.S.* III, p.772.

[63] *Absoluteness*, Eng.tr. p.168. At *G.S.* IV, p.9 Troeltsch remarks that 'the book is the germ of all that followed'.

course of history itself,[64] his thought now took a sharply Kantian turn to the analysis of consciousness, in the hope of finding *a priori* structures which would satisfy his earlier attempts to demonstrate the independence of religion and provide a basis for finding absolute norms from within the relativity of history.

2

From the start of his academic career Troeltsch had consistently repudiated Ritschl's use of Kant's distinction between faith and knowledge to ground religion in value-judgments. This metaphysical capitulation left religious belief without any ontological foundation and so undermined its claim to tell the truth about how things are. Troeltsch was shortly to argue that this rested on a misunderstanding of Kant, whose emphasis upon the practical character of religion referred simply to its separation from the exact sciences or speculation. That separation ought not to be understood to make the actual task of analysing religion superfluous; and in this analysis empirical and rational elements must be united. Neither does the separation refer to the establishment of the truth-content of religion, which for Kant requires analysis of the rational, i.e. *a priori*, laws of consciousness at work in the factuality of religious life. The real importance of Kant for theology is missed by those who appeal to him in support of a theology of value judgments: 'By placing all the emphasis upon the separation of theoretical and practical reason and stressing only the practical necessity of the values claimed by religion, they lose the necessity of the object to which these values are attached and plunge into the abyss of a theology based on human desires and illusions.'[65] Troeltsch soon felt confident enough about Kant to assert that he 'constantly stressed the need for an apriorist religious reason, and for the object given with this' and therefore struggled to combine the rationally necessary element with the empirical psychological reality of concrete religious ideas and feelings.[66] Making this combination is admittedly the major difficulty about Kant's position.[67] Troeltsch's point is that it is here, in the development of Kant's epistemology, that the philosopher of religion must work, rather than use Kant as a spring-board in the flight from metaphysics.

---

[64] See above nn. 32 & 33.
[65] *Psychologie und Erkenntnistheorie in der Religionswissenschaft*, Tübingen, 1905, p.28.
[66] *Ibid.*, p.33.
[67] *G.S.* II, pp.719, 760.

Ritschl had used Lotze in this way[68] and was followed by Herrmann in dependence on the Marburg school of neo-Kantianism represented by Cohen and Natorp. Troeltsch opposed this whole strategy by contesting the universal applicability of 'the purely phenomenological and causal view of history and human events that is demanded by Kantian doctrine, on the one hand, and even more emphatically by neo-Kantian doctrine, on the other, with its setting aside of freedom and the practical reason'.[69] He rejected this 'closed system of necessary causes and effects, so far as historical phenomena and the entire compass of human events are concerned' and thought that 'the entire life of the human spirit, in its relation to an intangible reality, requires an ontological foundation in principles independent of those appropriate to the causal-mechanistic approach'.[70] He recognised that 'to contest the application of a mechanising view of causality to every sphere of human life may, in addition to being a theological heresy, also be a philosophical one; or it may be that my attempt to demonstrate this point will be judged a failure. I maintain, however, that it is inadmissable to identify science with causal explanation, and that where such identification occurs, there is no room for religion in the real meaning of the word'.[71]

He was even prepared to argue 'that the Kantian doctrine of intelligible character and of motivation through the purely rational necessity of the good, and in particular Kant's philosophy of history, with its depiction of the development of a realm of moral reason, has broken through the rigidity of a purely phenomenological and causal view and made use of an ontological approach to human events'.[72] This suggestion was a little later worked out in Troeltsch's most impressive contribution to Kant studies: *The Historical in Kant's Philosophy of Religion, being at the same time a contribution to research on Kant's philosophy of history* (1904).[73] This kind of appeal to a more authentic Kant, or to the more correct historical interpretation of a shared piece of authoritative tradition, is a typical procedure by which modern theologians criticise their opponents.[74] The Ritschlians echoed the commonplace that Kant, as a figure of the Enlightenment, lacked a sense of history. They then exploited this supposed weakness to graft a supernaturalist understanding of history on to his critical

---

[68] See below, p.62f.
[69] *Absoluteness*, Eng.tr., p.31.
[70] *Ibid.*
[71] *Ibid.*, pp.31f.
[72] *Ibid.*, p.32.
[73] *Das Historische in Kants Religionsphilosophie*, Berlin, 1904.
[74] The tradition thus contested is more usually the New Testament or Luther.

epistemology. Troeltsch sought to undercut this dubious procedure by showing that Kant himself drew the consequences of the total historicisation of human thought and the insertion of sacred history into the general history of religion. Kant recognised the modern world's break with the traditional, miracle-based view of Christian history. He must, argued Troeltsch, be followed here too. The quasi-history of supernatural interventions must be abandoned in favour of real history, based as this is upon critical evaluation of the sources and reconstruction with the help of the principle of analogy.[75]

The possibility of finding in Kant the beginnings of a modern historical consciousness does not alter the fact that Kant himself developed his epistemology by reference to the methods of Newtonian natural science, and without consideration of the quite different logic of history. 'Whoever, in attempting to do justice to actual historical problems from the point of view of criticism, was detained by the purely natural science treatment of the life of the soul as a succession of causally connected phenomena, could not achieve a methodology corresponding to actual historiography, and still less a philosophy of history that provides structure, takes cognizance of historical development, and penetrates to the spiritual substance'.[76] As a philosopher of religion and compelled to 'approach his subject, religion, historically'[77] and 'free to recognise the new creations in the history of religion that are constantly being formed within the causal nexus',[78] Troeltsch found in the historical logic of Windelband and Rickert a way of avoiding the difficulties of Herrmann's position, dependent as this was on the neo-Kantianism of Cohen.[79]

The Baden school supplied what Kant lacked: 'a specifically historical logic that would culminate in a philosophy of history.'[80] Kant's concept of history had not provided a way to standards for evaluating historical developments', nor a way of 'apprehending a reality that has its life in history,[81] and Hegel's evolutionary metaphysics had broken down on the wheel of subsequent historical research. Rickert appeared to remain true to the actual procedure of historians and at the same time to provide a bridge from the methods of empirical historiography to the philosophy of history by means of which Troeltsch was hoping to solve the problem of finding normative

[75] *Das Historische*, p.134.
[76] *G.S.* II, p.715.
[77] *Ibid.*
[78] *Ibid.*, p.719.
[79] *Ibid.*, p.715.
[80] *Ibid.*, p.716.
[81] *Ibid.*

values for today. History and psychology alike had sharpened people's
feeling for the irrational in history and the collapse of absolute
idealism had been followed by an anti-religious positivism. But the
revival of critical idealism in the neo-Kantian movement was
stemming this flood; and when the Baden wing of the movement
turned its attention to history and the problem of values, Troeltsch
saw in this affirmation of both the rational or necessary, and the
irrational or contingent in history, a possible framework for a theology
based upon historical study. It is little wonder that he found in 'the
doctrine of Windelband and Rickert a redemption and liberation'[82]
from the one-sidedly psychological approach to the human sciences of
Dilthey and Wundt. He celebrated Rickert's *Die Grenzen der
Naturwissenschaftlichen Begriffsbildung* with the proclamation that
philosophy is once again becoming conscious of its proper tasks. Once
again, philosophy is beginning to take part in the elaboration of an
idealistic view of life, and indeed at that most important point where
the two problems touch: by recognising the peculiarity of the
historical world as over against nature, yet without abandoning the
historical world to the 'anarchy of values', but rather relating it to an
ideal value system.[83] Troeltsch's long and important discussion of
Rickert's book is entitled 'Modern Philosophy of History' (1903),[84]
and that title indicates where his own interests lay: in 'the problem of
the relation between history and norms, between development and
standards of development – the problem which the Hegelian
philosophy had placed in the centre of its thought' and which must be
'solved today without the Hegelian presuppositions which have lost
much of their cogency'.[85] Though the problem of deriving norms from
history 'confronts all of contemporary thought, it is most serious for
theology, since theology stands or falls with the possibility of the
attainment of universal norms and standards of value. As theology
relies increasingly on the historical approach, it must devote more and
more of its energies to the problem of the relationship of history to the
attainment of norms. Theology will accordingly be able to claim the
distinction of being the battleground on which the decisive battle is
being fought; the outcome of this battle will in turn affect every other
sphere of life. Unless religious positions can be regained and
strengthened, it will be impossible to establish norms in these other

[82] *Ibid.*, p.717. Cf. *G.S.* IV, p.10.
[83] *Ibid.*, p.679.
[84] 'Moderne Geschichtsphilosophie', *G.S.* II, pp.673-728.
[85] *Ibid.*, p.697. See also below, p.117.

areas. One's religious outlook ultimately determines whether norms will be accepted and obeyed.'[86]

Rickert, on the other hand, was not primarily concerned with Troeltsch's ultimately metaphysical problem. His sub-title indicated a purely epistemological interest: 'A logical introduction to the historical disciplines.' He wished to give an account of historical method which would secure its independence from the all-conquering claims of natural science. Whereas the latter seeks to generalise and attain laws, history is interested in particulars. Its material is selected and organised in such a way as to construct 'units of value' or 'value wholes' (*Wertganzen*). Values do emerge in history and it is the experience of value in the widest sense, not the personal evaluations of the historian, that determines the writing of history. 'Men structure historical reality by reference to what they consider important and essential, and that historical reality becomes history when the occurrences of the past assume their proper place in relation to these values, when they can be portrayed according to the degree in which they posit or negate these values.'[87] Historical reconstruction is based on objective scholarly knowledge of the development of human value-structures. It traces their development, structuring the flow of unique events in such a way as to exhibit the chain of individual value constructs.

Rickert shared the neo-Kantian distrust of metaphysics, and rightly insisted against Hegel that historical concepts, such as intellectual movements, the spirit of peoples, and trends have no independent metaphysical status; 'they simply formulate the fulness of historical experience and memory into concepts that facilitate the surveying and the understanding of this fulness without thereby abolishing the one true reality.'[88] But his assumption of a necessary relation of empirical reality to absolutely universal values, which we have encountered as a presupposition for the scientific necessity of history, and above all the conviction that 'all human values cannot be regarded as completely indifferent even from the scholarly standpoint',[89] provided Troeltsch with a point of departure for discussing 'the problem of the philosophy of history, i.e., the problem of an objectively valid value system'.[90]

Rickert's account of historical method presupposes a need, arising from the structure and organisation of consciousness itself, to structure experience by reference to the values which struggle to

[86] *Ibid.*, pp.675f.
[87] *Ibid.*, pp.691f.
[88] *Ibid.*, p.684.
[90] *Ibid.*, p.697.

emerge in the course of history. Troeltsch's problem as an ethicist and philosopher of culture and of religion concerns the relationship of our knowledge of historical value structures in the past and the construction of our own present values; how does the study of history help us construct norms which are objectively valid and obligatory today? A philosophical grounding of the values recognised as valid is required if history is to provide more than a chaos of value-systems, any one of which may be arbitrarily selected. The Hegelian solution of bringing to history goals already established by metaphysics destroys the significance of history, which lies in its individuality and particularity; goals must rather be abstracted from history itself.[91] A critical solution (i.e. one based on Kantian epistemology) must consider how knowledge is obtained; namely 'through judgments that, proceeding from a need of the consciousness, designate something as existent, and then relate this existent to the thoughts that necessarily flow from the consciousness, in order thereby to lift the existent itself into the sphere of the necessary'.[92] Empirical reality is considered either from the viewpoint of general laws (natural science) or of obligatory values (history) – i.e. the need to refer everything to some ultimate value. The conclusion is that 'knowledge rests ultimately on values and the norms to be derived from them. What ought to be is the key to what is; the acknowledgement of an absolute purpose of existence is the *a priori* of scholarship.'[93] The central position is occupied by the valuing consciousness, and reality is understood in terms of value. The epistemological subject or logical consciousness can only organise its knowledge from this standpoint, in which case 'it is absolutely certain that there must be an ultimate value. That which is so central to all knowledge, and which, specifically, first gives meaning to all historical knowledge, must also be real; that is, it must be capable of realisation. This, to be sure,' he adds, 'is a belief, and to this extent a religious thought.'[94]

Troeltsch draws from Kant the *formal concept* of an absolute value. It requires filling out with *content* on the basis of historical study. Here as elsewhere Troeltsch corrects and supplements Kant's thought with ideas derived from Schleiermacher,[95] Kant's 'absolute goal that is merely formal' with Schleiermacher's 'construction of a doctrine of goods based on the relation of spirit to nature'.[96] It was the excessive

---

[91] *Ibid.*, p.706.
[92] *Ibid.*   [93] *Ibid.*, p.707.
[94] *Ibid.*, p.708.
[95] *Ibid.*, p.623. At the same time he corrects Schleiermacher by Kant. See also *Psychologie und Erkenntnistheorie*, p.35, for this double movement.
[96] *Ibid.*, p.703.

formalism of Kantian ethics which Troeltsch considered a major difficulty about Herrmann's *Ethics* (1901), and it was in a discussion of this book entitled 'Basic Problems of Ethics' (1902) that he made clear his own position.[97]

Troeltsch shares the fundamental assumption of Herrmann's book that in the modern world it is ethics rather than metaphysics that must provide the framework for the study of religion. It is consideration of the ultimate values and goals of human life and action that gives rise to both religious and metaphysical ideas. Psychological, historical and epistemological knowledge unite to form a theory of value, and this may then be examined for its religious and metaphysical bases.[98] But beyond this initial agreement about the situation of theology today, Troeltsch rejects Herrmann's approach at a level which allows their disagreement to pose one of the fundamental choices confronting twentieth-century theology.

Herrmann modifies Kant with some christological emphases derived from Schleiermacher, but his view of Christianity as pure religion and morality centres on Kant's categorical imperative. Christianity is the realisation of ethical autonomy through trust in Jesus. The Church is relevant only as the bearer of Christian proclamation, not as an institutional organ of Christian action.[99] Cultural values such as the family, the state, society, science and art are reduced to preparations and materials for autonomy and must be sacrificed if they conflict with this.[100] Troeltsch also is indebted to Kant for making clear the formal necessity of the moral sphere. But for him the more important question about the relation of morality and religion concerns content. The religious perceptions which Herrmann rates so highly are far less important than the actual commands and values which stem from a particular religion's relationship to the divinity.[101] The ethical significance of Christianity will only become clear when these are compared and the Christian ones found to exhibit the balance of inner-worldly and transcendent goals which corresponds best to the actual nature of man. Christian morality, therefore, must be studied in a history-of-religions and philosophy-of-history way – which is the direction taken by Troeltsch's own studies.[102]

[97] 'Grundprobleme der Ethik'. *G.S.* II, pp.552-672, partially translated. See below, p.253, n.4.
[98] *Ibid.*, p.553.
[99] *Ibid.*, p.595. Herrmann's pupils in the dialectical theology followed him here.
[100] *Ibid.*, p.598.
[101] *Ibid.*, pp.670f.
[102] *Ibid.*, p.672.

Before considering in more detail how Troeltsch saw the historical study of religion and religions flowing into the philosophy of history, it is necessary to follow further the way in which he sought to establish an epistemological base for the reality and the study of religion.

The roots of the 'religious *a priori*', for which Troeltsch is best remembered by those who study the history of ideas through its slogans, are to be found in his renewed interest in Kant which was inspired by the Baden neo-Kantians' interest in history. The phrase itself does not occur until a lecture given at St. Louis in 1904: *Psychology and Epistemology in the Science of Religion.*[103] Troeltsch here counters the influential pragmatism of William James' *The Varieties of Religious Experience* (1901) with an account of a science of religion which faced the question of its truth. Kant's analysis of consciousness, developed to give a proper basis for normative knowledge for an age in which traditional authorities had collapsed, provided a foundation. He had corrected both rationalism's failure to give experience due weight and also empiricism's failure to consider *a priori* elements of consciousness that are independent of experience.[104] Troeltsch hoped to show that the formation of religious ideas was grounded in the structure of human reason itself. Human reason could therefore make religious judgments in the same way that it can make ethical and aesthetic judgments. It is a mistake to explain religion away as an illusion. It is rather a part of what it means to be human, even though not all men activate this aspect of consciousness.

Troeltsch insisted that his theory could not demonstrate the existence of the religious object,[105] and was aware that positivists and psychologisers would not take his theory of religion seriously.[106] He was aware of 'essential and serious difficulties'[107] in the theory, and soon stopped using the phrase; – it is remarkable how rarely it occurs in his writings. He admitted that he was 'going more than a little beyond Kant' in drawing out the 'metaphysical setting' of Kant's

---

[103] See nn.65. Sub-titled 'Eine Untersuchung über die Bedeutung der Kantischen Religionslehre für die heutige Religionswissenschaft'. Troeltsch again took up this theme in a memorial essay to William James: 'Empiricism and Platonism in the Philosophy of Religion' (1912).

[104] *Psychologie und Erkenntnistheorie*, p.25. Kant tried to unite Hume's truth with that of Leibniz and Plato.

[105] See below, pp.86, 111.

[106] *G.S.* II, p.756: 'For the pure psychologiser and positivist my theory of religion is just as grossly superstitious as papal encyclicals.' Quotations from 'Zur Frage des religiösen Apriori' (1909) *G.S.* II, pp.754-68 are from the forthcoming Adams and Bense volume.

[107] *Ibid.*, p.759.

position.[108] Its claim to be a legitimate development has not won acceptance. Kant's epistemology knows nothing of different *a prioris* for ethics, aesthetics and religion.[109] But the particular theory itself is less important than the whole attempt 'to satisfy the claims of both history and philosophy',[110] with the help 'of that school in modern thought which seeks to do equal justice to both the causal-psychological and the productive-rational elements'.[111] It is in the relationship between psychology and epistemology that Troeltsch considers the resolution of his problem to lie. The unity of psychological and logical consciousness is in his view 'the ultimate riddle of all reality and humanity ... the foundational fact of our intellectual life'.[112]

In the St. Louis lecture, and most impressively in an essay entitled 'Religionsphilosophie' (1904)[113] Troeltsch sketched out his ideal of a science of religion which is not science replacing or turned against religion but which preserves the 'sense for the presence of the divine in concrete, finite events and realities' which is 'fundamental to the phenomenon of religion'.[114] It combines the two sides to the study of religion, recognising the freshness and liveliness of religion, its mysteriousness and its irrationality, and so respecting its subject-matter better than the classical German idealists had done, by taking account of the advances made in history and psychology during the nineteenth century. But it was also to maintain their concern for the truth of religion, and refuse to be satisfied with a purely descriptive science of religion. It would criticise and regulate religious phenomena according to religion's own norms, distinguishing between mere appearance and truth by referring the psychological phenomena to a general law.[115] It would in this way be a means of critical purification and development of raw religious phenomena.[116] At this point philosophy of religion becomes theology, or (if the philosopher prefers not to take this step) it must make room for theology to build upon it, and face the question of something whose validity ought to be accepted.[117]

[108] *Ibid.*, pp.758f.
[109] See R. Köhler, *Der Begriff a priori in der modernen Religionsphilosophie*, Leipzig, 1920.
[110] *G.S.* II, p.754.
[111] *Ibid.*, p.756.
[112] *Ibid.*, p.709.
[113] In *Die Philosophie im Beginn des 20 Jahrhunderts, Festschrift für Kuno Fischer*, ed., W. Windelband, 1904, 1907.²
[114] *Psychologie und Erkenntnistheorie*, p.51.
[115] *Ibid.*, p.24.
[116] *Ibid.*, p.27. Cf. below, pp.92f.
[117] 'Religionsphilosophie', 1st ed., p.132, 2nd ed., p.452; below, pp.88 and 117-20.

The problem of fixing the basic presuppositions for a science of religion continued to exercise Troeltsch in his essay on 'Religion and the Science of Religion' (1906) translated in this collection. 'Its great question is the question of the nature of religious phenomena, the question of their epistemological and cognitive import, the question of the value and the meaning of the great historical religious formations.'[118] At the outset it is necessary to make a decision about which basic metaphysical approach to adopt. Of the four types available two, the Hegelian and the church dogmatics (doctrine of revelation) type, are as they stand clearly unsatisfactory, though both contain elements which must be taken utterly seriously.[119] The real choice is between critical idealism of the Kant and Schleiermacher type, and positivism – and it is a choice, not something that can be demonstrated.[120]

Having made this choice the student of religion is concerned with the four main disciplines which together constitute for Troeltsch the new science of religion which replaced the 'Religionsphilosophie' of classical German idealism.[121] Psychology of religion, i.e. the empirical study of religion, which for Troeltsch includes anthropology, has priority; this is the data. But then comes philosophical (epistemological) questioning about its validity and truth, which Troeltsch at this time thought he had in part solved by his theory of the religious *a priori*. The combination of these two sides provides the foundation of Troeltsch's science of religion. But he at once proceeds to speak of two other essential tasks: that of a 'philosophy of history of religion' and the 'philosophical treatment of the idea of God', i.e. religious metaphysics.

Attention to the positive historical formations (i.e. history of religions) follows naturally from the inter-penetration of the first two areas of study. Hegel's deductive metaphysics of the absolute must now be replaced by an inductive procedure which starts with empirical historical research. The aim here is to find a teleological law of development. Troeltsch is less confident than he was in his early essay on 'The Independence of Religion' (1895-6) about the clarity with which Christianity will emerge as the highest development, but it is the decisive form of religion in Western civilisation. Its significance and its future and its relationship to Eastern religions must therefore

---

[118] Below, p.88.

[119] On the merits of Hegel, see below, p.116. The essay on 'Religionsphilosophie' shows great sensitivity for the dogmaticians' perspective. See below, p.228-31.

[120] See below, p.83, and frequently elsewhere.

[121] His own terminology is not quite consistent, but see below, pp.114f.

be considered at this point. Then, finally, consideration of the idea of God in its relation to other knowledge may be expected to confirm the initial decision in favour of critical idealism.[122]

The third area of study specified in this account of his 'science of religion', the philosophy of history, redirects our attention to the important essay on Rickert, entitled 'Modern Philosophy of History' and to the longest essay in this collection, 'What Does "Essence of Christianity" Mean?', both of which appeared in 1903.

3

Rickert's account of historical method as the investigation of values, and his claim that this stems from a necessity of human consciousness to treat reality in this way, raises the question of 'the relation between the knowledge of historical value-structures and the construction of one's own present values'.[123] The 'values that are struggling to emerge and to assume form as life-relationships ... reside only in concrete realities that can be experienced and not in abstract concepts',[124] i.e. they must be drawn from history itself. But history confronts us with 'a chaos of value systems', and this poses the philosophical question of how to move from this datum to values which can be recognised as obligatory today. Can these values be philosophically grounded – or are we 'plunged into the abyss of relativism and skepticism'?[125]

Troeltsch's answer to the problem of the philosophy of history, which he believes to be true to Rickert,[126] acknowledges fully the inevitable personal and subjective element in the act of decision in which psychological and logical consciousness are united, but attempts to circumvent the change of arbitrary subjectivity. Standards and values cannot be deduced in naturalistic or Hegelian fashion from the causal succession, but must be 'constructed only according to one's best knowledge and conscience out of the most mature factual knowledge and the most personal commitment of faith'.[127] Since a subjective element is inevitable here, the dangers of subjectivism cannot be removed. They will only be overcome in practice through

[122] Troeltsch is clear about the element of personal judgment in his conception of the discipline. See below, p.83.
[123] *G.S.* II, p.696.
[124] *Ibid.*, pp.695f.
[125] *Ibid.*, p.696.
[126] *Ibid.*, p.712.
[127] *Ibid.*, p.711. A footnote at this point criticises Wundt and Vierkandt for failing to understand the apriorist personal element in this.

the maturity of those who reflect upon history.[128] 'Through scholarly circumspection and reflection, through knowledge of the broad scope and the development of history, this assessment is protected against the arbitrariness of the judgments of merely practical life, against the short-sightedness, isolation and self-satisfaction of uncontrolled and uncompared judgments. But even the most circumspect determination remains an individual act, whose objective necessity lies in the final analysis only in the certainty of the one making it that he, upon a careful weighing of all circumstances, feels compelled by his conscience to arrive at this particular judgment ... The endeavour to make judgments on the broadest basis, to attain the continuity with what has been attained, and to make decisions on the basis of well-considered comparisons gives such a decision its 'scientific' character, but this 'scientific' character does not eliminate the individuality of the decision. Everything historical, in spite of all references to absolute values, remains irrational and individual. This is the destiny and dignity of man.'[129]

This quite central emphasis upon 'decision' brings Troeltsch far closer than is usually realised to modern existentialist theologies, – and to Luther.[130] Reflection on the tradition leading to personal commitment can easily be transposed into the idiom of kerygmatic theology. Troeltsch himself was more interested in how this close connexion of history with ethics, 'the doctrine of the system of values that are to be recognised as valid', approximated to the thought of the

[128] As in the determination of the essence, 'the amateurs, the doctrinaire, the fanatics, the narrow-minded, beginners and specialists ... should leave the matter alone' below, p.143.

[129] *G.S.* II, p.712. Cf. pp.760f.: 'In practice all one can do is to make clear to oneself, on the basis of serious comparison, deliberation and absorption, the common thrust of these values, to enter into this thrust, and to think of particular values as approximations to an objective whose general direction is known even though its ultimate goal is not known. It is an act of the will – not an arbitrary whim but a fully considered decision – that dares to believe that the right path has been found. This act is indirectly confirmed by the possibility it affords of interpreting life by reference to this objective. The difficult problem of the absolute which is involved here – a problem which I have not ceased to think about since I wrote my book on the subject – cannot be further explicated here. But I believe that here also nothing is theoretically feasible beyond what is done in practice. Here the will that has become certain that its movement is correctly oriented decides by grasping what it recognises as the truth. It can present no further theoretical proof for the correctness of its material conviction. Such a proof – were it possible – would have been found long ago.'

[130] See below, p.163 for appreciation of how Luther intuited what was right. This interpenetration of correct historical and correct theological judgment is the crucial factor in this style of doing theology by interpreting and developing the tradition in the light of one's contemporary experience.

German idealists, particularly Schleiermacher and Fichte.[131] Whether or not one is persuaded by the epistemological argument for the existence of an ultimate value,[132] Troeltsch's historical interpretation and appropriation of the tradition in which he stands presents a clear model of how a theology rooted in critical historical study can proceed. It consists in a constant interaction between the tradition and contemporary experience. The tradition is studied historically and offers models and structures for interpreting experience; but at the same time it is subject to the critical judgment of the autonomous listener. It is impossible to say in advance whether the listener will be persuaded by a piece of tradition or will reject it critically. The truth and objectivity of the judgment to emerge from this confrontation of mind with history was underwritten for Troeltsch by his objective idealism. But he insisted against Hegel, that 'a goal for the world or for humanity cannot be metaphysically constructed and then applied to history; for truly, every such goal is always derived or abstracted from actual history'.[133] One begins by studying the history in its own terms and expects to find some help in establishing one's own norms for today. 'We impartially comprehend, survey, and compare these historical value constructs (of the past), and proceed to arrange them in a hierarchical order, which does not signify the coincidence of temporal sequence and level of value, but rather the construction of a standard that arises spontaneously from this comparison, and that carries personal conviction. This standard is found through taking from history the ideal contents of the values of life and energetically referring whatever attests itself to our judgment as important to the idea of ultimate values, in our own accustomed way.'[134] The value constructs of the past provide us with 'suggestive preliminary labours' from which we can learn as we make the decision or ethical act of uniting the realm of experience with that of necessary values and recognise a moral authority which claims us.

Whether or not the epistemological argument of Rickert and Troeltsch persuades us that 'the most intimate secret of the urge to know history is thus shown to be the relating of actual historical values to a value system that ought to be recognised as valid: this is the goal that necessitates mastering of the stream of diversity.',[135] it is surely true that we do in fact derive our values from critical reflexion upon history or the tradition in which we stand. We both question it

[131] *G.S.* II, pp.713f.
[132] *Ibid.*, pp.707f. See above, n.94.
[133] *Ibid.*, p.706.
[134] *Ibid.*, p.709.
[135] *Ibid.*, p.700.

and are called in question by it, and the fact that we can operate in this way will suggest to the idealist cast of mind that behind the veil of history stands something which is able to exercise a claim upon us. But Troeltsch's method is not restricted to idealists. Anyone who is convinced (and who is not?) that the tradition in which he stands contains valuable resources for ordering and interpreting his life, will proceed in the same way: ready to learn from the past, but also ready to criticise this tradition or develop it in new ways. It is only where Troeltsch attempts to give reasons for his results that the question must be asked whether his epistemological argument or his idealist metaphysics are persuasive. If they are not, it will still be necessary to proceed upon the lines he suggests – and to give as great weight as he does to the personal decision which can never be imposed upon another by external authority or decisive intellectual argument.

These two aspects of Troeltsch's proposals are clear in the following quotation: 'By entering into alien, or semi-alien, or past value constructions and exhibiting the geographical and historical relativity of our present value constructions, we find a constant corrective for our own value constructions; that is, we supplement and broaden our own being (which is inclined to become narrow) and we dissolve all naive attempts to isolate and absolutise that which is given. But this corrective, the need for which constantly drives us to history, would attain its ideal perfection only if it allowed us in a scholarly way to relate the abundance of historical value constructions to a system of values that ought to be recognised as valid.'[136]

Troeltsch himself did not remain satisfied with this attempt to unite the contingency and irrationality of history with the laws of consciousness and thus to establish normative values. Rickert's formalism seemed inadequate to the complexity of history, the further Troeltsch carried his historical studies. 'Geltungsphilosophie' provided a welcome liberation from a purely psychological approach to historical reality, but to transform reality into the product of the thinking subject is counter-intuitive. Troeltsch at once saw the need to supplement it with metaphysical considerations, and was soon to look for these upon lines suggested by Malebranche, Leibniz and Hegel.[137] The development of his thought in *Der Historismus und seine Probleme* (1922)[138] falls outside the scope of this volume, but it is worth noting its structural similarities with his earlier work. The problem itself has

[136] *Ibid.*, pp.700f.
[137] *G.S.* IV, p.10.
[138] *G.S.* III. For a recent discussion which shows how 'little had changed in Troeltsch's philosophy since his early writings', see G.G. Iggers, *The German Conception of History*, Connecticut, 1968, pp.174-95.

not changed, though the historical net with the help of which it is hoped to find valid norms for today is cast more deeply and less extensively: more deeply, as the connexions of any religion with its social context are better appreciated, and less extensively as attention is concentrated upon Western European culture. The 'cultural synthesis' towards which Troeltsch was working when he died was still to be based upon historical study of the tradition and the creative or 'axiomatic' act of decision with respect to it.[139]

The persuasiveness of Treoltsch's enterprise was widely assumed to have collapsed with the reaction against idealism within German protestant theology in the 1920s. But it is necessary to distinguish different elements in this reaction. Hostility to idealist metaphysics is an obvious feature of intellectual life in this century. Some of the objections raised against a metaphysics of history, however, do not affect Troeltsch. He was never an exponent of any form of evolutionary optimism, and was as aware as anyone of evil in history.[140] His position cannot be said to have been made implausible by the War, specifically. Mixed up with the new theology's rejection of idealist metaphysics was a far more questionable hostility to modern historical study and a refusal to allow history to provide the framework for theological thought. There were also elements of conservative or 'neo-orthodox' reaction to the entire liberal enterprise, which was at bottom a rejection rather than a correction of it.[141] On both counts it now appears that Troeltsch will be vindicated. Neither Barth's great alternative of a return to dogmatic method nor Bultmann's channelling historical work into a theology of existence, to name only the two most important of twentieth-century options, takes the modern secular world so seriously as Troeltsch did.

The effect of this new world's attitude to tradition upon a Christian's understanding of his faith received classical formulation here: 'I am convinced that biblical criticism, church history and the history of dogma have made their object so similar in all respects to other events that it could contain no miracle other than what is contained in all other events. It is the exclusiveness of Christian supernaturalism that I am combatting, because this exclusiveness is not demonstrable either on the basis of the inner experience of conversion or on the basis of the biblical traditions. But this exclusiveness is not merely incapable of proof; all history and

---

[139] *G.S.* III, pp.698, 771 etc.

[140] See below, p.189 and the notion of 'compromise' in the *Social Teachings*.

[141] The rejection of Troeltsch by the dialectical theology is a complex matter. See my essay 'Troeltsch and the Dialectical Theology' in the Lancaster colloquium volume, *Ernst Troeltsch and the Future of Theology*, ed. J.P. Clayton, London, 1976.

psychology contradict it. Thus my objections are not those of Spinoza and of the popular natural science of today but rather those of Hume and Kant. According to these, however, there are only universally scientific, rather than specifically theological, modes of understanding. The uniqueness of Christian theology lies, then, in the nature of its subject-matter, not in special methods of research and validation.'[142]

The succession to Schleiermacher, who denied that there is any specifically theological hermeneutics[143] is clear. The whole paragraph is an expression of liberal theology's critical edge which was more effective than its constructive proposals. The critique of supernaturalism is decisive. But the alternative of 'a religious orientation toward life apart from the church's miracle of redemption grounded in the saving death of Christ'[144] is clearer about what it denies than what it affirms. The main criticism to be levelled at liberal protestantism is not, *pace* Bultmann, 'that it has dealt not with God but with man'.[145] Barth could later acknowledge that the great idealists, whose metaphysics Troeltsch sought to revive, really still believed in God.[146] The problem of any idealist theology is rather the difficulty it experiences in giving account of the particularity of the Christian revelation. The weakness of liberal protestantism is its failure to associate its belief in God with its veneration for the historical Jesus in a manner which can claim adequate continuity with traditional christology and atonement theory. Symptomatic of this weakness is a tendency to allow legitimate criticism of the doctrinal tradition to pass into parody.[147]

One point in this collection at which this weakness in christology is evident is in the discussion of Hartmann.[148] Two separate issues, the centrality of christology for Christianity generally, and Hartmann's particular 'christology' are not kept apart. Troeltsch has no difficulty in arguing that 'christology interpreted as a mythical symbol of pessimistic pantheism' is simply not what the tradition means, and that it cannot claim any real continuity with it. Christology asserts the unity of the redeemer, not the creation, with God. Hartmann's

---

[142] *G.S.* II, p.766.

[143] F.D.E. Schleiermacher, *Hermeneutik*, ed. H. Kimmerle, Heidelberg, 1959, pp.15, 55.

[144] *G.S.* II, p.766.

[145] *Faith and Understanding*, London, 1969, p.29.

[146] *Church Dogmatics* II, 1, Edinburgh, 1957, p.73.

[147] See below, p.184. Some contemporary orthodox theology was that crude. Nevertheless, Schleiermacher's criticism of the two natures doctrine in *The Christian Faith* § 96 provides a better example of how doctrinal criticism should proceed.

[148] See below, pp.170-4 and 180f.

'suffering God and a painful world process' could perhaps have established rather stronger links with the tradition, but Hartmann does not explore these and Troeltsch can therefore disregard them. However, what must appear to most Christian theologians highly unsatisfactory is Troeltsch's own positive definition of the importance of christology as lying 'in the consolidation and justification of Jesus' authority and his position as an object of devotion in the cult, which in turn was and is only the presupposition and vehicle of what is really essential, namely the seizure of the living sin-forgiving and sanctifying Father in Christ' (below, p.173).

It is surely true that 'the relationship between faith and history can no longer be interpreted in the forms of incarnational christology, and that which can be experienced in the present has to be set above history. It is only for this reason that the old christology falls away and that the attempt is made to formulate the relationship to history anew' (pp.173f.). In a historically conscious age the relationship of faith and history certainly needs redefining. Christians today will understand the doctrine of the incarnation very differently from their predecessors. But that is not necessarily to reject it. Whatever his own errors, Hartmann scores a point in suggesting that 'the personality of Jesus, when freed from the christological myth, is grossly inadequate' (p.173) for a definition of Jesus' place in Christianity.

Troeltsch rightly pointed to the cult as providing grounds for 'the significance of the historical existence of Jesus for faith' (see below pp.182-207). But the worship that he could see was important for 'popular religion' played no significant part in his own 'religion of the educated'.[149] His lack of any inner relationship to sacramental worship precluded any recognition of the central place of the incarnation myth in Christianity. Other equally modern Christians would side with O.C. Quick and against Troeltsch in asserting that 'the sacramental outlook enables us to perceive how it is that both the philosopher and the historical critic are apt to miss the real point of the Christian faith'.[150] Of course the traditionalist must show that his own understanding of the incarnation and atonement, which should not be detatched from its ritual context, is compatible with what Troeltsch called 'the fundamental historicising of all our thought about man, his culture and values'.[151] In failing to attempt any such

[149] On this distinction, see especially the essay 'Religionsphilosophie', *op. cit.* 1st ed. pp.131f, 2nd ed., pp.451f.

[150] *The Christian Sacraments*, London, 1927, p.57. Quoted by M.F. Wiles, *The Remaking of Christian Doctrine*, London, 1974, p.82.

[151] *G.S.* III, p.102.

synthesis Troeltsch himself shared in the weakness as well as the very great strengths of liberal protestantism.

Anyone who criticises Troeltsch at this point is, of course, expressing a preference for an alternative theological position; one which values the classical Christian tradition of doctrine, ethics and spirituality more highly than Troeltsch did, or who considers that it is more viable in the modern world than Troeltsch believed. It is a matter of 'the extent to which one independently shapes continuity with the tradition or limits one's independence out of devotion to the tradition', (below p.170). Belief needs daring and much loyalty (below p.176). Troeltsch was more loyal to the tradition than Hartmann and more daring than Hengstenberg. Whether his 'liberal' theology with its weakened christology will support the traditional life of the church is a matter which Christian experience will decide. Troeltsch thought it would not, and therefore explored new forms of Christian community.[152] But what he said and did qualify him as a Christian theologian developing the tradition from the inside, despite the efforts of the more orthodox from Barth to Bodenstein, to deny him the name.[153]

It is clear from his doctrinal articles in *Religion in Geschichte und Gegenwart*[154] and elsewhere that Troeltsch's 'religious orientation toward life without the church's miracle of a redemption grounded in the saving death of Christ'[155] involves a massive critical reduction of the Christian tradition. But it would be inappropriate to catechise him on his lack of orthodoxy. Critical theology always involves reduction, and 'in the last analysis we are concerned not with Christianity but with the truth' (below p.175). This criterion demanded, in Troeltsch's opinion, one crucial concession to the intellectual world of modernity: 'At one point only is contact with today's scientific consciousness necessary and possible, namely with respect to the irrefutably given uniformity and homogeneity of human events. Herein lies the only contact with the scientific consciousness which I am demanding and, indeed, establishing.'[156] But that one

[152] See especially 'Schleiermacher und die Kirche' in F. Naumann (ed.) *Schleiermacher, der Philosoph des Glaubens*, Berlin, 1910.

[153] It is noteworthy that the hostility of W. Bodenstein's *Neige des Historismus* (Gütersloher Verlagshaus, Gerd Mohn, 1959) reaches a pitch in the discussion of the essay on the essence of Christianity concept, pp.95-8. See p.97: 'Troeltsch ist letzlich nicht Theologe, sondern indifferenter Kulturphilosoph, der am Christentum nur phänomenologisch interessiert ist.' A footnote cites E. Hirsch on what it really means to be a theologian.

[154] 1st ed., 1909-13.

[155] *G.S.* II, p.766.

[156] *Ibid.*, p.756.

point involved a revolution in theology, and the abandonment of any specifically theological method: 'There are only universally scientific, rather than specifically theological modes of understanding. The uniqueness of Christian theology lies, then, in the nature of its subject-matter, not in special methods of research and validation.'[157] The autonomy of post-Enlightenment thinking forces the church to abandon the external authority of dogma guaranteed by miracle. The only form of authority possible today is one which impresses itself upon our conscience – an inward certainty based upon experience. 'Here the will that has become certain that its movement is correctly oriented decides by grasping what it recognises as the truth. It can present no further theoretical proof for the correctness of its material conviction.'[158] Troeltsch does not deny the dangerous element of subjectivism inherent in his intuitional approach (below pp.166-9). A subjective element is inevitable in personal conviction, once unchangeable norms are no longer available. All that can be done is to keep it within limits. There is no criterion, given in advance, by which to decide whether or not a particular development maintains an adequate continuity with the tradition: 'It is precisely the living and creative characteristic of religion that its continuity asserts itself only in this continuous new formative process' (below p.170).

Troeltsch was convinced that his own 'free Christianity' was still Christian (below p.173). He was persuaded of 'the indestructibility and inner power of this orientation toward life', the content of which is God and the soul: 'All of our great idealist thinkers, with the exception of the radical pessimists, have felt and recognised that something absolutely indispensable to our existence inheres in this orientation. This is as true today as it was a hundred years ago. The old means of proof no longer exist, and with their passing the meaning of the Christian orientation toward life has changed. But the Christian orientation contains, today more than ever, a foundation of eternal youth that offers simplicity, health and strength to a generation languishing under capitalism, determinism, relativism and historicism.[159] Only we must attempt to reformulate this orientation, and to develop a new structure of support for it.'[160] This 'certainty with regard to the assertion of continuity can only be based on a conscientious, inward, personal conviction that one has taken up the

---

[157] *Ibid.*, p.766. See above, n.142.

[158] *Ibid.*, p.761.

[159] Troeltsch can use the word 'Historismus' in the negative sense of a destructive relativism, as here, as well as in the neutral descriptive sense of n.151 above.

[160] *G.S.* II, p.767.

genuine and real ideas of Christianity in one's conception of the essence and appropriated them and shaped them for the present time. He who finds this certainty confirmed in a continued more or less close relationship to the congregation, in his own religious life, in prayer and in moral activity, may be assured of the maintenance of continuity ... Christianity is affirmed when one has the Father of Jesus Christ present in one's daily struggles and labours, hopes and sufferings, when one is armed with the strength of the Christian spirit for the great decision in the world and for the victory of all the eternal, personal values of the soul ... ' (below p.170).[161]

4

Troeltsch's personal advocacy of his neo-protestant reformulation of Christianity demands that he be respected as a Christian theologian. Such respect will include assessment of his doctrinal conclusions. But he did not publish his lectures on *Glaubenslehre*,[162] and the weight of his publications suggests that he should be judged primarily on his attempt 'to develop a new structure of support' for his 'reformulation of the orientation' rather than as a doctrinal theologian.[163] Behind both doctrinal conclusions and 'structure of support' stands his conception of the theological task in the post-Enlightenment situation. 'Our central scientific interest will then shift to the philosophy of religion, with its definition – from the viewpoint of philosophy of history – of the nature (*Wesen*) and meaning of Christianity, and to general ethics, with its elaboration of man's final end (*Zweckbestimmung*), an end which can only be understood from a religious perspective. Dogmatics and moral theology thus become branches of practical theology in the narrow sense. In any event, this is how the total plan of my work is to be understood, and because its main points have already been sketched by our (German) idealist philosophy, I generally refer to it. I continue the approach, that prevailed before Hengstenberg and the Restauration.'[164]

That means above all Schleiermacher. It is Schleiermacher's conception of theology, sketched in the *Brief Outline on the Study of*

---

[161] Cf. also p.169 for Troeltsch's confidence that inner incompatibilities with the basic ideas of historical Christianity will soon be recognised as such and lead their adherents to withdraw from the Christian congregation.

[162] It was published in 1925, edited by Gertrud von Le Fort.

[163] His contribution as a doctrinal theologian, however, is beginning to be reassessed. See B.A. Gerrish and A.O. Dyson in *Ernst Troeltsch and the Future of Theology, op. cit.* There are plans afoot to translate the *Glaubenslehre*.

[164] *G.S.* II, p.767.

Theology[165] which Troeltsch took over with minor terminological alterations and referred to when he rendered to American readers his account of how theology should be done in a historically conscious ·age. In this essay, 'The Dogmatics of the "religionsgeschichtliche Schule" ' (1913) he insisted that there is, properly speaking, no history-of-religions *school*, but simply a *method* – the historical method applied consistently within the area of religion.[166] 'The movement signifies, in general, simply the recognition of the universally accepted scientific conclusion that human religion exists only in manifold specific religious cults which develop in very complex relations of mutual contact and influence, and that in this religious development it is impossible to make the older dogmatic distinction between a natural and a supernatural revelation.'[167]

In close adherence to Schleiermacher Troeltsch here distinguishes three[168] 'tasks of a dogmatics proceeding on the basis of the history of religions':[169] The first is 'to establish on the basis of a historical and philosophical comparison of religions the fundamental and universal supremacy of Christianity for our own culture and civilisation', measuring world religions 'by a standard which emerges in the course of this comparative study through the exercise of our own religious and ethical appreciation'.[170] This standard 'is not scientifically demonstrable as an objective reality, but neither is it any ready-made prejudice or irresponsible bit of arbitrariness. It is simply a decision which grows out of a sympathetic understanding of the facts brought out in this comparative study'.[171] Troeltsch's decision was in favour of prophetic-christian theism, and as a matter of 'developing our religious future' it was a *theological* activity, i.e. fundamental theology, the sphere in which the greater part of his work clearly belongs.[172]

---

[165] Eng.tr. by T.N. Tice, Richmond, 1966. The differences, however, should not be overlooked. Schleiermacher does not argue for the superiority of Christianity.

[166] *The American Journal of Theology*, XVII, Jan. 1913, p.4. S.W. Sykes has argued in *Ernst Troeltsch and the Future of Theology* (*op. cit.*) for a shift in Troeltsch's position in comparison with that of the essence of Christianity essay a decade earlier. See also below, pp.180f.

[167] *Op.cit.*, pp.180f.

[168] B. Reist, *Towards a Theology of Involvement* (London, 1966), pp.177f. takes Troeltsch's 'fourth aspect of the matter' as a 'fourth task', despite Troeltsch's comment (p.16) that it 'is not a specific task of this type of dogmatics, but throws light on the general character of the undertaking'.

[169] B.A. Gerrish (*op.cit.*) follows Schleiermacher in calling this 'historical theology' despite the common usage which distinguishes historical from systematic theology.

[170] 'The Dogmatics of the "religionsgeschichtliche Schule" ', p.10.

[171] *Ibid.*

[172] Troeltsch here refers in a footnote to his *Absoluteness* as an example of this.

The 'second fundamental enquiry and the second task of dogmatics' is concerned with the question, What *is* Christianity? It is the question of its ideal or *essence*, 'persisting in all specific manifestations', and 'the subject-matter and the normative principle of dogmatics'.[173] Like Schleiermacher, Hegel and Harnack, Troeltsch was prepared to offer his own thumbnail sketch: 'Christian religious faith is faith in the rebirth and elevation of man alienated from God, affected through the knowledge of God in Christ and resulting in his union with God and his fellow men, constituting the kingdom of God.'[174] As Troeltsch here observed, his 'historical writings have in general been devoted to the task of indicating this synthesis or of setting forth the various definitions of essential Christianity at different times'. Again, it is a *theological* task, because 'this essence is actually the subjective, personal interpretation and synthesis which present thinking derives from the entire situation with reference to actual living issues and for the purpose of directing future activity'.[175] But as in the first step the theological activity is based upon general scientific work, in this case history.

Thirdly, there follows 'the exposition of the content of this essential Christianity, the development of the specific conceptions implied in Christianity concerning God, the world, man, redemption (spiritual elevation), social communion (the kingdom of God), hope (eternal life),[176] i.e. church dogmatics, or, better, *Glaubenslehre* – 'since it does not set forth permanent and unchangeable truths ... this title would clearly indicate the confessional and subjective character of the undertaking'.[177]

Dogmatics is '*the exposition of a normative Christian religious system*'.[178] A dogmatics written on history of religions principles, a historically conscious dogmatics, or 'historical theology' will involve these three parts. Troeltsch's duties as a professor of systematic theology led to his giving lectures on the third part, but it is clear from his published work as well as his non-publication of the *Glaubenslehre* that he saw his own vocation to lie in the first two rather than the third, the 'scientific' rather than the 'church' area of theology. Both tasks of scientific theology themselves involved the adoption of a personal stance, but they were rooted in historical and philosophical study as practised outside Christian theology, and could make a claim to truth that was

[173] *Ibid.*, p.12.
[174] *Ibid.*, p.13, retranslating the German given in a footnote.
[175] *Ibid.*
[176] *Ibid.*
[177] *Ibid.*, p.17.
[178] *Ibid.*, p.6.

independent of any claim to revelation. *Glaubenslehre*, on the other hand, had no such intellectual status. It was necessary for the church, the most important task of practical theology; and it required some intellectual skill in its exponents. But it is not itself 'an essentially scientific discipline'; it has a practical purpose.

It is in this light that Troeltsch understood Schleiermacher's doctrinal classic, *The Christian Faith*. He thought it stood in some tension to Schleiermacher's basic outlook in philosophy of religion and philosophy of history and could only be understood as 'a systematising and classical formulation of the rhetorical and dogmatic means of expressing religious feeling, for the technical needs of the preacher ... [It] fixes no dogma but is simply a handbook for preaching, a systematic arrangement of the means of expression which have proceeded and still do proceed from the ground of life they all share, the religious power which flows from Christ. This is why it is only intended to serve the church's needs at a particular moment ... '[179]

Troeltsch distinguishes rather sharply between the more conventional church theologian who composed *The Christian Faith*, and the philosopher of religion and of history from whom Troeltsch derived his own programme. The transition is epitomised in the shift from the philosophical ethics (*Ethik*) to Christian morality (*Die christliche Sitte*). The former elaborates man's final end from a religious perspective, whereas the latter is a branch of practical theology and not Troeltsch's particular concern.

The sharp distinction between 'scientific' and practical or 'church' theology, is discussed in the essay 'Half a Century of Theology: a Review' (1908) – (below, p.56f). It had been given prominence by C.A. Bernoulli in a book entitled *Die wissenschaftliche und die kirchliche Methode in der Theologie* (1897). The real contrast, Troeltsch insisted in his review article,[180] was between historical method and the old supernaturalism. Bernoulli associated the 'church' method with Schleiermacher, and contrasted it sharply with the scientific method, which owed most to Hegel. Troeltsch was sympathetic to the author's thesis, but understood 'church' to refer not to the practical interest as such (which he shared) but to the pre-Enlightenment view of the church as a divine institution containing supernaturally guaranteed doctrinal truth. Schleiermacher only shared it to the extent that his christology contained a remnant of supernaturalism.[181] He did not

[179] 'Schleiermacher und die Kirche', *op.cit.*, pp.27f.
[180] *Göttinger Gelehrte Anzeige*, June, 1898, pp.425-35.
[181] *Ibid.*, p.428.

carry out his own programme consistently but accommodated his theology to the tradition, and this is most clearly visible in his christology. Troeltsch associated himself with the criticisms made of this by Baur[182] and Strauss,[183] from a more consistently historical standpoint.

Granted the difficulties inherent in Schleiermacher's attempt to unite the historical and the ideal in Christ, it is far from clear that Troeltsch was right to assume that the only possible way forward was to break with the traditional Christian confession of Jesus as God. 'It is immediately evident', writes Troeltsch, that a historical critical point of view brings the personalities and the facts of the biblical history, particularly the person of Jesus, into the relativity of historical events and into the uncertainties attached to tradition. Tradition thus cannot be the specific and immediate object of faith, as was the case in the absence of historical – critical scholarship. Then Jesus was identified with God in order that he might be an immediate object of faith. Critical procedure, on the contrary, means that the God of Jesus is the object of faith and Jesus himself is transformed into the historical mediator and revealer. This consequence, from the very beginning, emerged as the inevitable correlative of historical criticism. Through the *religionsgeschichtliche* broadening of the historical-critical method it has been extraordinarily reinforced. Under these circumstances dogmatics has the task of setting forth the Christian faith in God, or in other words the conceptions involved in essential Christianity in complete self-dependence without any intermingling of historical elements. It sets forth our faith in God as something existing in present experience and renewing itself with each individual in the experience of redemption.'[184]

Troeltsch recognised that from the beginnings it has been belief in Christ which has made of Christianity an independent religion, and that within the church this has remained the centre both of dogma and cult.[185] He insisted 'that there is no other way to hold together the Christian community of spirit than through the common confession of Jesus, that it is impossible to keep alive the distinctively Christian idea of God apart from seeing its life-giving embodiment in Jesus, and that all the greatest and most characteristic ideas of Christianity – the idea of a grace that grasps and conquers us, of a certitude available to us,

---

[182] *Kirchengeschichte des neunzehnten Jahrhunderts*, Tübingen, 1862 (rp. Stuttgart, 1970) pp.183f.

[183] *Der Christus des Glaubens und der Jesus der Geschichte*, Berlin, 1865, Eng.tr. forthcoming.

[184] 'The Dogmatics of the "religionsgeschichtliche Schule" ', *op.cit.*, p.14.

[185] 'Schleiermacher und die Kirche', *op.cit.*, p.28.

and of a superior power (*Kraft*) that elevates and overcomes us –
depend on a religious appreciation and interpretation of Jesus as
divine revelation. To separate the Christian belief in God in every
respect from the person of Jesus would mean to cut this belief off from
all its historic roots, from every means of expounding and illustrating
it, from any greatness exceeding the measure of the average
individual, and thus ultimately to dissolve the belief itself.'[186] Jesus is
the focus of Christian piety and cult, but he is this as a dead man, the
founder prophet whose memory is revered and whose influence is still
felt, not as one who is ontologically one with God. In the *Glaubenslehre*,
christology ('Jesus Christ as object of faith') is strikingly prominent;
it even precedes 'the Christian concept of God'. But this centrality and
importance of Jesus for faith, 'the connexion of faith to history, must
be understood purely in psychological terms' (p.84). The religious
interpretation of Jesus is no different in kind from the religious
interpretations of the history of Israel and the church.

The patristic, immanent Trinity is discarded. An economic trinity
remains, simply as a formula for connecting the historical and the
religious in Christianity. It is not part of the Christian doctrine of
God. Jesus is a living and effective symbol of faith, the central and
fundamental revelational personality, redeemer in the sense of model
and authority for redeeming certainty of faith, the revealer – but not
himself God. The most important question at issue between liberal
protestantism and classical Christian orthodoxy is whether or not the
admittedly historically conditioned doctrinal interpretation of Jesus
as 'of one substance with the Father', must now, in the light of our
modern historical thinking about Christianity, be rejected.[187]

Troeltsch believed passionately in God, and in the significance of
Jesus of Nazareth, and wished to hold the two together. 'Christian
theism and personalism, Christian belief in an elevation and
redemption to a higher kind of humanity born of God, may indeed be
linked to a religious appreciation and interpretation of Jesus' person.'
But this is 'in no way any longer the christological dogma of the
church'.[188] Troeltsch saw no conceptual possibility, within a modern
historical view of reality, of fusing belief in God with the traditional
theological evaluation of Jesus – which is what the doctrines of the
essential Trinity and the Incarnation are about. A modern Christian

---

[186] 'On the Possibility of a Liberal Christianity' (1910), Eng.tr. in *The Unitarian
Universalist Christian*, 29, 1974, p.30.
[187] On Troeltsch's distance from orthodoxy, marked by his inability to go beyond a
psychological interpretation of the significance of Jesus, see *Glaubenslehre*, p.117.
[188] 'On the Possibility', *op.cit.*, p.32.

must therefore discard these doctrines, together with traditional views of the atonement and the sacraments.

Troeltsch was aware of the magnitude of his break with orthodox Christianity. He also recognised that it was an open question whether the new version of Christianity would be able for long to support a specifically Christian faith and life – 'the fundamental question whether a Christianity thus based on new foundations and presuppositions is at all inherently viable or not ... or whether it is merely the last echo of a disintegrating Christian piety'.[189] For most of his life he was optimistic about the chances of neo-protestantism being able to mediate what was true and valuable in Christianity for the modern world, and thus combat the great cultural crisis confronting Western civilisation. He was also convinced that the new version of Christianity, while abandoning the traditional christology, retained 'the innermost motif of that dogma', which he defined as 'the Christ-mysticism of an inner bond by which the community is united with the head, from whom the members derive life and strength and whose representation as the revelation and symbol of God constitutes the chief element of a properly Christian cultus'.[190]

In a sympathetic account of 'Troeltsch's Conception of the Significance of Jesus' G.E. Wolfe attempted 'to show that the Christ-mysticism advocated by Troeltsch is *in essence* the same as that of Paul and John; that, at all events, it commends itself as quite adequate for the maintenance of the Christian faith and life'.[191] Whether it is in fact adequate for this is not necessarily the same question as that concerning the relationship of Troeltsch's position to that of Paul and John, though it is a relevant criterion for judging Troeltsch's claim to be maintaining an adequate continuity with them. The discontinuity with Paul and John is more striking than the continuity. Troeltsch cannot share the Nicene Creed's ontological seriousness about the early church's 'identification of Jesus with God'. The reason he gives, that 'tradition cannot be the specific and immediate object of faith', though true in itself, does not justify the break. Of course the relationship between tradition and revelation is irreversibly transformed in a historically conscious age. But the pre-critical identification of these, which Troeltsch rightly rejects, need not be replaced by the Enlightenment's sharp separation in which the historical can serve only for illustration and can never become an eternal truth. Troeltsch's 'Jesus as symbol and rallying-point' is not God, and his identification with the historical Jesus is at most a

[189] *Ibid.*, p.27.
[190] *Ibid.*, p.32.
[191] *American Journal of Theology*, XX (1916), pp.179-204. See p.202.

practical necessity.[192] The reason is plainly that the only theological ontology which he could offer was a religious metaphysics in which a historical figure could not possibly be called God.

The road taken by Troeltsch remains the most natural road for anyone whose introduction to theology is dominated by the modern historical study of early Christianity. That is what gives him such paradigmatic significance. Anyone who finds the resultant break with Christian orthodoxy intolerable will be compelled to retread the liberals' path. Is it indeed impossible in a historically conscious age to think through Christian belief in God in the closest possible connexion with a more traditional evaluation of the person of Jesus? It is in this context that Karl Barth's massive attempt to overcome the dualism between time and eternity presupposed by nineteenth-century liberalism can be fully appreciated.[193] If Barth's enterprise fails to avoid the sands charted by Troeltsch, the question remains for systematic theology today, how to do justice to the truth perceived by both these giants.

5

Troeltsch's inadequate christology was the one legitimate cause the dialectical theologians had for rejecting him.[194] His chief claim upon our attention resides not in the substance of his doctrinal position, but in his method for doing theology in a historically conscious age – which means within the context of the history and scientific study of religions and religion. His readiness to express a personal theological position, and his 'scientific' or intellectual endeavour to 'develop a new structure of support' for this in a science of religion which could be generally accepted as a road to truth regardless of particular religious beliefs, have been discussed. It is now necessary to consider the importance, both for Christian theology in a historically conscious age and for the study of religion, of his account of the way in which believers do in fact interpret and develop their tradition. This corresponds to the 'second task of dogmatics' outlined in 'The Dogmatics of the "religionsgeschichtliche Schule" ', and is the theme of the essay on the notion 'essence of Christianity' (below p.124-79).

[192] See B.A. Gerrish, 'Jesus, Myth and History: Troeltsch's stand in the "Christ-Myth" debate'. *Journal of Religion*, 55, (1975), pp.13-35.

[193] The fruitfulness of considering Barth in this light (and thus indirectly as an attempt to answer Troeltsch) has been shown by R.H. Roberts, *Eternity and Time in the Theology of Karl Barth* (Ph.D. Diss. Edinburgh, 1975).

[194] See my argument in *Ernst Troeltsch and the Future of Theology*, ed. J.P. Clayton, London, 1976.

It may be described as the central core of theological work in an age
when there is no longer a specifically Christian theological method,
but only a specific subject-matter – the Christian tradition. What
Troeltsch sketches out here is not especially dependent upon his debt
to Rickert. He actually mentions the concept 'the essence of
Christianity' and its similarity to Weber's 'ideal types' and
Burckhardt's universal historical concepts, in the context of criticising
Rickert's deficiencies.[195] Neither is it dependent upon Troeltsch's
metaphysics of spirit according to which 'history is ceaselessly striving
to realise values which have an objective, inner necessity' (below
p.143).[196] The more he emphasises the uncertainty, and the decisive
character of the intuitive act of faith involved in binding oneself by a
deliberate act of self-commitment to the truth and values which have
power to hold us, the further he is moving from a Hegelian type of
necessary correlation between mind and reality to an authentically
Reformation view in which only God can give any guarantee of the
rightness of our decision, and where that guarantee is beyond our
sight.

   Troeltsch's account of the way in which a believer may interpret his
tradition in the light of his contemporary experience (including the
view of rationality which he accepts) then looks very similar to what
several kerygmatic theologians practise. The main difference is that
Troeltsch makes no pretence of restricting himself to a set of canonical
documents (below p.146). The tradition as a whole is to be
interpreted, though as for Schleiermacher (*Brief Outline*, § 69-105),
within the tradition, beginnings, or the 'classical period' do have a
special status (p.147). Above all, since tradition is, to post-
Enlightenment man, *only* tradition and never to be identified with
revelation, any part of the tradition is open to *criticism*. This last point
is especially important and receives illuminating treatment in a
section on 'the essence as criticism' (pp.137-45). Troeltsch recognises
his affinity with the Reformers who 'acted with an instinctive
appreciation of what was historically essential and what was
demanded of the present' (p.163). It now appears absurd to suggest
that such criticism 'is only possible for Protestantism, which is based
precisely upon the principle that personal insight into what is
essential in Christianity is able to evaluate selectively the mass of
actual historical manifestations' (p.145). But Troeltsch can certainly
claim that 'the presupposition that there is a right to criticise the
historical development' is one 'which has flourished on Protestant soil'

[195] *G.S.* II, p.723.
[196] Cf. *G.S.* II, p.764: 'An active presence of the absolute spirit in the realm of the
finite ... '.

(p.167). The explicit application of such criticism within the biblical part of the tradition is largely the result of the Enlightenment, though it is adumbrated in Luther's canon criticism. Troeltsch calls his critical interpretation of the tradition 'immanent criticism' or 'criticism of historical formations in terms of the ideal which lies within their main driving force' (p.142). 'The historical is measured by the historical, the individual formation is measured against the spirit of the whole conceived intuitively and imaginatively' (p.142). This is what, in a different idiom, Bultmann calls *Sachkritik*.[197] The main difference is that whereas Bultmann fails adequately to distinguish between a purely historical and a theological *Sachkritik*.[198] Troeltsch avoids that mistake by distinguishing the purely historical from the 'dogmatic, normative concept of the essence' (pp.177-9).

The main problem confronting any theologian who refuses to absolutise any part of his tradition, is to establish the grounds on which he may criticise it. At the theoretical level Troeltsch's answer perhaps says all that can be said. In practice, however, it is difficult to strike a balance between criticising the tradition and allowing the tradition to call contemporary assumptions into question, or between freedom with respect to the tradition, and submission to its authority. How far can Troeltsch be said to acknowledge the authority of specifically Christian claims? It was one of Barth's main objections to 'culture protestantism' that it failed to bring the critical edge of the Gospel into play against a civilisation ripe for judgment.[199]

This criticism in fact touches Troeltsch less than most of his contemporaries.[200] He insisted that 'the greatness of religion consists precisely in its opposition to culture, in its difference from science and utilitarian social ethics, its proclaiming supramundane and suprahuman powers, its unfolding of the imagination and pointing to what lies beyond the world of sense. A religion reconciled with culture is usually nothing but bad science and superficial morals; it has lost its religious salt'.[201] Nevertheless, it is difficult to find in Troeltsch's

---

[197] Variously translated content criticism, material criticism of the content, objective criticism, theological criticism, doctrinal criticism, critical interpretation, critical study of the content.

[198] I have discussed this in *The Nature of New Testament Theology*, London, 1973, pp.42-52.

[199] E.g. 'Evangelical Theology in the Nineteenth Century' in *The Humanity of God*, London, 1967, p.12.

[200] Contrary to the impression given by Barth (see preceding note) Troeltsch was not one of the ninety-three intellectuals who supported the Kaiser's war policy.

[201] *G.S.* II, p.100. See also B.A. Gerrish, 'The Possibility of a Historical Theology: An Appraisal of Troeltsch's *Glaubenslehre*' in J.P. Clayton (ed.) *Ernst Troeltsch and the Future of Theology*, London, 1976.

work a satisfactory explanation of why or how religion can stand out against contemporary fashions or proclaim God's judgment. It requires a more real Lord than Troeltsch can offer to say, 'Thus saith the Lord'. A more substantial christology is apparently needed to sustain these typical religious attitudes within Christianity. The critical distance between the Gospel and the world is likely to be lost if 'belief in Christ and the idea of the church (which) from the start have been the basic Christian doctrines and require each other'[202] – are reduced to psychological and sociological necessities. It is above all through the christological definition, reflecting the church's distinctive faith in a Lord who is more real than Troeltsch can allow, that Christianity resists dissolution into its cultural context, and may call into question the civilisation of which believers are themselves a part.[203] This christology, that calls Jesus God, cannot be apologetically grounded. It is axiomatic for orthodox Christianity, and provided that it is possible to make sense of it, may remain so. It is not necessary to abandon it, out of respect for a metaphysics which cannot make sense of it.

Troeltsch, however, did abandon it, so far as scientific theology is concerned, because he built his own dogmatics upon an apologetic that proceeded from historical and scientific data, instead of starting with the Church's faith. It was then natural for him to define the historical starting-point more broadly, and instead of investigating the Christian tradition, to consider the whole of Western culture. His awareness of Christianity's fusion with its social contexts led him to see Western civilisation as his subject-matter. The perspective was no longer that of the 'essence of Christianity' essay, and Troeltsch's subsequent development raises the question whether the theological method adumbrated there must be abandoned when one accepts Troeltsch's more mature view of the complexity of Christian history.

Troeltsch was right to insist upon the extent to which all forms of Christianity are culturally conditioned. This is nowhere more obvious than in the history of Christian social ethics. There can be no evading Troeltsch's broadening of the historical perspective, and it certainly complicates the already complex task of interpreting a tradition. Further variables are introduced. But Troeltsch's development of Schleiermacher's account of how to do theology in a historically

---

[202] 'Schleiermacher und die Kirche', p.28. Troeltsch rightly adds that this correlation is 'a clear sign that the purely dogmatic element can never be independent of the sociological element'.

[203] The Barmen declaration is an example of christology providing a sticking-point for the Church.

conscious age remains the most obvious way forward. The historically given, and exceedingly complex, Christian tradition has to be interpreted ever anew in the light of contemporary rationality and experience. The tradition may, for particular purposes, be defined even more broadly, to provide a framework for discussion with other religions and ideologies. In principle God-talk must embrace the whole of reality. The method remains the same: Historical study leading to evaluative judgments in which norms are sought from within history itself.

This approach to theology is the natural one for those whose training has, following Schleiermacher's precept, been dominated by historical study. Troeltsch's formal delineation of method in theology has proved more permanent than his more frequently discussed attempts to provide a modern substitute for the old natural theology. Theologians must always be in dialogue with the philosophy of their time. As the climate changes, particular attempts at mediation soon appear dated; Troeltsch was aware of the relativity of his own efforts. But his aims and methods have survived wherever critical history is taken with full seriousness. Our only question is whether this historical approach to theology does not require a stronger christological anchor, if the distinctiveness of Christianity and an adequate continuity with past interpretations of the tradition are to be maintained. Troeltsch's conviction was that the traditional affirmation of the divinity of Jesus Christ as the second person of the immanent or essential Trinity is incompatible with a historical method and world view. That is open to question. If this conclusion can be resisted, Troeltsch's method can be carried even further than he himself took it without the cessation of a specifically Christian theology.

6

The prerequisite for interpreting the Christian tradition and working out a new account of Christianity's essence was further immersion in historical work. This Troeltsch undertook, notably in *Protestant Christianity and Church* (1906)[204] and *The Social Teachings of the Christian Churches* (1911).[205] A lecture on 'The Significance of Protestantism for the Emergence of the Modern World' (1906) later enlarged and

---

[204] *Protestantisches Christentum und Kirche in der Neuzeit* (in: *Die Kultur der Gegenwart*, I, IV, 2nd ed. 1909).

[205] *G.S.* I, Tübingen. Baron's bibliography in *G.S.* IV dates it 1912. Eng.tr. by Olive Wyon, London and New York, 1931. Reprint: New York, 1960.

published in English under the title *Protestantism and Progress* (1912)[206] and also *Augustin, die christliche Antike und das Mittelalter* (1915)[207] may be grouped with these two major works of 'the most eminent sociologically oriented historian of Western Christianity'.[208]

It is clear from the earlier large work that although Troeltsch argued (below, p.177) for a stricter separation of historical and meta-historical concerns than Harnack had achieved, the writing of history was always a matter of achieving clarification on the problems of the present. This involved for him understanding and justifying the deep cleavage between the Reformation and modern protestantism. The medieval elements in the Reformation were therefore emphasised: 'Luther read in Paul only answers to catholic problems, to the question about the certainty of salvation.'[209] He adopted the catholic scheme but gave it new content: Grace remains central, but is now subjectively appropriated by faith; the formation of a Christian culture which embraces all life is still the ideal, but is achieved by a different ethic; the concepts of the church as an objective institution of salvation possessing absolute truth, and of authority, remain in force – though now it is a state church, and authority is bound to the Bible. For two centuries, therefore, the middle ages experienced a second blossoming within protestantism.[210] This is not to deny the existence of 'modern elements in protestantism' – especially the dissolution of the sacramental idea and the rise of religious subjectivism. But it required the external onslaught of modern secular culture to effect the transition to neo-protestantism.

Troeltsch's own deep sense of the tension and even opposition between religion and church was powerfully expressed as early as 1895.[211] It here recurs as 'the conclusion: protestantism's insight into an inner antinomy between religion and church; they cannot dispense with but neither can they endure each other. All that can be learned from this conflict is to make present again and again the pure Christian idea which is independent of any church, and so keep the

---

[206] *Die Bedeutung des Protestantismus für die Entstehung der modernen Welt*, Eng.tr. of second (1911) edition by W. Montgomery, London and New York. Reprint: Boston, 1958.

[207] Troeltsch considered this monograph 'a very important supplement (to the *Social Teachings*) and close to my heart. New studies on the history of medieval thought should really proceed from here', *G.S.* IV, p.12.

[208] This dictum of Talcott Parsons is quoted by J.L. Adams, 'Why the Troeltsch Revival?' *The Unitarian Universalist Christian*, vol.29 (1974), p.15. See also *JSSR* I (1961), p.103.

[209] *Protestantisches Christentum*, p.258.

[210] *Ibid.*, p.265.

[211] 'Religion und Kirche', *G.S.* II, pp.146-82.

life of the fellowship pure from the dangers of ecclesiasticism'.[212] That is all that can be done to avoid the dangers inherent in the church idea. There is no possibility of avoiding some form of church organisation and cult, if religion is to be effective.

The great variety evident in the history of Christianity is justified in Hegelian fashion: 'The idea must, as Hegel says, be allowed to underlie the different media of representation in pictorial form and it must possess an inner movement that enables it to give different answers to the problems of different ages, different peoples, strata of society and individuals, while at the same time preserving the unity of the spirit. But this means a complete change in the concepts of truth and revelation within protestantism. Modern protestantism no longer believes in the idea of revelation as held in early protestantism and catholicism (these differ only in content). It believes in the elevation, deepening, purification and empowering of human life through the personal powers which proceed from Jesus. It can therefore tolerate different churches alongside one another, and in each church it rebels against official doctrine. This is why the real life of protestantism is to be found outside the church, even though the church itself is acknowledged to be valuable and indispensable.'[213] It is the disciple of Richard Rothe[214] as much as the social historian of protestantism who is speaking here.

Troeltsch was able to contemplate with equanimity drastic changes in Christianity both at the level of organisation and of dogma. He recognised that religious beliefs are temporally, and to a large extent sociologically, conditioned. A revolution in Western culture was bound to affect the form of Christianity, and this would be reflected at the level of belief. The main importance of this history of protestantism is the emergence of a 'history of culture' approach to Christianity. It had already been adumbrated in 'Die kulturgeschichtliche Methode in der Dogmengeschichte: Die Bedeutung der *lex naturae* für Katholizismus und Reformation' (1901),[215] and it reached its full fruition in *The Social Teachings of the*

---

[212] *Protestantisches Christentum*, p.397.

[213] *Ibid.*, p.398.

[214] See Troeltsch's Heidelberg memorial lecture: 'Richard Rothe', (Tübingen, 1899).

[215] *G.S.* IV, p.739-52. This is a review of E. Seeberg, *Lehrbuch der Dogmengeschichte* II. In an essay on 'The theological and religious situation of the present' (1903) Troeltsch wrote that Harnack's *History of Dogma* 'has hardly said the last word. The more one searches in the history of religions for religion itself and practical achievement, and the more one sees dogma and apologetics as only the reflexions of the actual ground swell, the more the history of Christianity is drawn into the

Christian Churches and Groups. Although the influence of Max Weber should not be exaggerated,[216] the broadening of Troeltsch's historical perspective in the light of his friend's sociological theory is a mark which distinguishes this latter work. Whereas the sects had received only a brief mention in 'Religion und Kirche' (1895)[217] they are now recognised to represent a form of Christianity which deserves to be studied in its own right.

Max Weber had in 1897 moved to Heidelberg from Freiburg where he had had close connexions with Rickert and the Baden neo-Kantianism. From 1898 to 1902 he was a sick man, but in 1904 he was able to accept an invitation to the St. Louis congress, and he and Troeltsch made the American trip together.[218] The relationship developed and led to their taking flats in the same house in 1909. A break between them occurred in 1914 over a clash of opinion arising from their para-military duties.

Weber's most famous work, *The Protestant Ethic and the Spirit of Capitalism,* was published in 1904-5, and his shorter essay 'The Protestant Sects and the Spirit of Capitalism' in 1906. Troeltsch's *Social Teachings* began to appear in 1908 and was complete in 1911. In his autobiographical sketch he explains how he came to see the problem of intellectual history in a quite different way, and became immersed in sociological studies: 'The whole range of ideas in the philosophy of history and theory of development had to date been treated one-sidedly as history of ideas, as with Hegel and Dilthey. It had to play a large part in every philosophy of religion. Now it was changing. New problems emerged out of all the existing solutions. At the same time I came under the spell of that overwhelming personality Max Weber who had long been well aware of these wonders which for me were just

surrounding history of religion and into the general history of culture. This then involves our knowledge of the social movements' *G.S.* II, pp.17f.

[216] While acknowledging the importance for Troeltsch of Weber's Church-sect dichotomy as an analytic tool J. Milton Yinger adds: 'For the most part, however, Troeltsch is not concerned, as is Weber, with the development of a scientific methodology for the investigation of stated hypotheses. The importance of his work rests, rather, upon the exhaustive treatment that he has made of the complex history of Christianity – a complete and penetrating "intellectual history" which interprets the development of the church in terms of its total cultural setting'. 'The Sociology of Religion of Ernst Troeltsch' in: H.E. Barnes (ed.) *An Introduction to the History of Sociology,* abridged edition, Chicago, 1966, p.312).

[217] Two footnotes to the republication of this essay in *G.S.* II (1913) (pp.146 and 171) insist that it requires supplementing with the results of the *Social Teachings* where 'I have in the meantime learned to reckon far more highly the significance of these other groups. Official theology thinks in a much too restricted manner in terms of the churches alone'. The omission of 'and Groups' in the English translation is unfortunate.

dawning. And at this point I was captivated by the Marxist doctrine of infrastructures and superstructures. Not that I simply considered it correct, but it does contain a mode of questioning which can never be evaded, even though each separate case must be examined individually. Its mode of questioning was how far the origin, development, change and modern plight of Christianity is sociologically conditioned, and how far it itself operates as a formative sociological principle. These are extraordinarily difficult questions and scarcely any useful preparatory studies had been done on them. And yet it was no longer possible to speak of a purely history of doctrine or history of ideas approach to Christianity, once this problem had been grasped.'[219]

The *Social Teachings* grew from an attempt to review an unsatisfactory book which revealed the sorry state of the subject. The result was 'a history of Christian church culture, a full parallel to Harnack's *History of Dogma*, in which all religious, dogmatic and theological issues are considered only as the basis of their effects in social ethics or as a mirror and reflex of the sociological contexts, varying in intensity according to the period. In order to limit a theme that was all too large, I was content to throw light upon these ideas which emerge simply from the social teachings of the churches and sects, i.e. their ethics and social theories. More exact research on the real practical conditions was beyond my powers, given the scope of the whole. The work revealed the pressure which the original utopian and eschatological ideal exerts like some powerful welling spring upon the layer of rock above it. It showed, too, the dead weight of non-religious factors, the compromises, new revolutions, deviations and finally the crippling of the Christian church culture with the implementation of modern political, economic and social conditions'.[220]

Troeltsch was in retrospect aware of the book's deficiencies: 'Above all, there is no independent chapter on Anglicanism. But what had been gained was a truer picture of the historical reality than either the church supernatural or the modern history of ideas accounts were able to give.'[221] The merits of the *Social Teachings*, the importance of the church-sect-mysticism typology, the debt to Weber from whom the notion of Calvinism's 'inner-worldly asceticism' is learned, are

[218] See his obituary essay, 'Max Weber' (1920), reprinted in *Deutsche Geist und Westeuropa* (Tübingen, 1925).
[219] *G.S.* IV, p.11.
[220] *Ibid.*, pp.11f.
[221] *Ibid.*, p.12.

well-known and require no further introduction.[222] It 'is a great pioneer work. If it is at many points inadequate, the reason is frequently that it has itself inspired many other superseding studies'.[223]

But what did it mean for Troeltsch himself? 'With all this I had clearly somewhat outgrown the theological faculty' and its practical tasks of educating clergy and teachers.[224] This introduction can break off at this point – but not because 'the *Social Teachings* represent Troeltsch's taking leave of theology altogether. He had as a theologian nothing more to say'.[225] That judgment was common throughout the ascendancy of the dialectical theology in Germany.[226] It does not correspond with Troeltsch's wider view of theology and its concern with the whole of reality.[227] Neither his acceptance of an additional teaching commission for philosophy at Heidelberg in 1910, nor his move to a personal chair in philosophy in Berlin in 1915[228] were understood by him to imply a desertion of theology and religion. The need to defend German culture during the war and the desperate need for social and intellectual reconstruction afterwards explain the direction of his political writings after 1914.[229] His more important work on the philosophy of history and culture stands in a direct relation to his earlier theological work, as has already been noted. He commented that his 'studies in the theory of history' were 'thoroughly in the direction of my most original interests. My philosophy of religion required above all clarification of the question about the essence and criteria for judging the development of the history of religion. The attempt actually to carry this idea out in a particular stretch of history brought me into the midst of a host of sociological

---

[222] B. Reist (*op.cit.*) discusses its methodology, the two protestantisms, church and sect, and the notion of 'compromise'. R.H. Bainton, 'Ernst Troeltsch – Thirty Years Later', *Theology Today*, 8 (1951), pp.70-96, provides an excellent critical discussion of the substantive historical judgments the work contains.

[223] R.H. Bainton, (*op.cit.*), p.96.

[224] *G.S.* IV, p.12.

[225] W. Bodenstein (*op.cit.*), p.122.

[226] See below, pp.212f, and 'Troeltsch and the Dialectical Theology' (*op.cit.*).

[227] Cf. *G.S.* II, p.227.n.

[228] On the refusal of conservative churchmen to allow him into the theological faculty see U. Pretzel, 'E. Troeltschs Berufung an die Berliner Universität' in *Studium Berolinense* (Berlin, 1960), pp.507-14.

[229] See especially, 'Das Wesen des Deutschen' (1914), 'Der Geist der deutschen Kultur' (1915), 'Deutsche Zukunft' (1916), etc. The more permanent of Troeltsch's contributions were collected in *Deutsche Geist und Westeuropa* (1925). After the war his most important political comment was contained in his *Spektator-Briefe* (1918-22), published as a collection in 1924.

problems. And when accordingly one proceeded beyond the religious realm into the whole of culture, I only then saw, just as Schleiermacher once did, how clearly I was dependent upon the close connexion of philosophy of history with ethics. From all these points there emerged before me, as the essential problem of my present situation, the theoretical and philosophical side of history, its relationship on the one hand to professional empirical research and on the other to a theory of cultural values or ethics. It is the problem that I had already raised in several essays of my Volume II (*Gesammelte Schriften* II) and begun to answer, at this point in complete union with Schleiermacher'.[230]

It is possible to see in *Der Historismus und seine Probleme*[231] 'a secularised form of the theology of his preceding period',[232] or, in Troeltsch's words, 'the old problem of absoluteness taken up on a much broader scale and tending towards a totality of cultural values, not just one's religious position'.[233]

It is not necessary to conclude that 'the idea of the cultural synthesis represents the self-dissolution of Troeltsch's thought'.[234] However little sympathy one may have for the notion of 'Europeanism' – and Troeltsch's concept was less parochial than it sounds[235] – it remains true that one has to formulate values and ideals for the present on the basis of studying the past. If the truth and value contained in one's tradition cannot fully be metaphysically undergirded, they can be affirmed on the basis of a historical and comparative study that poses a challenge to take one's stand on what appear to be the best options available in a pluralist world. Troeltsch was aware of 'the necessity of an activist philosophy of history, which takes up a position and does not merely contemplate the panorama of history'.[236] Ethical decision and religious faith in the ideas which penetrate real history, however, remain essential ingredients even when the horizon is widened to include the whole of culture.[237]

Troeltsch did not live to complement his 'formal philosophy of history' with a 'material philosophy of history' which would supply

---

[230] *G.S.* IV, p.13. Cf. *Glaubenslehre*, p.130: 'No contemporary theologian sticks so closely to the method and meaning of Schleiermacher and feels himself in such inner agreement with him' – while avoiding his inclination towards monism.

[231] *G.S.* III, Tübingen, 1922. Reprint: Aalen, 1961.

[232] W. Bodenstein (*op.cit.*) p.187. The link with the 'essence of Christianity' discussion is made explicit at *G.S.* III, pp.118f.

[233] *G.S.* IV, p.14.

[234] W. Bodenstein (*op.cit.*), p.192. The phrase 'cultural synthesis' is Rickert's.

[235] *G.S.* III, pp.703f. See especially pp.715f.

[236] *G.S.* IV, p.14.

[237] *G.S.* III, p.693.

the content of his cultural synthesis of modern Europeanism. The five lectures destined for English audiences in 1923, and published as *Christian Thought* (1923)[238] provide only a few hints. The most important of them, 'The Place of Christianity among World-religions', takes up the problem of *The Absoluteness of Christianity*, and indicates the change involved in Troeltsch's having meanwhile abandoned the notion of the 'supreme validity'[239] of Christianity. The three lectures on 'ethics and the philosophy of history' continue to give a central place to the act of decision.[240]

These studies and projects 'go far beyond the originally religious starting-point' of Troeltsch's work.[241] But the starting-point was never lost from sight. 'If life and strength remain, I would then like finally to return to the religious sphere and bring my philosophy of religion to completion. That is my first love, and the religious element remains too at the centre of the present cultural synthesis which has to be drawn by the philosophy of history. Without this there is no naivety and freshness.'[242]

Life and strength did not remain, and the part of Troeltsch's construction which was actually written is too suffused with religion and metaphysics for the taste of most subsequent philosophers. It has been admired more than it has been imitated.[243] But neither the *Social Teachings* (*Gesammelte Schriften* I) nor *Der Historismus und seine Probleme* (*Gesammelte Schriften* III) require introduction or advocacy.[244] The intention of this particular selection from his Heidelberg writings on theology and religion, is to suggest that there is more to be learned from *Gesammelte Schriften* II than is generally appreciated.

The selection would give a distorted picture if it did not include one of the several masterly historical analyses of the contemporary situation for which Troeltsch was appreciated even by those who repudiated him. It also includes an example of what falls outside the scope of *Gesammelte Schriften* II (on the religious situation, philosophy of religion, and ethics): one of his more specifically doctrinal essays – which perhaps vindicates the repudiation of Troeltsch's doctrinal

[238] Ed. F. von Hügel. Reprint: Meridian Books, Inc., 1957.

[239] *Höchstgeltung* is frequently translated 'supremacy'; 'Prime validity' would also be possible. See above, p.11.

[240] See pp.65f., 68, 98, 107.

[241] *G.S.* IV, p.14.

[242] *Ibid.*, pp.14f.

[243] E.g. F. Tönnies, 'Troeltsch und die Philosophie der Geschichte', in *Schmollers Jahrbuch*, 1925. J.P. Stern, *Values in History*.

[244] Characteristic of the lack of appreciation for Volume II is J. Milton Yinger's comment on the collected writings – 'Volumes I and III of which particularly have established him as a scholar of the first rank' (*op.cit.*, p.307).

theology, if not of Troeltsch the theologian. But the core of this collection consists in the methodological essays on the notion 'essence of Christianity' and on a science of religion. If they are as topical today as the editors believe, there may be some justification for suggesting that like Luther, Hegel and Marx, Troeltsch should be found to provide new stimulus through renewed attention to his earlier work. In this case no rediscovered manuscripts are forthcoming. But by bringing well-known ones[245] to a wider readership, English translations may be hoped to facilitate the reassessment of a theorist of religion and theology who could have much to teach a later generation.

[245] All four have been recently reprinted in German, the first and last in paperback (Theologische Bücherei 43, Munich; Siebenstern-Taschenbuch, 138).

1

Half a Century of Theology: A Review [1]

Fifty years ago the much appreciated founder of the *Zeitschrift für wissenschaftliche Theologie* [Journal for Scientific Theology], Adolf Hilgenfeld, introduced it with a review of developments in the church over the preceding ten years and an account of their relationship to the task of theology. The main issue then was the separation between church and state planned in the constitutional proposals of 1848 – i.e., church politics and the religious policy of the revolutionary movement. There was also the political and ecclesiastical reaction: the setting up of an independent constitution for the church. This transferred the government of the church in Prussia from the king as constitutional head of state to him as the leading person in the church. The church was to be administered by the new independent authority, the provincial synod (*Oberkirchenrat*). The result was independence for the church *vis-à-vis* a denominationally neutral state, and the maintenance of orthodoxy through the power of the king.

Hilgenfeld, rather like Eduard Zeller at the same time, showed the serious dangers inherent in the 1848 programme. The free development of Christianity would be inhibited by the sectarian spirit of autonomous churches. It would do away with the theological faculties and, with them, with the mutual enrichment and adjustment between theology and other academic work. He also showed the dangers and consequences of the church's reaction: above all the removal of the legal basis, achieved through the union, for a theology and teaching not tied to any particular confession. It opened the way in Prussia and elsewhere to domination by a harsh dogmatic neo-Lutheranism. Finally, as consolation in difficult times, he pointed to signs that the flood of reaction was subsiding, especially to the well-known programme of the Prince Regent, later Kaiser Wilhelm I. He saw this as heralding a return to normality, and new hope for a purely scientific theology and modern advances in religious teaching. On these grounds alone he believed the future of protestantism to be

[1] First published in *Zeitschrift für wissenschaftliche Theologie*, LI 1908.

secure, and with marvellous tenacity and courage he fought for it in his journal through difficult years.

1. *Church viewpoints have receded within historical theology*

At the start of a new series of the journal, we may look back over the period since that essay, and the path theology has taken. In marked contrast to the earlier account, the chief characteristic of the situation is the decline of the church's voice in the whole of public life, above all in the interests and intellectual horizons of educated Germany and across the whole spectrum of academic work. The churches have not, of course, disappeared. Even now they exercise some quite considerable political influence. And, apart from liberalism's winds of freedom and modernity in the 1870s, which affected even the church and theological debate, they have become no less conservative. The Roman church was victorious in the cultural struggle and has gained a dominant position in Germany. Protestant orthodoxy has entrenched itself liturgically with a uniform service-book, and constitutionally through the management of synodical elections. It is making an increasing impression on the school laws and the control of schools. But despite all this the churches are not really a matter of debate. Ordinary academic and literary activity passes them by, and gets on with its own problems and tasks quite independently. After an arid unphilosophical period in which pure positivist facts and the degeneration of history into scraps of specialist information was cultivated, a new religious movement is making itself felt. But even this pays little attention to the churches. Only occasionally can the sounds of the cultural struggle be heard, or Voltaire's *écrasez l'infâme* translated into the new idiom of a Haeckel. There may be a variety of reasons why church matters are ignored, and they will not all be good and far-seeing. But the fact is indubitable. It is there for all to see, and is expressed in the public's quite astonishing indifference and ignorance about anything to do with the church. Whatever school, confirmation class and religious instruction in secondary schools may do, this ignorance is intentional and basic. Again and again the educated and liberal world perceives with naive astonishment that these ecclesiastical powers, ignored and assumed to be dead, in fact determine our internal politics in every nook and cranny. Church and religion have become a private affair – and not only among communists (*Sozialdemokratie*). They are tolerated with the indifference and indulgence that simply accepts people's irremovable peculiarities instead of engaging in a fruitless windmill-jousting against them. But the presuppositionless character of all scholarship and education is taken as self-evident. Where the extraordinarily difficult tangle of problems about this is recognised, the assumption remains as a matter of course that at any rate it cannot be 'the church's' presuppositions which lie at the basis of our culture and science. Rather, these assumptions themselves have first to be tested critically and independently established. A century in which people of different religious persuasion have mingled, boredom with the periodic upsurges of their petty warfare, the unforgotten horror of ecclesiastical reaction combined with political reaction, the evident intellectual ossification of catholicism and the special apologetic pleading of the majority of protestant theologians – all that, together with an enormous development of independent academic work and a concern for social problems that pays no attention to the church, has led to this result. And this result, we repeat, stands in a peculiar contrast to the strong political influence of the church's point of view and its powers in Germany.

But this intellectual situation has had a very great influence upon academic theology throughout this period. Theology, too, has become far more indifferent to the problems of the church. The special position of theological faculties as state institutions and members of large academic corporations has given it a relative independence over against ecclesiastical influences. This independence is produced and maintained partly by the state having an interest in there being a measure of intellectual equilibrium, partly by the irresistible influence of an academic environment, and partly by the theologians' own scholarly concern for truth. They consider protestantism to be the principle of free research in religious matters, or, where it is not dared to interpret protestantism historically in this sense protestantism is itself transcended: intellectual honesty and truthfulness as such are considered a religious demand, and consequently as demanded by Christianity also in so far as it is truly religion. This, however, has given theological science a new character. It is in fact non-confessional, and only protestant in that it sees intellectual freedom as a protestant requirement and in that its liberation from historical protestantism does not involve coming closer to catholicism. It has accepted the normal scientific methods of its sister faculties and works with them under no presupposition other than the profound inner significance and independence of religious life, and within this especially of Christianity. Apologetic tendencies have generally receded. One can read research on the Old Testament, New Testament, church history and history of doctrine that intends simply to show how it happened or may have happened. It dispenses entirely with relating them apologetically and dogmatically to the present. This change is immediately perceptible wherever one looks back at the older literature. A strong theological, apologetic or polemical interest in evaluation is always apparent even in radical and liberal works. Scientific theology today, on the other hand, is resolutely unconcerned about the practical and dogmatic implications of its results. It lacks special theological presuppositions and methods, and all party political spirit is absent.

The change can be expressed by saying that theology is no longer liberal but scientific. It does not fight for a normative, allegedly pure understanding of Christianity to be set up against orthodox or confessional corruption. It does not try to show that conservative versions of Christianity are wrong and that the new scientific versions agree with the authentic spirit of Christianity and the requirements of science. It has nothing to do with church parties and church reforms. All it wants is free space to do its work, the right to exist for the sake of the clergy who learn from it, and the spread of its writings throughout the educated world. Whether this is in every respect an advance is another question. But it is a fact, and very largely an unsought for and unconscious fact arising from the general academic atmosphere from which theologians cannot be shut out and which does not stop at theology. It has penetrated deeply into quite conservative work and in scientific theology has made the struggle between opposing opinions and schools calmer and seemlier. There is now agreement about methods and basic principles and even to some extent results, which fifty years ago seemed impossible. The further away we go from the central dogmas the more this spirit is victorious in every camp. The Old Testament has been almost entirely surrendered to it and in church history and the history of doctrine only primitive Christianity and the Reformation remain controversial.

2. *The church's apologetic interests have been maintained within systematic theology*

Now while on one side ecclesiastical orientations, both liberal-reforming and orthodox-conservative, have receded markedly, the practical relationship of theology to the church has become all the stronger on another front. The more the really scientific research was felt to be without relevance (directly, at least) to the church's concerns, the more necessary it was for those disciplines that could to do justice to the situation of theology as at the same time a practical, i.e. church-oriented, science. Not only does it have the task of educating young theologians. The whole size and scope of its existence are based simply on the fact that the phenomena it investigates are an essential and existing part of our practical life.

The inevitable radicalism of scientific work is what sharpened our perception for the special and atypical conditions pertaining to a practical and religious field of study. This has in fact led very largely to a total separation of scientific and practical work. The former is largely indifferent to the latter, and practical theology is left to make what it can of scientific theology or else practical theologians utterly despise this, feeling it nothing but a hindrance, and carry on simply with the Bible, confession and church work.

Everyone familiar with the real situation knows what a frightful gulf exists here, despite the existence of many clergy in practical work who continue faithfully to work scientifically and often suffer seriously from this development. But this kind of separation is easily explained only as a product of circumstances. It is not in the least a necessary consequence of scientific theology in and for itself. At any rate it cannot be so designated by theology unless it wants to sign its own death-warrant as theology. This is what Franz Overbeck did. He thought it would mean the death of Christianity and of religion generally if they subjected themselves to scientific scrutiny. He saw his theological chair as simply a shield behind which he could the more securely set about his work of destruction in cold and dispassionate aversion to Christianity.

That is of course quite an exception. Total exclusion of religious faith from scientific work is only a possibility for those who for special reasons have killed or let die their notion of religion. Those in whom religion continues to live will never be able to see things in this way. They will always be convinced that the different sources of knowledge must somehow coincide and harmonise. However much purely historical interest and methods are objectified and made independent there still remains, therefore, a practical religious interest, and with it a view of theology as a science which seeks normative religious knowledge. It has had to take up the question as a matter of principle and still must. Granted that theology is in the first place a purely scientific activity subject to ordinary methods, it must also elaborate that side of itself which leads into practice, and which has its own ecclesiastical significance and intent.

But this question has led to a characteristic division of interests within theology. One part is the servant of pure science and only serves the church indirectly. The other part serves the church and practical work; it directly and as a matter of principle assumes the special task of mediating between science and practice. It is obvious that the first part falls to the historical disciplines and the second to dogmatics and ethics. The separation of history and dogmatics, the purely scientific free development of the former and the latter's practical mediating way of working without a strictly scientific attitude, is the result of this changed situation. Every student senses this as he moves from historical and exegetical studies to dogmatics and ethics. A different spirit rules in each of the two groups. It is clear too from the whole development of theological publications. Historical and exegetical research forms an enormous and increasing flood and addresses itself to the general interest. The narrow trickling stream of dogmatic works waters only specifically theological plains. Originality, freshness and forward driving power, the mark of real science, are to be found in the former. The latter contains practical interests, mediation and compromise. Dogmatics has everywhere abandoned the demonstration of scientifically valid general truths in favour of personal, subjective convictions of a confessional sort, and seeks to harmonise these with the church's dominant tradition and forms of expression.

The natural separation of dogmatics from a history which works purely scientifically, and as a matter of course turned its attention to practical tasks is in the first place an unintended result of this development. There is also the general weakness of the philosophical and metaphysical spirit to consider. It no longer dares gain valid knowledge about the transcendent either inside or outside theology, and is satisfied with personal certainties. Their precise dogmatic formulation and expression is no longer so important, and this indefiniteness and uncertainty about dogmatic statements helps bring together to some extent the different and conflicting points of view. This tendency results in part from people being sick of the struggle between groups and parties and sick of the theological frictions, which do more than anything else to discredit religion. The quickest way to overcome this evil is indefiniteness at a theoretical level and standing together in practice.

3. *The dogmatics of Schleiermacher and Ritschl have a mediating character*

What thus came about as a result of the situation itself was naturally made a matter of principle and theory. It would all have seemed just a miserable and unprincipled coward's way out unless inner reason and necessity for the development could be found – one which still provided an inner connexion despite the split. The practical and mediating position of dogmatics assigned it in the first place by its actual development had to be based on theory and principles. In short, that was achieved through the 'agnostic' theory about the nature of religious knowledge.

This formula is well-suited to illuminate both procedure and context. It was minted by the papal theologians in opposition to similar movements on catholic soil. In the language of protestant theology it is called the distinction between theology and religion – a distinction which is held to indicate the difference in principle between modern theology and the old churchly theology, against the dogmatisms of orthodoxy and of more recent types of theological and religious rationalism. This dogmatic agnosticism signifies the impossibility of exact and adequate conclusions in the area of religion. The basis for its knowledge is said to reside in its practical, confessional and feeling character, and all statements containing or communicating this sort of knowledge are said to be inadequate and symbolic.

The word 'knowledge' is used here only in an improper, non-theoretical sense. It means no more than that access to the real grounds of life is possible in this sort of practical and symbolic attitude too – in fact that it only really takes place in this form. That was already the position of Kant and Herder, and to a much greater degree Schleiermacher. As regards popular and practical religion it was also the position of the Hegelians, though by coupling it with academic religion they made it practically ineffective. So it was already the broadly axiomatic assumption of the great founders of modern theology and the science of religion that only in this way could religious thought and knowledge get off the ground in the new situation, and that only in this way was the still indispensable link with the tradition considered possible. Tradition was then treated not as binding doctrine or rational truth but pictorial and pliable material, expressing incommensurable experiences and real life. It could then be fitted to and reconciled with advanced thinking. As early as that, very radical historical and exegetical thought cut loose from dogmatics and theology. The latter based the case for its significance and truth on practical necessity and achievement. Its possibility and compatibility with a scientific world of ideas was based on the merely symbolic character of dogmatic statements as appealing to the imagination.

On this basis dogmatics was seen in principle as the presupposition of practical theology. Schleiermacher even assigned it to practical theology (although he actually said 'historical' theology). He gave it the job of differentiating and reconciling scientific thought and religious proclamation. It was only possible to pose the task in this way on this assumption of that dogmatic agnosticism, that surrender of compelling and adequate knowledge, i.e. the assumption of a religious epistemology which makes religious 'knowledge' independent of rational knowledge by referring it to its own sources.

This religious epistemology makes it possible for religious knowledge to compromise with rational knowledge because it surrenders any theoretical scientific knowledge that is really adequate to and actually objectively grasps the transcendent world.

This was the theoretical justification for making room for science in general and the historical exegetical disciplines in particular and for the practical mediating type of dogmatics. It allows the tradition to be treated in a harmonising way and at the same time religious thought to be broadened out and developed. It does of course mean that there is bound to be extraordinary scope for variation amongst individual dogmatic positions. A theology built on these foundations took away from the spiritual authorities the power to compel assent. The different trends had to be accommodated in practice and find common expression. If knowledge was so subjectively based only those who possessed its subjective presuppositions could share it. This meant that any existence of a church depended on the voluntary accommodation and tolerance of different groups. It was bound up with a new concept of the church which based it not on having dogma in common but on a practical religious union in the general substance of religious life. It made dogma fluid, restricted only by the wish to be connected with the substance of christian life. That demanded a church without dogma.

But then, for all its formally conservative posture, the new way of treating the religious world of ideas had in practice a profoundly transforming effect upon the christian world of thought. Schleiermacher's faith was the religious interpretation of the world and life as influenced by the religious power proceeding from Jesus. It saw in the overcoming of a consciousness of guilt and in the reconciliation with the suffering in the world through faith in God, the power to lead a life united with God. This life would find its particular ethical and theoretical form in a way that preserves its individuality and autonomy.

This programme of Schleiermacher's[2] was not at first taken up and fulfilled. The movements of the period had brought the renewed dogmatism of pietism and orthodoxy, and the Hegelian school's sublimated dogmatism of religious philosophy or metaphysics. The theology of mediation which allegedly continued the tradition of Schleiermacher had limited the variability of expression in dogmatics

[2] For more details see Süskind, *Christentum und Geschichte bei Schleiermacher*, 1911. This shows how deeply Schleiermacher himself still allowed practical presuppositions to influence his historical theology and philosophy of religion, even though in itself this separation from a purely scientific and no longer church and theology standpoint is the meaning of his whole construction.

to a gentle oscillation of its statements around the biblical terminology, and to simply less precision about dogmatic statements. It performed the task of mediation too as a careful attuning of a natural with a supernatural theology, guaranteed by the experience of sin and redemption. The two dogmatisms reconciled here were no less dogmatisms for both sides being defined as inexactly as possible and 'inner experience' coming in at the decisive moment in place of the dogma of the Bible and early church.

In the struggles around the middle of the century orthodoxy and the so-called theology of mediation were victorious within the church, and liberal and speculative dogmatics was overcome. The wider non-theological world turned away from liberal and conservative dogmatics equally and left a church dominated by orthodoxy to its own devices. Even where it was considered politically and socially necessary and was exploited for conservative ends there was very little interest in its inner essence.

Despite this, scientific theology which was relatively independent of the church and open to the general influences of the scientific atmosphere continued to construct its own purely scientific positions. It became ever more independent by devoting itself to exegetical and historical research using normal scientific methods. D.F. Strauss had sharpened its conscience in this area. The radical surrender of the theological history to the general principles of historical method has gradually penetrated further as a result of the decisive influence of Strauss, even though people do not usually like to appeal to him and he himself made it difficult for theology to testify to the gratitude it owes him.

Strauss was of course not the only man to point in this direction. Old Testament studies in particular had already taken the same path independently. By following these impulses more than anyone the Tübingen school then became the standard-bearer of the science's future development. The dogmatic or metaphysical presuppositions of this school had of course gradually to recede before this line could be vigorously pursued. But then it too became a source of that powerful quickening of purely historical thought and research in the field of theology, which now presents itself as purely historical and scientific in the above-mentioned sense.

But this brought back in a significantly strengthened form the situation into which Kant and Schleiermacher had in their day introduced their agnostic theology. What was at first a purely factual need to find a place for practical and mediating work, and the way that dogmatics was in fact turning its attention more to the tasks of practical theology, led again to a theory which assigned practical interests to a dogmatics oriented on the agnostic view and able to formulate and guide practical life.

The significance of the Ritschlian School is that it opened up this way out of the situation. It owed its extraordinary success to having shown on the level of theory and principle the way out of a real emergency. It was quite right that with this basic position and by the impressive way it thus summed up the practical and ethical essence of Christianity, it should have dominated the dogmatic development of recent decades. It is in principle an unphilosophical and anti-philosophical theology.[3] It only employs as much philosophy or epistemology as it needs to avoid competing with philosophy and metaphysics. It liked to appeal to Kant and to the emerging Neo-kantianism of the period which sharpened Kant's essentially critical attitude to the point of harshly denying all and every metaphysics. Schleiermacher also had emphasised this aspect of Kant's thought. Now all they took from Kant was the demotion of knowledge of nature to simply a science of phenomena, and the denial of metaphysics. They either ignored or contested the positive theory about religion held by Kant and the neo-Kantians. Instead of this they turned to history. But here too, they were only concerned with free scientific history so long as it found in the great centres of Christian history nourishment for constructing religious ideas and provided justification for an agnostic anti-metaphysical theology.

Biblical research was expected to supply the dogmatician with the basic ideas of practical religion from the Bible, or rather from the teaching of Jesus for which the rest of the Bible was only commentary. History of dogma was to show how philosophical, metaphysical and orthodox dogmatic theologies contradicted the Bible and were bankrupt. The history of Protestantism was meant to show the foundations of a theology free of metaphysics in the way Luther thought. Everything else could be left to research to do with it what it liked.

Just as Carlyle recognised that philosophy cannot decide the big questions of real life and fled to hero-worship in the hope of making effective the suggestive impression of great historical movements and personalities, here too history was clung to. It was not without reason that these circles liked to appeal to Carlyle, while restricting his hero-worship to Jesus, Paul and Luther, and lifting these heroes out of the

[3] A very characteristic example is F. Traub, *Theologie und Philosophie*, 1910, which reproduces this theology as the school requires. It signifies the expulsion of the philosophical spirit from theology, though not by means of the orthodox belief in miracle but by an agnostic theory about religious experience or religious (that is, of course, simply Christian) certainty.

normal profane course of events. The general modern historical spirit is therefore taken up, but in silent agreement with a biblicist Lutheranism only the Christian high-points are brought out, and both the factuality of these and their absolutely unique religious significance are guaranteed by the practical religious effects which flow from them.[4] That is truly overcoming history (*Historie*) with history, just as the basic anti-philosophical stance is an overcoming of philosophy by philosophy.

Having thus secured its independence against actual history and against speculation, the new dogmatics has the job of burying both orthodox and liberal dogmatics with their assumptions of possessing real knowledge. It formulates instead a unitary practical and religious guide for life drawn from the preaching of Jesus, Paul and Luther. It cannot produce knowledge of the transcendent but a guide for practical life. It is simply a religious interpretation of things and the world gained from an experiential certainty about Jesus' revelatory and redeeming significance.

It takes up in a sense, and far more than Ritschl himself realised, the basic position of Schleiermacher. It takes up the proper principle of mediation on an agnostic basis. Religious ideas are said to be based on practice. They are not dogmatically or metaphysically adequate. Since they do not claim to be objective knowledge they are flexible and only subjectively binding. They are able to take full account of both the community's tradition and of the state of scientific knowledge of the world. Yet they are said to be or to contain truth because they rest on a practical experience or on the preaching of Jesus, the authority of

[4] Of course not all representatives of this view go along with such a dubious notion as the guaranteeing of factuality by a religious impression. Harnack, for example, has never shared it. At this point the historians of the school separate themselves from the systematicians. Nevertheless, the historians too, with such a weighty researcher as Harnack at their head, treat those points of history given prominence by religious value-judgments very differently from the rest of history. They thus make those high points into objective religious authorities and designate their effect as perceived by religious experience as the establishment of redemption amongst unredeemed humanity. This is Weinel's procedure too in his *Biblische Theologie des Neuen Testaments*, 1911, which for just this reason was accorded the most emphatic agreement by Harnack. It is in fact the theologised historical method of Carlyle and it fits in very nicely with metaphysical agnosticism. But despite its superiority to Carlyle in technical and philological-historical respects, it stands much further distant from the normal historical method than the great Scotsman did. Something similar is already apparent in Schleiermacher. See Köhler, *Idee und Persönlichkeit*, 1910, p.81. How much more sharply systematic theologians define the border dispute against ordinary historical methods can be seen, as well as in Herrmann's work, also very characteristically in Reischle, *Christentum und Entwicklungsgedanke*, 1898, pp.29-35, and *Der Glaube an Jesus Christus und die geschichtliche Erforschung seines Lebens*, 1893, pp.24ff.

which is established in this way. It is again the grand idea of mediation in the true sense. It knows that mediation means abandoning a properly scientific character. But it also knows that religion is not a science and cannot be transformed into one.

This dogmatics emerges in place of the minute harmonising and soothing imprecision of the theology that calls itself theology of mediation and that falsely exploits the name of Schleiermacher for its own designs. Its mediating and practical character is admittedly less consciously a matter of principle than that of Schleiermacher who had allowed attention to scientific knowledge to cut very deeply into his theological constructions at every point. He had intentionally characterised the link with the church's language and tradition precisely as a 'link' and a reinterpretation for the sake of preserving it. The negative stress against metaphysics receives more attention than the positive view of faith's ideas as symbolic and appropriate to the imagination. The correlative relationship of the two ideas is seen less sharply than it was by Schleiermacher; so modern dogmaticians are less conscious and aware of conforming to the modern view of the world and of re-interpreting the church's tradition.

In the case of Ritschl this conformity to the modern world-view took place more tacitly. In the formation of his theological ideas he too always pays attention to the view that natural and spiritual reality proceed on a self-contained immanent and causal course. His re-interpretation of the church's tradition was done more instinctively and with less awareness that he was giving it a new shape. But here too biblical and church expressions like kingdom of God, reconciliation, justification, redemption, world dominion get quite a new meaning. Only the form, not the substance, is conserved. In all this he well and truly takes up again the formal position of Schleiermacher.

The real difference from Schleiermacher is simply that the construction of theological ideas is attached not to religious experience being symbolised in the present subject, but fundamentally to the symbolic expression already given to his religious experience from Jesus. This is then considered normative for all religious consciousness which imitates and is based upon it. In other words, Ritschl twists Schleiermacher's subjectivism and spiritualism so far as possible back into a Lutheran biblicism. Instead of the religious self-consciousness developed from the community there is the objective authority of the preaching of Jesus interpreted in a Pauline and Lutheran manner with all that is merely 'background' or 'inessential' cut out. The whole thing then looks more objective, though the basic theory of agnosticism is itself not in the least given up. Ritschl also differs from Schleiermacher in that the scientific picture of the world he espouses is not, as it was for Schleiermacher, the monism of identity philosophy. He emphatically opts for a dualistic theism which allows the moral realm of freedom victory over nature. The personalist and dualist elements in Christianity can therefore emerge more naturally than in Schleiermacher's very forced amalgam of these with his deterministic monism.

Again, in his conception of the christian idea Ritschl stressed even more than Schleiermacher its active character in shaping the world ethically. He thus brought christian ethics closer to the practical ethical problems of modern Christianity. Schleiermacher thought he had settled these, as far as a specifically christian ethic was concerned, simply by the strengthening of the religious consciousness through life and fellowship with·Christ. But despite all these changes made by Ritschl, the overall position is still unmistakeably Schleiermacher's idea of dogmatics as the foundational division of the church's practical theology: a discipline which uses and presupposes scientific knowledge and method and yet is not itself a science, but something better and higher which can never be transposed into the form of a supernatural or natural science. It interprets on the basis of the continuing impression of the person of Jesus and in the form of pictures of God, the world and man, the ethical and religious ascent to God. These pictures do not establish a scientific explanation of the world but an ethical and religious milieu for the christian community. They help express and extend this milieu.

Even more than in Ritschl, Schleiermacher's type emerged in the work of Herrmann, the most significant theologian to continue the Ritschlian line. For him Christian faith is a trust in God gained from the impression of Jesus' personality, in self-condemnation of evil and reliance upon God's loving will. In all other matters this trust could be formed and verified quite freely in whatever way looked possible. Christian faith is here making people autonomous beings by a faith in the Father of Jesus Christ which overcomes the consciousness of guilt and worldly anxiety. Beyond that there are no rules about doctrine or morals. Dogmatics is simply to show how this faith in Christ emerges. This origin connects it sufficiently closely to a decisive basic substance for it to remain Christian no matter what its symbolic forms and ethical effects.

In this way the older liberal theology which around the middle of the century had generally speaking represented the scientific spirit in theology, was joined on the dogmatic side by a new tendency in addition to the anti-speculative study of history. Just as history-writing gave up the dialectical law view of a necessary development of the Christian idea, so too dogmatics stopped identifying the Christian idea with the scientific and philosophical knowledge of God and relied instead on the sovereignty of specifically religious feeling. It thus regrouped the parties on the right and on the left, becoming more alive religiously but not more conservative. Its conservatism is only apparent. Herrmann's paradoxes in particular can teach us how radical an impulse is contained in this abandonment of firm and adequate knowledge. On the other hand, this biblicism grounded purely in history and feeling was so unsafe against general historical methods that these could burst through at all points with far more radical consequences. With Harnack biblicism is ready to flow into pure history of religion.

4. *The new dissolution of this mediation between historical and dogmatic thinking*

Those, then, are the two main tendencies in scientific theology over the past half century. On the one side stands historical theology, born of the influence exercised by Hegel's idea of development and continuity. This has more and more cut loose of its metaphysical basis in panlogism and stripped off the practical and apologetic viewpoints of the church. The Enlightenment thinkers, the Herder-Eichhorn school, then above all Vatke, De Wette, Strauss and the Tübingen school have brought about this development. It is continued today in an enormous literature of research on the Old Testament, New Testament, church history and history of doctrine. Theologians and non-theologians are engaged in it and the same methods are considered valid as in research on the Buddha, Mohammed and Zoroaster, or for illuminating the religious world of late Greek syncretism. As a matter of fact this co-operation with linguists has been extremely significant and driven research more and more successfully to break free of specifically theological presuppositions.

On the other side stands the agnostic theology of mediation, strengthened by renewed recourse to Schleiermacher. That is, the dogmatics of the Ritschlian school which as a matter of principle aims to mediate and serve the church in a practical way. It does not actually reject metaphysics but it will not allow philosophy to make any contribution to religious knowledge. It constructs its religious metaphysics upon the basic idea in which Jesus gave symbolic expression to his faith in God for his community. This knowledge is guaranteed in a practical way by feeling.

There are of course several other positions in addition to these two main groups. Pietistic biblicism and the credal orthodoxy of confessionalism continue to flourish. There are also still traces of speculative rationalism to be found. But the first two stand in conscious opposition to all the principles of modern thought and construct an objective dogmatic knowledge on the basis of a miracle (however secured). The third have been able to assert a belief in their speculation and also the agreement of their speculation with the Christian idea only within continually diminishing circles. The broad tendencies to be found in the results of modern intellectual life are and remain, therefore, the two mentioned before: a fully free historical research that knows no specifically Christian presupposition, and Schleiermacher's and Ritschl's type of systematic theology which gives up the claim to scientific dogmatic knowledge and from this agnostic position engages in mediation. It varies considerably due to its subjective character. (Lipsius' position also is related to this group.) Under the cover of agnosticism this theology continues to develop the religious world of ideas and also preserves so far as possible continuity with the tradition's world of ideas. The two tendencies have at many points come into conflict and have not always even come into contact. But on the whole they have operated as groups which supplement one another and which could co-exist and be seen as the two main branches of theology, each with its own particular trends and interests. In this respect the inspired sketch of Schleiermacher's *Brief Outline* was victorious and in essentials established. History is completely free and shows the great historical and religious figures and personalities; dogmatics makes effective for the community the life content presented in them on the principle of conservation and mediation, interpreting the historical data in a religious way for faith.

Neither group of course has remained untouched by far-reaching changes and developments. In these developments their points of opposition which were at first concealed or ignored or settled in minor individual arguments have broken out, formulating and bringing about an awareness of the new, broad problem involved in this division. That is the change in situation which the past two decades have brought.

The two tendencies in theology could co-exist peacefully in Schleiermacher's sense for as long as history could presuppose as self-evident that the religious consciousness was perfected in Christianity and that Jesus' historical significance lay in his incorporating, and within his community continuing, the absolute ideal of religion; for as long, also, as dogmatics required nothing more from history than the picture of a creative central religious personality and his historical effects. It could then, according to its own independent needs, link these up with the dogmatic interpretations and call them accounts of what was subjectively experienced in a living relationship with Jesus' religious power. But neither the first nor the second condition remained fulfilled. Schleiermacher could still assert this kind of balance, given the state of historical knowledge at his time. Later on Ritschl could only maintain it by twisting things somewhat. In his teaching about the stages in the history of religion, in his *Life of Jesus* which described Jesus as the perfect religious genius, and in his basic view of church history as a life-context proceeding from Jesus and expressing the effect of him in each individual's subjectivity according to time and circumstances, Schleiermacher could secure the harmony of his systematic theology with the history of religion and of Christianity. Ritschl, on the other hand, had on the whole to leave the far more refined, relativising, analytic and sceptical historical research of his day to itself. He took the central point, the personality of Jesus, out of the rest of history by means of a value judgement of faith, and designated it a miracle of revelation set in contrast to the rest of history. He could therefore no longer direct dogmatics to a free subjective interpretation of what is received in and from Jesus. He had instead to tie it to the external authority of Jesus. This was sometimes established purely historically and positively through the decisive significance of the historical and factual element instead of the allegedly rational and general, and sometimes through the supernatural concept of miracle which was supposed to be secured by means of an 'inner experience of Jesus'. But that then tore apart too the connexion which in Schleiermacher existed between Christianity and the non-christian development of the religious consciousness. Christianity was taken out of the development of the religious consciousness and without a plain foundation in the miraculous was treated in obvious isolation as disrupting the fabric of history. Even at the time of Ritschl and his immediate pupils that was a very difficult and complicated affair. But since then the matter has become progressively more difficult and complicated.

History became more and more free of any particular, Christian presuppositions. It transformed church history into the history of the Christian religion and the various church formations emerging from it. It transformed the history of doctrine into the history of the movement of religious ideas issuing partly in church formulae and thus creating in the different churches different centres of authority while in the same continuum free religious thinking continued to develop. It transformed biblical research on the history of the literature and biblical theology into the history of Israelite, Jewish and early Christian religion. It saw everything flowing like an endless movement of inter-twining threads, mixing at all points with general cultural situations, so that the history of Christianity was woven into the general history of culture and ideas. But seeing Christianity in its natural and historical context necessarily involved seeing it on analogy with and in connexion with the history of religion generally. Its history had to be illuminated from the general laws and tendencies of the development of the religious consciousness.

Not only were points of analogy and similarity brought to light, but also at every point the existence of a material link with other religious developments. Light was cast upon the religion of Israel from its connexions with the ancient religious traditions of the orient. Late Judaism, the matrix of Christianity, was found to be penetrated by all kinds of gnostic, oriental and hellenistic influences. The emergence of primitive Christianity was seen to be marked by relationships to and contrasts with the great oriental and Hellenistic movements of religious syncretism. The problem of the origins of Christianity became a problem in the history of religions, a question of the interaction of different influences and of the measure of originality possessed by Jesus and his great chief apostle.

This question then raised new difficulties for all the old problems concerning the sources and the tradition. The synoptic problem had seemed settled and resolved by distinguishing between the original documents and the authentic words of Jesus, but now it became a live issue again. The entire research seems today to be beginning all over again with new questions. The position is on the whole familiar enough, and it is quite certain that the whole situation will become progressively more complicated the more that linguists make their indispensable contribution to this problem. Usener and Paul de Lagarde have given decisive stimuli in this area. There is also of course in many cases a more or less explicit animosity against Christianity which likes to give double emphasis to all that Christianity owes to external influences and whatever is uncertain in the tradition, and makes this the starting point for daring new explanations. But even that has in fact simply pushed research forwards. Details can be left on one side. What matters is the scope of the whole thing in principle, and that is clear enough. This line of research is called quite simply the history of religions school.

There emerged from this two quite extraordinarily difficult consequences burdening all theology.

The first is historical critical uncertainty about our picture of Jesus. It not only shows the task of writing a life of Jesus (which exercised the previous generations) to be insoluble, but also undermines the entire Jesus tradition at its religious core in the words of Christ. The older liberal theology produced in works like Keim's *Life and Character of*

Jesus what was assumed to be a strictly historical presentation, and so gave an opening for dogmatics to interpret this historical picture for faith. In the last twenty years or so the lives of Jesus have dried up. Dogmaticians no longer link their work to one of these. Ritschl considered the task insoluble and preferred to speak of faith's impression of Jesus, secured by the apostles' interpretation of him.

The consequences of this standpoint were made clear by Kähler's complete scepticism about historical knowledge of Jesus and his insistence upon submission to the apostles' teaching about Christ. But then the real problem is raised, concerning the relationship of the apostles' faith in Christ found in the tradition to the real Jesus. How far does even that part of our tradition found in the gospels transmit the community's christological dogma instead of the real Jesus? Dogmaticians thought they could be satisfied with the faith in Christ expressed in the christological dogma of the apostles. The historian on the other hand was more concerned with how the apostles' christological dogma, so fundamental for the church, emerged from the actual proclamation and activity of Jesus.

From this point the tradition was treated even more sceptically to the point of doubting even whether Jesus called himself Messiah at all. The tradition of Jesus' sayings was shattered and the difference between Johannine and synoptic tradition again removed. Any more exact and definite knowledge about what was historically past was thus disputed. On the other side the genesis of the apostles' christological dogma and the Christ cult became the real problem. The older liberalism had solved it by seeing this as the product of the dialectical development of the religious idea within Christianity. But now variegated alien influences of the mythical and gnostic type were brought in, in the attempt to explain it. The older liberalism thought it was able at all points to identify authentic tradition by means of criticism and to reconstruct as a dialectical process internal to Christianity the advance from Jesus' proclamation to the apostles' christological dogma. This made it possible for dogmatics to link the historical kernel of the Jesus tradition and the dogmatic kernel of christology. But that position is now disappearing. In its place there have arisen new still unsolved historical problems which make it very difficult for faith to attach itself to so uncertain a reality, or else tempt people to the most sensational and radical solutions in which the church's view of its own origins is completely false and legendary and to be replaced by the modern critic's discovery of the real order of events. Since it shares the same methodological premises and since the tradition is so obscure, it has become progressively more difficult for scientific theology utterly to rule out these sensational constructions. We will have to be prepared for yet sharper attacks at this point.[5]

This first main point concerns the historical foundation of Christianity and the historico-religious statements in its systematic theology. The second, however, extends to the whole of Christianity itself and the whole content of its world of religious ideas. Not only its origins but its whole subsequent development too seems equally woven into the total fabric of historical life. Isolation is decreasing at all points. The older liberalism had derived the entire history of Christianity out of a dialectically necessary self-movement of the Christian idea and so maintained in modern forms the old independence and isolatedness of Christianity within life as a whole. Modern church history and history of doctrine, on the other hand, shows it to be interwoven into all the movements of life as a whole. At important points it is determined not by its dialectic but by its surroundings and the general historical situation. Since what are called economic or sociological methods have been applied to the history of Christianity this two-way influence appears very much more strongly than in a simple history of doctrine approach.

The result is then the disappearance too of the kernel idea which drives this dialectic on and had simply to be distilled from it. Christianity becomes a thoroughly complicated and in many ways contingent whole. Its present and future form will be shaped anew from its total context and so it becomes again and again a living organism. But this entanglement of Christianity in the wider context of the history of religions with all its analogies and real connexions, and in the currents of ordinary practical and intellectual life, places it completely in the stream of the historical process. The question then arises how far its religious idea and power is in any respect ultimate, perfect and absolute. The concepts of revelation and redemption asserted by the older liberalism and by Schleiermacher, though in the form of absolute religion breaking through rather than as a miracle opposed to all the rest of history, is thus threatened by being drawn into the fluctuations of revelation in ordinary spiritual life. It becomes a question how far Christianity as such is a definitive religious phenomenon which completes everything. It therefore becomes a question too how far it is to be seen as revelation and redemption in the absolute sense.

Of these two problems my opinion is that despite its threatening appearance at the moment the first is less far-reaching. It will finally

[5] Consider only Albert Schweitzer's history of criticism, *The Quest of the Historical Jesus*, 1906, Eng.tr. 1910.

turn out here as with other religions that the personality of the founder prophet is the decisive point of origin. Once the problems recently thrown up have been worked through and the environmental factors in the emergence of Christianity closely researched, the fireworks of sensational hypotheses will cease and the primitive church's view of its origin will be seen to be right in essentials. Christianity arose not through a misunderstanding or through some alien redeemer myth being attached to a certain 'Jesus', but from the life and personality of its hero. I have no doubt at all that this will stand firm despite the certainly very urgent problem of how the christological dogma emerged in the community and where it came from. I also definitely believe that the main traits of the preaching and tradition can be sufficiently known for anyone who attributes to them a basic religious significance to find here a point of contact for a continuing religious development.

At the moment things look particularly confused and unclear. But they cannot remain like this for ever. Research will make advances and when the dust has settled enough will remain of the old picture for Jesus at any rate still to be seen as the source and power of faith in Christ and so of Christianity – even if the historian as such can no longer describe him as 'absolute central personality' or 'opening up a new stage of humanity' or 'sinless and religiously perfect man'. As I see it, the decisive difficulty rests rather in the total conception and evaluation of the position of Christianity as part of the history of religion. This new picture in which different historical currents flow into each other does at any rate constitute a new problem. I have tried in my work on *The Absoluteness of Christianity and the History of Religions*[6] to formulate it as a result of the development of theology, and to answer it. This is the main question, and one's judgment upon Jesus and evaluation of him will always depend essentially upon our answer at this point. Someone who sees in Christianity the permanent upmost plateau of man's religion will naturally also see and seek in its founding personality deeper forces than someone who sees in it nothing but a passing phase of religious formation made up of the accidental confluence of various streams, or someone who wants to make his contribution to the devaluation of this religious formation by uprooting its historical foundations. On such important main points historical research cannot be completely separated from the imponderables involved in evaluating what such a fact has brought

---

[6] Second ed. 1912. The difference between the two editions reflects the continuing advance of the questioning. I recently read somewhere that this book is 'recognised to have posed the question in an unfortunate manner'. 'Uncomfortable' would perhaps have been more correct.

into the world. But as regards the practice of a purely historical method based on analogy this matter is of no significance.

Those are the problems which arise from historical and purely scientific theology. The practical and systematic mediating theology of the Ritschlian school has also for its part produced a number of profound internal difficulties of its own. It was formerly possible to build upon the epistemological philosophy of religion basis of its presupposed agnosticism. This is what the master himself had done, satisfied at this point with a few *aperçus* and a firm declaration of will. A religious agnosticism which means to count as knowledge – not scientific or explanatory knowledge, but one that interprets reality in a practical and religious way – is not such a simple theory. 'Knowledge in religious value-judgments', as the theory is called, fails above all to bring out the objective elements in these value judgments. It also fails to show the character of the religious ideas in which they are objectified and so the pictorial and symbolic nature of this knowledge. That has been done in part by the very important Paris school of theology, the symbolo-fideists, as they are called. It has also been done in Germany by Lipsius and by the series of successful Schleiermacher revivals resulting from Ritschl's work. Others, like Herrmann, have been aware of the need to concentrate this agnostic-gnostic theory of knowledge upon an objective central point. Relying strongly on Kant they have conceived it as simply a religious interpretation of reality in the sense of making people capable of ethical autonomy by a trust in God gained by reference to Jesus. This concentration and simplification sees the proper object of knowledge in the assertion of a theistic belief in God and the autonomy which proceeds from it. It really looks only to the personality of Jesus and his faith in God for the expression of its ideas and in any case subjects him to very considerable variations.

It is therefore clear that this theory about religious knowledge still has a number of very problematical gaps in it which can easily plunge it back into uncertainty. There is then another aspect from which it looks no less uncertain. Ritschl himself had allowed attention to the modern picture of the world – i.e. its causal nexus of events and the immeasurability of the world making anthropocentricism impossible – to influence his thought considerably, though without making this explicit. He re-interpreted the biblical and history of doctrine concepts which he appropriated as far as possible along these lines. But on the one hand it became ever more obvious that forced and unhistorical interpretations were being offered here and that in fact his procedure was silently to conform traditional Christian ideas with those of modern science or modern ethics. On the other side it became clear that this bringing into conformity never went far enough. The most burning questions of the modern life or death struggle of religion received no answers, or merely pretend answers.

For example, Ritschl calmly continued to assert an anthropocentric view – the creation of the world for the sake of man. He did not concern himself in the least with evolution. The elements of modern knowledge had to be carried much farther into the construction of Christian ideas than was the case with the master. This would involve re-shaping them. Or else all questions of world-view must be laid aside and a far more consistent return made to a purely religious and ethical interpretation, leaving the question of world-view much more open than Ritschl left it.

The first alternative is evident in all the countless discussions about apologetics and metaphysics which have come from the Ritschlian school. The dogmatics of H.H. Wendt gives characteristic expression to the outcome. The latter alternative is energetically and winsomely adopted by Herrmann. On the one hand he allows full validity to the enormous world in its mechanical causal nexus of events and leaves it alone, and then allows the religious man simply a religious and ethical autonomy which is based on experience of God's holiness and love in the picture of Jesus, and total indifference to the question of world-view which is left entirely to science. Dogmatics then becomes a psychological guide towards gaining this experience by reference to Jesus, and the surrender of all constructive religious and ethical thought to the autonomous subject, even though of course that cuts off rather than satisfies all questions.

Finally there are – and this is the most important thing – the most difficult questions for this dogmatics arising from the development of historiography – the turn of historical theology towards history of religions. This operates at the level of both main points already mentioned: with respect to the problem of secured historical knowledge about Jesus and his significance for emergent Christianity, and also with regard to the problem of 'the absoluteness of Christianity'. I have indicated that the first problem was already a very difficult one even for Ritschl and could only be resolved by sheer assertions. He more and more withdrew from the means by which Schleiermacher had resolved this problem – i.e. a philosophy of religion based upon historical development and reaching its climax in Christianity. Instead he went back to isolating Jesus' preaching of the kingdom of God and Paul's faith in Christ which is alleged to have grown directly out of that, through judgments of faith and value. Herrmann then utterly banished every kind of philosophy of religion, and using experience of Jesus as his criterion set Christianity as the only religion over against everything non-Christian as being non-religion. That set him free of the problematical consequences of an evolutionary history of religion which puts Christianity on the same level as other religions. But that has then made the matter even worse. The lee-way between allowing freedom to purely historical research and faith's religious and ethical interpretation of Jesus has, despite every effort to make statements of faith independent of historical research, become smaller and smaller. The latter has become more and more dependent upon the first. This situation has in many cases led to a definite religious subjectivism which is mainly concerned with personal religious experience and considers everything historical as merely stimulation and sign-posts. Or it leads to a traditionalism which proceeds not from the isolated person of Jesus but from the whole historical substance of Christianity. Or to a personality cult which ascribes to every great religious personality a persuasive power to elevate and to communicate, and which values Jesus simply as the central pedagogue.

Particularly interesting in the case of Herrmann is the struggle between history-writing and subjective mysticism. He stresses increasingly the personal certainty of the religious life in itself. It can only be found as one's own truth and one's own experience. But it needs a power supply from history and a foundation outside itself. At the same time Herrmann has recourse again and again to the 'impression of Jesus' which can be got from the gospel, independently of all historical work. Someone who has at this point become certain of his cause does not need to concern himself unduly about what other people consider necessary on historical grounds. This 'impression' then implies a special metaphysical position for Jesus established through judgments of faith. These are quite extraordinarily difficult statements and their difficulty will increase in proportion that their real sense is understood. If on the other hand the main thing in the person of Jesus is located in the material content of Christianity's religious and ethical ideas, i.e. upon what is called the 'principle of Christianity', then again these are plunged into the most violent motion by researches in sociology and social history, and especially by practical social problems. The harmony between spirit and nature so often called Christian by the older liberalism, the unity of life in God with its strong intellectualist and aesthetic colouring has as good as disappeared and sounds like a dead phrase.

The Lutheran ethic of vocation and position in society, was renewed by Ritschl. It has made particularly clear the gulf between this conservative ethic that accepts the status quo, seeing it as a matter of estate, and the total social regrouping and totally new tasks of the present, which force Christianity also to completely new reflexion about its ethics. But everything here is at a very early stage and Gottschick's excellent *Ethics* only marks the break-through of the new ways of posing the questions. My researches on *The Social Teachings of the Christian Churches* currently in press show what profound changes and interweavings Christian ethics, apparently the most solid kernel of the Christian principle, has undergone. But above all the general history of religion, unconcerned with dogmatic boundaries, reaches out for Christianity even more energetically, and draws it into the general history of the development of the religious consciousness. This happens not just at a theoretical level but in concrete particulars. Facts are what count here now, not theories. Christianity can be shown to contain in its make up elements of all the religions in its environment. It is itself a confluence of the great currents at the turn of the religious era. It can no longer be isolated, but must be placed in the continuity of the development, however highly its special character and newness are evaluated. Dogmatic turn-pikes and boundary stones no longer frighten off researchers, and dogmaticians are more and more under pressure from historians.

Scientific theology, therefore, is on all fronts in a state of most profound and difficult turmoil. Since it is not allowed to operate in the practical life of the church, dominated as this is by conservative or at best mildly conniving practice, it has taken on even for young theologians what is without doubt an almost disturbing character. Its great, free, forwards-striving character is hardly felt any longer. Instead we hear more about the problems it creates and the conflict with the forms and authorities of the church. Talented and strongly educated, free personalities fresh for the future are urgently needed. But it is hard to win them for theology or to keep them there. We are certainly approaching hard times despite the great and high tasks posed especially by the present for a free religious life.

5. *The significance of general philosophy of religion for solving this split*

To draw the consequences of the situation for the further development of theology exceeds the framework of this sketch. I want only to underline the really main basic problem. This is to be found in the juxtaposition of a purely scientific historical theology and a practical mediating dogmatics. The real problem of the situation cannot be understood in any other way, given how things are and their internal constitution. All historiography is bound to ordinary historical methods. Theological pretend history which sees things here under other laws and presuppositions than in non-Christian areas stands condemned by its endless evasions and untruths. On the other side, every conceivable dogmatics must take account of the special character of religious knowledge. It must give up the claim to scientific and adequate knowledge and continue and use the powers of the tradition. The relation of the two and the possibility of their co-existence is a matter of life and death.

Despite its obvious short-comings, C.A. Bernoulli's book *Über die kirchliche und wissenschaftliche Theologie* is well worth pondering. He has quite rightly picked up this problem as the central one. The latest attempt at dividing up the whole theological field, that of Paul Wernle,[7] is basically concerned with the same problem.

It is in fact this essential and fundamental problem which is at the heart of contemporary scientific theology and prevents it from being truly content about its great mission. Bernoulli's solution of a completely presuppositionless historical research without any kind of religious basis running parallel with a practical church dogmatics that absolutises certain historical data and that has no scientific value and can even allow its positions to be scientifically incorrect, is just not possible. Bernoulli has meanwhile been consistent and said a firm goodbye to theology. But he laid his finger on the sore point. This is where help is needed. All scientific theology must at this point produce a programme which enables it to be scientific study of the total historical phenomenon of Christianity and at the same time support for a living religious preaching.

Remedy and clarity are only possible if both branches of work going their separate ways are given a common stem and so too a common presupposition. Historical theology cannot be presuppositionless in the sense of regarding the historical knowability of Jesus, the complete erroneousness of the church's own view of its history, the non-Christian origins of the apostles' teachings, and the validity and continuity of Christianity as ever open questions or possibilities that have continually to be reckoned with. It must of course raise these sorts of questions, but it must somehow finally make up its mind about them and then either dissolve itself and Christianity or else finally feel free to consider the large basic issues of the knowability of Jesus and his abiding religious significance, and the prime validity of Christianity, as a matter of general presuppositions.

These results have to be achieved partly on a basis of its own work and partly from broader general investigations. I have no doubt that it will recover the knowability of Jesus and so the possibility of a religious valuation of him from its own work. It will regain these as

---

[7] *Einführung in das theologische Studium*, Tübingen, 1908.

fully legitimate presuppositions won on the basis of honest and uncorrupted work. The religious valuation itself does not belong to it. All it can indicate is a state of affairs which is certain and clear enough for a religious valuation to be able to be attached to it. The main question, however, concerning the validity of Christianity itself is not a purely historical one. It is a matter of philosophy of history or philosophy of religion which can only be tackled in a scientific way from the perspective of a general theory of religion and a theory about its graduations as perceived by the philosophy of history.

Here, too, there is no question of an arbitrary decision or some sort of notion of an exclusive miracle justifying the affirmation of Christianity. It is rather a matter of a comparative valuation proceding from a view of the whole of historical life so far as we can know it. Here too we have to struggle for the presupposition as men with autonomy; we can not just subject ourselves to it. But having attained it we have as a matter of principle a conception which serves as a foundation for all that follows. All historical research can then proceed completely freely within it. Here again, this presupposition can either be won or it cannot. If it cannot then of course a specifically Christian theology providing normative knowledge is no longer possible. But if it can, we have in full freedom made a fundamental decision about values which gives a basis for all that follows and upon which a special and independent research into Christian history can have its significance for systematic theology. The emphasis then rests upon the religious content alive in the present, but its historical emergence is for that very reason of more than merely scientific interest. The historical elements find a significance internal to the religious world for forming the religion of the present. But faith's interpretation of the history undertaken for this purpose must conform to the results of research.

We are just as much led back to this sort of a general science of religion by systematic theology and ethics. The whole theory of agnosticism – recognising that religious knowledge exists in the symbolic and inadequate expression of religious experiences, and conforming to the modern world-view and latching on to the forces of history – all that can only be obtained, grounded and guided along the right lines by a general theory of religious knowledge. If dogmatics is to be a normative science and real knowledge instead of a lazy and in the worst sense practical compromise that weakens everything, then that can only be based upon a careful theory of this nature. It will then on the one side be able to make an internal valuation of everything in the tradition and at the same time carry on developing independently and freely harmonising and fusing itself with modern knowledge. Just as we found, in speaking of historical theology, that the foundation came from a philosophy of history that proceeded from a consideration and graduation of the whole of man's religious life, so here too, in the discussion of systematic theology, it comes from a comparative theory about the psychological quality of the religious consciousness and its value as knowledge, and is again based upon the whole fulness of phenomena.

Both problems, however, unite for the task of creating a general science of religion or philosophy of religion that does not aim to construct a knowledge of God by philosophical means but rather which investigates the religious consciousness critically and analytically to discover its general laws and graduations of value. The intention is to determine in this way with complete scientific freedom the position and significance of Christianity amongst the great formations of religious life. The possibility of such a philosophy of religion, the solution of its task in the sense of recognising the prime validity of Christianity; that is the common presupposition shared by the purely scientific historical theology and by the practical mediating agnostic dogmatics.

The purely scientific character of the first comes from the scientific character of the historical methods which have been successfully developed for getting to know historical actuality. The agnostic, only conditionally scientific character of the latter comes from the agnostic character of all religious knowledge as such. It consists in conserving and continuing already created symbols and in conforming to the growing sum of knowledge. It therefore is by nature both free and creative and also bound to the tradition. But both these branches sprout from the same stem of a general investigation in the philosophy of religion, the result of which, establishing the prime validity of Christianity, does not need to be proved again and again. It can be taken as recognised. Only on this presupposition is theology and an internal as opposed to merely opportunistic justification of theological faculties possible. Only then does their existence depend not merely on the passing historical and geographical accident that we are in fact Christians, but upon the recognition of a special inner value of Christianity itself.

If we look closer, this demand for such a discipline was already made by Schleiermacher, the man who separated scientific historical work from the practical mediating disciplines and so created and recognised the whole situation.[8] In making this separation he

---

[8] See Süskind on the admittedly very aphoristic account of this philosophy of religion as a critical discipline in the *Ethics*, and on how it is concealed by a 'philosophical theology' that is very tied in its presupposition in the *Brief Outline*. In

presupposed a common root which he called philosophical theology and which in emphasising more strongly its presuppositionless character we are calling philosophy of religion. He only sketched out this discipline and his treatment of it in *The Christian Faith* is only indirect. But the broad sweep of his thought with its foundations in philosophy of religion and the branching-off of the two large main branches from this common stem has never really been seriously carried through by the theologians. Only the Hegelian theologians have done so, but they have then dealt with the philosophy of religion in a way that is intended to remove the separation again and at the same time make dogmatics into the expression of a scientifically demonstrable metaphysics. The programme has never been carried out in Schleiermacher's own sense. It remains to be realised and it is the task of scientific theology today to take it up in complete freedom and with the broadest scientific education. This is what is needed rather than swamping with more and more talk Schleiermacher's brilliant but extremely fragmentary sketch, and especially his veiled development of it in the Introduction to *The Christian Faith*. Scarcely one stone of Schleiermacher's own teaching can remain upon another, but his programme remains the great programme of all scientific theology. It only needs working out, not replacing by new inventions. It is also to be hoped that philosophical thought which today itself stands increasingly before the question of religion will off its own bat solve this problem in a similar sense by evaluating the historical element. From that side too some understanding for this task will then re-emerge, instead of despising the Church at a theoretical and literary level while at a practical level submitting to its domination.

Only in this way will we again find a programme for scientific theology and one which has the advantage of being not a new invention nor a clever fad but an old fundamental idea of our great master and a requirement that has grown organically out of the situation. This will again give a central point for the groups and tendencies in scientific theology which are today totally disoriented and in need of something new to unite them. This central point will be able to overcome the split and false estimation of the distances. It makes possible the most free and rich individual movement and particularity. This will then lead to a justification for the practical life of the church which only a desolate and ineffective anarchism or the

the Introduction to *The Christian Faith* this philosophy of religion can at most be looked for as the latent background. All that is now admirably discussed in Süskind's book. I have described the ecclesiastical domestication of Schleiermacher's theory of religion in my essay, 'Schleiermacher und die Kirche'. See *Schleiermacher der Philosoph des Glaubens*, ed. F. Naumann, Berlin, 1910.

pessimistic aversion towards the historical church can forget as is usually the case today in our scientifically educated world. We shall then be able to say of theology too: *non scholae sed vitae*. This will then find its life in its proper setting, in a fellowship that believes in the future, in living revelation, in increasing clarity and increasing love.

2

Religion and the Science of Religion[1]

Like all cultural sciences today the science of religion inevitably has to cope with the difficulty that the decisive, basic presupposition of its work needs to be determined right at the beginning, and that this presupposition then controls the whole treatment throughout. The issue is how one is to consider the great cultural creations of the human mind. Does one recognise in them the independent dispositions and powers of the mind, giving form from their own inner necessity to their own ideas and values? Or does one see in the mind nothing more than the formal power to shape a system of generalisations out of positive facts as far as possible objectively conceived, and to make this system serve the aims of human survival and the advancement of the race? In the first case we have before us mysterious, unconditioned tendencies and impulses of the reason, appearing constantly in new forms, out of whose autonomous spontaneity spring up the great cultural formations of family, state, society, law, art, science, religion and morals. In the second case we have above all the regular and homogeneous linkage of the objective facts of the external world, and in the inward world no mystery other than the ability to recognise the laws of nature and to use them for maintaining the life of the species. The first is the position of idealism, which not merely conceives of reality as being grounded in mind to begin with, but also considers mind to be furnished with qualitatively creative powers for the production of specific spiritual values. The second is the position of positivism, which in the first instance recognises only assured facts and the ordered connections between them, and then turns these facts over to be processed by the will, for which processing the only criterion is the assertion and completion of human existence itself. It is the age-old opposition between Platonism and realist empiricism, although each in its own way has now assimilated the modern concept of nature. In more modern terms it is the contrast between Kant and Hume, and to relate it even more to

[1] The title of this essay was 'Das Wesen der Religion und der Religionsgeschichte', i.e. 'The Nature of Religion and of the Science of Religion'. Troeltsch added a bibliographical note which is appended at the end of this essay (Ed.).

the present, it is the contrast between the positivism of the Comte and Spencer school against the interpretation of mind offered by Hegel and those akin to him.

There are indeed yet other fundamental presuppositions which claim to control the science of religion at its root and which have often been passionately applied to it. One is that of materialism based on natural philosophy. Another is the similarly based pantheism, which can admittedly be taken in a thoroughly idealist way, but which then even more, by the naturalistic idea of mathematical necessity, robs the life of the spirit of its qualitatively creative and pluralistic characteristics. From the point of view of materialism follows the metaphysical inadmissibility of the objects believed in by religion, and therefore the task of explaining religion as a psychologically motivated illusion. From the second point of view arises the demand to recognise in all religion only the purely pantheistic form as true, and to declare all theistic and pluralistic religious ideas to be psychologically motivated illusions. The absurdities in which both of these theories get the cultural sciences tangled, and the disinclination towards all metaphysics engendered by such conflicts, have of themselves destroyed the power of such presuppositions today, particularly for the science of religion. Materialism is no longer seriously considered in this context, and as pantheism is under suspicion of being a fantasy just as much as every other religious idea it too is at any rate no longer a self-evidently viable scientific presupposition. Today the dominant influence is that of positivism which renounces any kind of metaphysical causation theory and in particular any metaphysics of the relationship between spirit and matter. It meets the contemporary interest in the natural sciences by restricting all cognition to the ordered linkage of facts and by excluding all romantic and nativistic sources of knowledge, and yet it leaves an independent basis for the cultural sciences in that mind has the ability to make use of knowledge gained for the purposes of individual and corporate well-being. The only clear alternative to this is an idealism which stresses, not an abstract metaphysical teaching about the mere phenomenality of the physical world, but rather the concrete conception of mental life as being a power which brings forth what is ever again new and quite different. The nature of the continuity between these manifestations of the spirit, and their relationship with the basis of material nature, are secondary questions in this context. In the present state of the discussion the decision between these two has to be taken right from the start. The decision will be in principle either a matter of personal conviction, depending on how one reacts to these forms of life and their own account of themselves; or it will be based on the fundamental dogma that true science consists only in the ordered relating of positive facts and that the autonomy and spontaneity of mind may be allowed only so much as is compatible with this basic presupposition, while everything further is left on the corpse-strewn battlefield of human illusions.

The outline of the science of religion to be given below takes its stand decisively with the first point of view. It rejects the second because it is contradicted by one's objectively based impression of the ideal contents of culture; because its fundamental dogma is a naturalistic presupposition with no compelling foundation and cannot be exclusively valid even for the physical world; and finally because the remnant of spiritual autonomy and spontaneity retained by positivism is in contradiction to its own presupposition and is unmistakably the remnant of a much richer spiritual reality which could not be quite eradicated but was simply starved as far as it could go.[2]

If this account is correct, then we should reject from the start the positivistic theory of religion. It sees in religion absolutely nothing other than an activity of human thought which links together the phenomena with the human will so as to make this knowledge serve the aims of the human individual and race. Religion is taken to be nothing but the way in which, in the absence of objective scientific methods, reality was ordered and interpreted, and the images of the powers and forces of this reality linked with the objectives of the human species. Religion would thus be a primitive science of the basic human psyche, with an associated ethical and social teaching, a way of thinking which personifies everything as spirits finally producing the idea of God, and whose naive transference of human and personal intentionality into the wider non-human reality makes these gods into the promoters and guarantors of human ends. For this period of thought it is indispensable and beneficent, unavoidable and natural, but it disappears therefore necessarily with the change in human thought from personifying fantasy to depersonifying science; with the

---

[2] I have shown in an essay on William James how the task of the philosophy of religion can be formulated from a positivistic standpoint which values more highly the spontaneity and the independent wealth of content of mind, and which finds in Comte and Spencer too much constraint imposed by what was originally a rationalistic and mechanical concept of nature. For this reason James terms his position not positivism but pragmatism. I have shown there that in this way the distance from idealism can be reduced, but that it is necessary to oppose this view too by asserting the idealist standpoint. On this question see also Windelband's 'Der Wille zur Wahrheit' in *Präludien*, 1911. [N.B. Troeltsch's article referred to here has been translated as 'Empiricism and Platonism in the Philosophy of Religion'; see Appendix: Troeltsch in English translation (Ed.).]

change from a cosmic, anthropomorphic generalisation of the values of human life to the recognition that human intentionality is found only in man himself and in his own promotion of the welfare of the species on the basis of scientific knowledge.

The whole science of religion becomes under these circumstances an evolutionary investigation of the thought-forms of the primitive mentality and its gradual transition to positive science and a scientific ethic based thereupon. Its only theme then becomes one of rise and decay. Its task is purely historical and psychological – an account of the psychology of peoples. The objectively systematic concern can only be to ensure that the important social functions fulfilled by this phenomenon, without which it would not have taken on such great importance, are not neglected on its dissolution but are emphatically taken over into modern, positive science.

Initially it is not a question of refuting this theory but rather of denying the presuppositions on the basis of which it claims to be the only possible one. The way must be held open for religion to be fully apprehended. It must be possible to analyse it in its own terms. It must be examined at least provisionally as a completely independent phenomenon, which it claims itself after all to be. It must not be made subject from the start to general theories which prescribe in a prejudicial way what in religion is justifiable and what is not. Such would be a violation of the analysis right at the beginning, and such a violation is affected by the positivistic theory. According to this theory one knows to begin with what religion is and what it can only be: namely, an intellectual error of the primitive mentality which has managed to survive so long because of its great importance for social cohesion and its connection with the human need for happiness.

For this theory there is no other mental procedure beyond the inter-correlation of facts and exploitation of such thought for the species' desire to assert itself. Religion too has to be thus accommodated under these principles, with account taken of its origin under the special conditions of primitive thought which had not yet gone beyond the stage of personification and learned to distinguish between human goals and the universe indifferent to them. If this ready-made prejudice is rejected and the possibility of qualitatively individual mental dispositions and constructions is recognised, then religion does not need to be conceived of in advance as a merely historical and temporary problem with respect to its origin, development and decay, but can also form a real and permanent element in its innermost nature and in its meaning for culture. In that case one does not already know without further ado what religion is. On the contrary, a knowledge of what it really is can only be determined as a result of the analysis to be made. And what it is can in the first instance be recognised only out of itself, out of the investigation and comparison of its own statements about itself, and out of the relationship which it claims to have towards other cultural elements and which these display towards it. One is then not bound from the start with knowledge about what it cannot be and in particular that it cannot possibly be what it claims to be. The analysis owes no allegiance to a fundamental view of things which predetermines the whole conception of the matter from fixed assumptions, but on the contrary it can draw out from the subject matter itself its own inner nature, in accordance at least in the first instance with the way in which it understands itself. It is a quite secondary question as to how this own nature of the subject-matter itself is to be located among the rest of reality, whether it is able there to assert itself, and what modifications it there seems to or must undergo. The huge collection of facts which has now been brought together, especially by the positivist approach, and which has indeed often been quite meaningfully interpreted in so far as it is a question of the characteristic *forms of primitive thought*, is in our perspective only the source materials for the real enquiry to come. The question is what is the religious quality among all these varied and manifested phenomena which are generally referred to as religion? How can one seize hold of the religious factor in them, and what meaning, what depth of development and what implication does this religious factor have in its emergence through history? Only then can the further questions be considered about truth content, developmental laws and objectives, and the relationship between this element of culture with other elements of culture.

On the other hand however the general presupposition of idealism posited here does not imply anything more than the possibility of seeing in religion a qualitatively individual and creative power of spiritual life. It by no means entails an interpretation of religion determined in advance or the unfair insertion of philosophical postulates of a metaphysical kind into the religious ideas. Rationalism at all times has tended to read supposedly rationally based concepts about the nature of the world into the religious ideas as if they were what these contain by way of truth, so that it appears, on these presuppositions, that no other truth content than this could be found to remain in religion, if indeed it is allowed to have any at all. This treatment founders, however, partly on the scepticism with which just such metaphysics as this is nowadays greeted, and even more on the embarrassment and violation which accrues all round as a result of the way in which religion is then conceived. For this reason the sensitivity of recent thought to everything factual, concrete and empirical, has steered research emphatically towards the examination of religious phenomena as these are available in the realm of historical, psychological reality. The philosophy of religion has become the science of religion. From a branch of metaphysics has emerged the independent enquiry into the factual world of the religious consciousness. Out of the highest general science has appeared a new specific science. In so far as positivism for its part has wished to see this, in so far as it characterised metaphysical philosophy of religion as a scientific watering-down of the really more powerful religious ideas, its contribution has advanced the matter. Only that interpretation must be rejected which grows out of the presupposition of positivism and conditions every further apprehension from the start. Neither the semi-materialistic metaphysics of positivism nor an idealist metaphysic, however formulated, should be allowed to undertake in advance the interpretation and criticism of the religious data and thereby, from such a prejudicial treatment of the religious data, pre-define the task of the science of religion. With respect to both of these it is therefore a matter of scientific research into religion finding its independence. It should press upon the phenomenon of religion neither an interpretation of its truth, nor of its untruth. Only the initial possibility and probability that religion is a qualitatively distinct aspect of the spiritual life of man is to be maintained. Without the presupposition of such a possibility and probability the investigation does indeed become idle. The importance of the idealist presupposition lies in the fact that the independence which the religious self-consciousness claims for itself is possible in terms of an idealist theory such as has been described. Without it one is tied down in advance to the impossibility of an epistemological or cognitive value in religion, whereas with it the possibility of establishing such a value is left open but without the sense in which it might come about being in any way prejudged.

Thus within modern science there has gradually formed a science of religion which is an independent specific science similar to logic, ethics and aesthetics. It is something different from the philosophy of religion in the older sense, which was always a philosophical treatment, criticism, interpretation or even destruction of the religious phenomenon, from a point of view which saw real, concrete religion as nothing but an annexe, as a more or less accurate realisation of the philosophical content, or as an illusion to be explained in this way or that. What is required is an analysis of the religious consciousness as an independently characterisable form and direction among the creations of human consciousness, and the sifting out of those indications of epistemological and cognitive content which can be drawn in the first instance from the phenomenon itself.

Critical idealism, as the doctrine of the creation of all life formations through consciousness, and as a critical demarcation between qualitatively different creations of consciousness found side by side, is the general presupposition required here as for all science, and it cannot be developed secondarily *within* the science of religion any more than within any other specific science. It is enough that this idealism, which arises out of the most general and abstract considerations, and leaves open the possible validity of religious ideas, should meet together with the inner self-awareness of religion with respect to the truth-content within itself, and that these two should be mutually confirming in so far as they allow the possibility of this truth-content. Everything else must remain open.

If on the one hand the science of religion presupposes philosophy in this way, on the other hand it leads again back into philosophy, just as does every other specific science. As the natural sciences flow out into the philosophy of nature, historical science into the philosophy of history, ethics, logic and aesthetics into general philosophical reflection, so too with the science of religion. The recognition of the truth-content of religion, however the science of religion displays it to be constituted, comes into relationship with all the other aspects of knowledge. It receives a conditioning from these which can only take place when they are brought into synopsis, and then in return it has its own effect upon these others with an integrative theme of its own, which only from this point can be brought to bear over the whole field of knowledge. The truth-content of religion can only assert itself and take on the form of its most general meaning in the context of such a final concluding treatment. At this point the science of religion turns over into the philosophy of religion, or if the expression is not taken in the sense of a confessional authoritarian dogmatics, into theology.

Between the two poles, however, lies an independent field of work, that is, precisely the science of religion in its concrete particularity. Its great question is the question of the nature of religious phenomena, the question of their epistemological and cognitive import, the question of the value and the meaning of the great historical religious formations. If the result seems to demand a stepping out beyond all these historical formations, then the practical outcome is a contribution to the uprooting of the prevailing religions and to the creation of religious unrest, in which new religious formations arise and perhaps a surrogate for real religion is produced. If on the other hand the enquiry seems to have to tarry with one of the great historical formations as a valid culmination, then it becomes the scientific basis for the theology of this religion. Such a theology must then see its free and living task in a consideration of its own history, as a revelation of the highest religious values, and in working through its religious thought-world for the purpose of practical proclamation. In so far as such a theology is a science it finds its basis in a science of religion and a philosophy of religion of this kind.

1. *Naive religion and religions treated scientifically*

The science of religion therefore does not produce religion or give birth to true religion, but it analyses and appraises religiosity as a datum. In order to treat religion scientifically in this sense, it is necessary above all to attain a view of religion which is still independent of scientific interpretation and processing. As far as possible, the object of study should itself be our informant, without being distorted by our scientific classifications, comparisons, explanations and interpretations. Against this is admittedly the difficulty that religion in its own real life is luxuriantly tangled up with scientific conceptions and interests and points of contact. This means that even if a serious attempt is made to hold back one's own interpretations and scientific theories, one cannot thereby directly grasp the essence of religion as something free of all scientific admixtures. Primitive religion is in the main just as strongly marked by primitive scientific thought as is every cultural religion by more highly developed thought, by philosophy and by popular modes of explanation. Indeed religion is criss-crossed with a wealth of other kinds of interest too, ethical, artistic, legal, political and social. But in these cases the distinction is easier to draw, or at least more familiar to us, than when the religious functions of the idea of God are merged with its rational functions directed towards the explanation of the world, or with the aesthetic functions connected with the concrete elaboration of the idea. If the essence of science lies in comparing, correlating and connecting up a set of phenomena in order to arrive at general concepts which control and illuminate particular cases, then the essence of religion freed from scientific pre-determination must lie in its naive loyalty to the direct pressure of religious fervour without any artificially contrived interconnections and general overviews. We have to seek religion in its naive, direct expressions, which go no further in their links with the rest of life and thought than is necessary for these to be mastered and influenced. For naive religion such matters as the unity and interrelatedness of reality, comparisons with other religious ideas and apologetics with respect to them, and consolidation by linking up with generally current objective views of the world, all these are quite remote or of little real interest. Naive religion will be found everywhere where the feeling for science and generalised accounts of things is little developed, where religion is not overwhelmed by the comprehensively interpretative fantasy of myth, and where there is nevertheless a strong religious sensitivity. The world of religious ideas is everywhere analogous in certain main outlines, and when it was powerfully created by primitive man unknown to us in prehistoric times, it must have emerged out of a naive and strong pressure. Where this creation can still be observed in its dying phases we shall frequently surmise the presence of naive religion. Thus the really primitive peoples and the most ancient periods of history open to philologists and archaeologists will give evidence of naive religion, although at the same time care must be exercised not just to take personificatory thinking, or indeed myth, as being religion or to interpret every case of religious practices as being real religion. Admittedly all divine or demonic powers are always conceived of at this level in terms of the generally current world-view, but this does not imply the converse that all conceptions of invisible powers which determine events are religious. They only have religious meaning in the cult and through the cult, and a cult is only to be found when these powers have delivered themselves of a revelation or a proclamation which initiates the connexion with them in the cult. The religious idea only arises in so far as particular events or impressions suggest that the power revealed in them has religious meaning and demands religious intercourse whether temporary or permanent. One can only speak of naive religion in so far as such a belief in a revelation and a cultic relationship possesses a strong, simple and direct validity. We approach naive religion to the extent that we can hope for the possibility of getting at the nature of this cult and the feelings which precede and accompany it. In cults, prayers and liturgies, in so far as these have not just come to be carried on as mere conventions, lies the meaning of the primitive religions, a sense which brought into being not only countless small and changing examples but also the great cultic centres and ideas of God. Thus while the mere ethnographical and anthropological study of religion can only be used with caution as indicative of naive religion, it does nevertheless incomparably refine our sensitivity to it. This is because in this area scientific enquiry and technology are still too little developed to confuse the natural self-assurance and the natural instinct of religion. Admittedly mythical thought too is a kind of science, and moreover one which tends to swing over into artistic fantasy. In both these directions it has overrun religion often enough. But the interconnexions of myth are very loose and therefore it is easier for a quite naive expression of religious faith to appear distinctly through it.

Naive religion is also to be found in the great specifically religious personalities who usually spring from classes of people not burdened by science, and whose whole life and work is nothing but a complete devotion to the religious idea which holds sway for them, admitting of neither doubt nor proof. Here belong the founders and the reformers, the prophets and seers, the preachers and missionaries, who may indeed be more or less reflective with regard to their own inner religious experience and to the dialectics of the religious idea, but who in religion itself perceive only the religious thoughts and who are so certain in themselves that they need little or no backing up by generally recognised truth or knowledge. Admittedly the idea of God is itself even in such cases quite naturally linked in many ways with received ideas and may even be identical to them. It is found within the general framework of the view of the world current at the time. Nevertheless what matters every time is the initiative of communication on the part of the divinity, enlightenment, revelation, the sense of being grasped by a truly divine mode of being, and then consequent upon this prophecy, prayer, communication and unity with the divine being, processes which are accompanied by characteristic and specifically religious feelings and moods.

Very important data are those one-sided or exclusively religious personalities, sects and groups, among whom the effects of scientific ways of thinking sit but loosely or are absent altogether, and who also have not yet lost their religious innocence by any struggle against science. These are the enthusiasms and the eccentricities so utterly despised by earlier research into religion and which are now by contrast almost over-esteemed. One must distinguish carefully here between an over-refined or a starkly postured enthusiasm, and the genuine article. In any case one should not become too involved with this dangerous material for fear of producing a caricature of religion. For the sources of religious sensitivity run freely at the other extreme even in the most intellectually detached thinkers, and if one can only learn to distinguish the religious motifs of their thought from the rest it is possible to learn about the characteristic nature of religion particularly well by observing *them*. It is possible to consider the whole history of philosophy from the point of view of how far it is influenced by the side-effects of the great historical religions or of personal religious intuitions. This in turn gives a basis for determining the difference between the religious and the purely intellectual. It is here that just such thinkers as Plato, Plotinus, Augustine and Spinoza are of the greatest importance, because it is above all in their quest for unity of understanding that we can most instructively observe the nature of the religious in its recalcitrance towards comprehension by the intellect.

Finally the inner experience and self-observation of the enquirer himself must be brought into consideration, and in particular all those aspects of it where he knows himself to be without sideward glances and secondary interests, and especially without philosophical speculation, and is aware that he is feeling and immersing himself into the religious impulse alone. What is required, as in research into art, is to grasp the phenomenon as far as possible in its most instinctively sure self-revelation, that is, to gain a 'pure experience' of it, the sort of pure experience which by contrast with those which have already been scientifically interpreted is always necessary as a starting point for new orientations and scientific insights. Certainly the immediacy of the experience is easily spoiled by self-observation. Yet every religious person knows the amazing variety of intensity in the various religious moments of his life, and it is a question here not so much of direct self-observation but rather of the recollection of this gradation and of the moments of deepest intensity and immediacy. Everyone knows that these moments are to be found in prayer and in meditation. To these above all a theory of religion must do justice, if it is to be not a mere metaphysical system for the intellect, but a theory of religion as it really is.

In the manifestations referred to above is to be found the most obvious and most appropriate data for research. If one holds to these one is likely to grasp the characteristic and essential features of this sphere of culture. With all this it can admittedly almost never be a question of completely pure naivity. Yet it will be so paramount that the enquiry is at least steered towards the most essential and leading phenomena. But this distinction between naive and scientifically reflective religion should not be taken as a judgment of value. Naive religion, so far as one can locate it, indicates for us the essential characteristics of the phenomenon; but this does not in itself mean that it is more authentic, more pure or more true, as compared with scientifically reflective religion which would be less authentic, counterfeit, and confused with alien admixtures. On the contrary, naive religion is usually marked by an antipathy towards the acquisition of clarity and harmony through science, and therefore tends to be one-sided, cultureless, overwrought or mentally confined, inharmonious and confused. Only the few really great figures are an exception here because for them the naive religiosity is combined with an equally naive, noble, pure and clear spiritual disposition with no trace of selfishness of dogmaticism. Science and the acquisition of science are strangers to them, and purely scientific thought has no way of appending itself directly to them; yet they have the seal of genius of which Schiller said: science can teach you nothing, may she learn rather from you. Similar to these are some lesser spirits who give themselves over to the religious impulse purely and unreflectively, and who yet precisely because of this submission leave the rest of life which they do not understand to its own devices, in the hands of their God. In general, however, this is not the case with naive religion. It requires everywhere the correctives of scientific education and disciplines, quietness and harmony, objective knowledge of the world and balanced appraisal born of tolerance. It needs everywhere a broadening of vision over the rest of the world and a harmonisation with what is contained in the world. Indeed the latter is a requirement which arises even for the purest and greatest religious revelations, if they are not to issue in mere philistinism and narrow sectarianism among the masses whom they excite. Christianity became what it is only through its alliance with classical antiquity, while among the Copts and the Ethiopians it turned into a caricature. With us too cultureless Christianity easily tends to become a priestly clericalism or petty sentimentality and pomposity. Islam was enriched by the influence of Persian and Greek culture, and under the influence of the Turks it became a destructive philistinism. The distinction between naive and scientifically reflective religion is important therefore only for laying a basis for scientific enquiry itself. Such a basis attempts to clarify what is essential and characteristic in religious life in order not to obscure the picture in a superficial way or to approach religion with uncomprehending destructiveness.

The science of religion therefore has like all science a practical objective, namely to organise and clarify what itself grows in naive and tangled form and to harmonise and to balance out one-sided tendencies with other factors in life. It increases in importance with the richness and complexity of life in general. It does not then create or discover true religion, but it does contribute to the development of what is given in so far as it is able to be developed at all. The purpose of scientific work on religion is therefore entirely and necessarily to influence religion itself. Religion like every other sphere of culture needs to be harmonised and adjusted with the rest of life, and it can only in this way learn to separate kernel and husk and to bring the kernel into ever new and fruitful relationships with the other areas of life. Science was born last among the powers of human culture and all the other great movements preceded it as the creations of naive and powerful forces. But science grows because it is inevitable, because naive isolation can nowhere be maintained, and because the labour of a consciously functioning intellectual culture consists in linking and harmonising the various components of civilisation.

The freshness and energy of every feature of life derives from naive forces and their creations, and the living continuance of these powers depends entirely on contact with them or renewal of them. But from science we derive order, clarity, peace, contextual balance and mutual fructification. The scientific regulation of the relations of the naive forces to each other is as important as their original production. For this reason science itself must first learn to distinguish itself from the naive forces and their creations, but must then go to work on the formations which it finds before it with full energy and clarity. That this exercise does not leave religion unchanged is only to be expected. Even with respect to religion, science is not the art of washing a fur without wetting it. Religion which undergoes the influence of science will become other than it was, and must do so. This is the seed-bed of all the difficult and unavoidable struggles between religion and science, and of the distinctions between naive religion, culturally developed religion and formations lying between the two. What is required is so to manage these struggles that on the one hand the specific character and natural power of religion is not broken and on the other hand the blessing of scientific balance, harmony, tolerance and understanding is not trifled away.

2. *Initial attempts at a scientific treatment of religion*

Things being thus it is not without reason that attempts to process and influence religion scientifically are as old as civilisation itself. It is not a matter of the spontaneous and unconscious merging of the religious ideas with the general pictures of things, such that sometimes religious ideas penetrate thought in general and sometimes the world-view penetrates the religious ideas in an inextricable way. This happens quite naturally as soon as the attempt is made to express and interpret the religious ordering of things which founds the cult. Rather it is a matter of conscious labour towards the unification of the various cults and conceptions of God which come up against each other, and of the conscious harmonisation and linking of the religious ideas with other knowledge of the world.

(1) As far as our present knowledge of history goes the great productions of priestly speculation in India, Babylonia and Egypt take first place here. The various cults and deities found side by side or linked together already through political conquest are unified and traced to a common root. A pantheon is created in which the

individual divinities are linked together by heredity and kinship and thus traced back to a highest primal god. Unity and coherence is brought in by the doctrine of a theogony, of an original sharing and splitting, or of a pattern of inheritance as in a family. At the same time the cultic myths are systematised, harmonised and reinterpreted and the whole myth is re-edited as a kind of theology. This becomes a corpus of wisdom restricted to priests and specialists and not reckoned accessible to ordinary participants in the cult. From this point on speculation takes still further steps, leading to a speculative monotheism which radically reinterprets the popular mythology. The individual divinities are emasculated into mere particular manifestations of the divine being as such, and are considered as being so many names or forms of revelation of the one deity. Popular polytheism does not disappear, but above it hovers the priestly interpretation. Sometimes there may even be made an attempt at practical reform in this direction, in which a monotheistic cult is introduced revering the primal ground and unity of all divinities under a particular symbol, and allowing one single supreme divinity to swallow up all the other gods. This is how the famous attempt at monotheistic reform of the Egyptian Akhnaton is to be understood. With this too is connected the assimilation of the general view of the world to the religious idea. This again is partly to bring about unity and coherence, so as to present religion to the intellect in a state of comprehensive coherence with reality as a whole. Partly too it counters contradictions and objections which might arise against the religious ideas on the basis of the general understanding of the world. And so from theogony we progress to cosmogony, to the doctrine of the creation of the world as the result of divine activity, and to the exhibition of divine sway in all the happenings of the world. A mythical cosmology arises, the doctrine of an upper, divine world and a lower, human world. These are thought to correspond intimately with each other so that what takes place in the upper world is repeated in the lower world, and this gives rise to astrology and systematised divination. Indeed the amazing influence which Babylonian science, in this sense, came to exercise over the ancient world is today clearer than ever, even if the age of this Babylonian speculation has often been over-estimated. The oldest speculations of the Greeks also follow this path, except that in this case they are not in the hands of the priests but of free thinkers and literati.

(2) Another form of scientific harmonisation between various religions, which because of their differences and contradictions demand unification and can only maintain themselves by being keyed

in with something more general, is syncretism. This appears wherever the naive presupposition of autochthony and complete separation from all foreigners and barbarians has broken down, and where a cultural unity of diverse peoples arises. In syncretism the various divinities of different peoples are regarded as being nothing but different names for deities who are in themselves identical. A detailed and laborious attempt is undertaken to identify the various national gods with the corresponding foreign ones and to harmonise and combine the myths, so that it all appears as being the same religion which simply expresses itself all the time in various languages with various names for the gods. What is called Hellenism, and again the fusion of the Greek and Roman divinities, are the finest examples of this. While the priestly speculations of Babylon and Egypt united the deities of the areas over which they held sway, the Hellenist-Roman mixture of the gods brought together the deities of the various national and cultural systems. But once the path of reduction has been trodden in this manner it is not far to the idea of reducing the various identified deities with a common basis and of linking them up in this way with cosmological speculations. This happened on a grand scale in the time of the great confluence of peoples and cultures within the great Roman empire. After Stoicism had led the way a major attempt at this was Gnosticism. It tried to unify the various deities and cults in the perception of a fundamental unity to the world out of which there came theogonic and cosmogonic emanations. Believing and using the various myths without any attempt at historical criticism and applying Stoic and Platonic philosophy in a fantastic speculation, Gnosticism is a precursor of those attempts which have been undertaken in modern times with a much clearer historical conception and stricter metaphysical thought by Hegel and Schelling.

(3) In order to get nearer to the heart of the matter it is best to remain on the subject of religious myth. This came to be elaborated as a theory of the world and of events, it was fitted together with the scientific explanations of the world, then critically purified from among these, and the resultant speculation was declared to be the truth content of the cruder popular forms of faith and of cult theology. In these cases the importance of myth comes to be greater than that of the cult, which in this process itself remains unaffected in its popular and state-determined form. It involves the separation of myth and cult and the beginning of the divorcing of an intellectualised religion from the popular religion. In this sense all philosophy and speculation springs from myth and remains in company with it just as long as philosophy does not undertake a quite different evaluation and

explanation of things, and as long as the origin of religious myth does not itself become a problem or fail to count without question as a generally valid conviction and revelation. Thus in particular did Greek philosophy grow up out of speculative interpretations of myth. For this reason although it left myth ever further behind it, it nevertheless maintained a point of connection with it in all its main forms, apart from the purely sceptical and materialistic systems. This dissociation is even more interesting among the Indians where exegesis and meditation made of the old cultic songs of the Vedas a book of wisdom propounding an audacious pantheism, thereby leading to the cutting loose of brahmanic theory from every form of popular religion and cultic community. Thus arises a philosophical religion without cult, a religion of pure thought. Where such religion recognises the cult it lends it mystical and symbolic interpretations which divest it of its real character as cult. It either takes up a position opposed to the popular religion as in the case of the Eleatics, or it interprets the popular religion allegorically as in the case of the Stoics, and in some circumstances may combine with this a syncretism which goes on to see the real truth-content of the syncretistic identifications as lying ultimately in metaphysical concepts. The philosophy of religion becomes itself a philosophical and scientifically validated religion; though at the same time it must not be overlooked that aspects of concrete, positive religion remain influential in such a philosophical religion. It is only through a self-deceit that such elements can be made to appear as axiomatic scientific truths which merge with other scientific truths or which can allegedly be deduced from them. Seen in this light the history of philosophy emerges as being largely a series of transformations of religious motifs which in fact stem from the positive religions. But in so far as these motifs are raised into the sphere of the rational and of what is conceptually of general validity, they are altered in their nature and torn loose from their historical and positive context so that they may share in the essence of all that is rational and in the autonomy and general validity of knowledge.

(4) In all these cases the object of the attempt to comprehend religion scientifically is the finished product of the religious life in myth and cult. This product is built into the more general systems, and more or less altered to fit, but the inner, living religious process itself is not made into an object of consideration. This happens in those quite different systems which arise from listening in to and describing religious moods and from the analysis of these moods and the technique of their stimulation. We have here in the first place

Indian mysticism, cultivated in certain branches of Brahmanism and artificially interpreted out of the sacred writings of the popular polytheistic religion. For this mysticism not even the pantheistic theory is decisive but rather enlightenment in practice and the confirmation of theory in personal experience. Not only does the concreteness of the cult disappear here, but also that of the myth and of any theory which reformulates it. Only the process of the origination and influence of the religious mood with its submission to the divine is seized upon and this is described in the full depth of its content. This represents the first psychological analysis of religion, and since it flees from all concrete expressions it sees religion as something which as a matter of course is timelessly and everywhere the same, while any historical reference to the stimulation of external events disappears. But such a psychology in turn still needs a firm foothold in a general view of the world, and so out of the mystical psychology of religion and the technique for bringing about the states in question there arises also a metaphysics which bears the well-known traits of the crudest and most audacious pantheism. Only the divine is real, and in religious devotion the appearance of a single, finite world of the senses is destroyed. A similar development may be seen with Greek mysticism. In this case mystical exaltation is linked by Plato with the philosophical doctrine of elevation to the realm of ideas as the true foundations of reality, and by the Neo-Platonists with the metaphysics of the various levels of reality and the return of the thinking spirit to the only truly real ground of the world. For the latter in particular this doctrine was a psychological analysis, a practical technique of religious stimulation and a reduction into the most general metaphysical foundations of the world. They made of it a power of influence for centuries, and a source on which Christians, Mohammedans and Jews drew for their analysis and techniques of subjective religiosity.

(5) There arose already in Greek thought an influential theory drawing upon the ethical elements woven in with the religious consciousness, namely Stoicism. Stoicism sees the essential kernel of religious ideas as being the concept of a general law to be obeyed by every rational being intending to maintain his dignity over against accident and sensuality, sorrow and misery, and which binds together all rational beings in a community of reason independent of all the accidents of race and blood. The metaphysical basis for this ethical law is then given through contamination with a pantheistically conceived general law of the universe, or with the law of nature in general which only emerges as a specifically ethical law for human

beings. The stoic theory of religion becomes a theory of an ethical law of nature, of the ethical law as an issue of the divine law of the world and of nature as a whole. In Roman and later Stoicism are found once again strong links with the idea of God in an ethical and theistic sense. This theistic-moral interpretation of Stoicism begins with Posidonius and became through Cicero a powerful influence for centuries. The concrete religions, cults and deities were treated as symbolic cyphers for individual manifestations of the universal law and could be interpreted quite syncretistically as a varied nomenclature for those manifestations. This theory was also taken over by Christian theology, though the syncretistic application of it was left aside, and used as a scientific account of the 'natural' religion and ethics which Christian theology presupposed and therefore as a foundation for its own theory of religion. For this reason the Stoic theory has achieved an exceptional degree of influence and often enough it has swallowed the theological theory of religion back into itself again.

(6) Next comes the illusionist theory of religion, a psychological analysis which also seeks out the spiritual motivations and pre-suppositions for the formation of religious ideas, but this time on the basis of quite other fully developed metaphysical assumptions which exclude the possibility of religion being true. This appears in mature Greek culture and is based upon a purely mechanistic metaphysics which has no more room for the gods, and upon a purely immanent hedonism which has no longer any perception of transcendent values. For this analysis neither the mystical conditions and feelings nor the ideas about the gods, the religious explanation of the world, cultic practice, or the motivations of fear and hope are taken into account. Religion appears as the result of unscientific fantasy, the product of fear and hope, as a construction and an institution for political ends. The practical result of such theories of religion is supposed to be the freeing of the emotional life from disturbances wrought by supersensible phenomena and incommensurabilities. This doctrine was stated particularly impressively by the school of Epicurus, and the explanation of myth along these lines by Euhemerus gave the whole system the special name of Euhemerism. The doctrine was revived in the Renaissance, and for similar reasons it has been quite richly developed by the modern groups which avow materialism and positivism.

(7) The last of the great theories is that of exclusive supernaturalism or of the doctrine of revelation. It was fundamentally elaborated in Judaism, then further developed by Christianity and

Islam. The extent to which the position was and is similar in Parseeism and Buddhism cannot easily be gauged in the present state of our knowledge of these religions. However that may be, it has had a quite specific development on the basis of the Jewish root. The religion of Israel is the only monotheism which is popular and not the result of speculation. It is an ethical monotheism which finds its final principle in the unity and the autonomy of the ethical divine will, and is thus not a speculative shell drawn over a persisting polytheism but the aggressive, radically anti-polytheistic religious power of a people. Thus the truth it bears takes on the character of a general validity and coherence, and the idea of a divine revelation beside which all other alleged revelations seem counterfeit. The holy scriptures in which this divine will is set down become the exclusively true and sacred source of knowledge, and the history of the chosen people of Israel becomes a quite special history of revelation and miracle compared with which all non-Jewish miracles are fables or demonic deceit. The deification of history which belongs intimately to the Jewish conception of God gives to the otherwise not unusual idea of sacred inspired scriptures a special perspective and position, such that the scriptures and the sacred history evidenced within them form a comprehensive and all-illuminating system of revelation and philosophy of history. According to this the will of God for the world is the fulfilment of his holy moral commandment; the greater part of mankind is fallen; only to the people of Israel is it granted to be the elect bearer of the truth and the leader of the repentance and return of man to God. This theory was then further developed particularly by the emergent scientific theology of the Christians and combined with the inheritance of the cosmology and philosophy of religion of antiquity. The revelation is more than a mere revelation. It begins with an effective preparation since the beginning of the world and finds its completion in redemption through Christ, a redemption consisting of the full knowledge of God, full union with God and full certainty of eternal blessedness after the annulment and forgiveness of sins. This process of salvation including in itself the Jewish idea of revelation is then finally set into the metaphysical framework of late antiquity, into the doctrine of the emanation and return of the spirit from the divinity back again to the divinity. In its departure from God the human spirit fell in sin and then was left to the mercy of its own natural forces and the inextinguishable remnant of reason. The leading power in the return to God is first the revelation in the narrower circles of the patriarchs and then of Israel, the salvation being prepared by directly miraculous initiatives and communications of the divine reason, until the full being of this latter finally takes human form in the incarnation of Christ, opens the way through the foundation of the Church and of its sacraments for all to participate in this saving incarnation of reason, and becomes the deification of man. The basic concepts of this theory are: the common idealistic metaphysics of emanation and return, the philosophy of history which divides mankind into those under original sin and those who are redeemed, the recognition of a profane revelation in heathen science, the location of the complete sacred revelation in the divine man, and the construction of the Church as the organ of salvation and of the fulfillment of reason. The theory was destined for a tremendous role in the history of the world, and in its further development it learned to support its fundamental concept of the divine reason with ever more elaborate philosophical means. Admittedly it was the miracles of salvation history, characteristic of the direct revelation and communication of God, which remained the finally decisive evidence for central religious truth. All else was thought of as human and therefore at best only indirectly divine knowledge, mostly obscured by sin. Thus it had little effect on the outline of the system as a whole when the protestant reformers broke up the framework of neo-platonic metaphysics, and no longer thought of the saving incarnation as being essentially an incarnation of the divine reason identical in principle with profane revelation. They retained the theory of original sin, the explanation of non-Christian relative truths of religion and ethics in terms of natural reason, and the apologetics of miracle, with its direct communication from a God who suspends nature as the evidence of absolute truth. Indeed the old outline returned again in a more modest form even among the protestant theologians and apologists down to the so-called 'positive theologians' of modern times. It represents a violent isolation of one's own religion over against all others by means of an exclusive supernaturalism, and then a new correlation of the two in a theory of natural and supernatural revelation. Thus this theory too ends up by gathering everything together under one coherent viewpoint, and is also significant in that from among the existing elements of the religious consciousness it stresses most highly the idea of revelation and authority. The religious philosophy which takes its point of departure here is a strictly constructed doctrine of supernatural authority which takes various forms. For the catholics it is based on the authority and the miraculous character of the Church, for the older protestantism it is based on the Bible, and for the orthodox protestants of the present it is based on the miracle of conversion which vouches for all other miracles. It is theology in the narrower, technical sense of the word, just as this is found too among the Jews and Mohammedans.

3. *The major modern systems*

By contrast with all these presuppositions and intellectual procedures of antiquity and the middle ages the modern world has created a new basis of scientific thought in the modern natural sciences and in the modern critical and evolutionary view of history. There are many points of contact with the science of antiquity, but nevertheless a completely new basis has been established. As a result of changes in the most important branches of knowledge the theoretical consideration of principles, that is, philosophy itself, has been set upon new presuppositions. This applies to philosophy in general and also to the science of religion in particular. In order to clarify this it will be helpful to characterise the major systems which have been built up on these new foundations. These new ideas have been emerging since the seventeenth century. First come the attempts of the great metaphysicians to find a scientific validation and formulation for the idea of God, it being assumed that this idea of God correctly understood will be more or less identical with that of the Christian revelation. Examples are Descartes, Spinoza, Malebranche and Leibniz. Next come the efforts to get away from the welter of different confessions and institutionalised revelations, by means of a psychological analysis which would establish a kernel of truth common to all religions, and which would at the same time be compatible with the new metaphysics aligned with the natural sciences. This was found in the ethical consciousness and its metaphysical correlates, and Christianity was seen as a kind of divine introduction to this truth of nature. This was the position of deism and its representative philosopher Locke, while closely related were the Scottish philosophers of feeling and Rousseau. Finally came the return to the mystical elements of the religious mood, apparently reflecting the experience and the perception of the unity of God and of the world, overcoming the dichotomy between these two in a saving way. This view is without time and without history, and it recognises everywhere and identically in all real religions, and in mystical Christianity, the real meaning of each and every religion. This is found in radical pietism and spiritualism and in the renewed neo-platonic mysticism. In addition there is no lack of radical religious scepticism, in which no room is left for the supernatural alongside a self-sufficient nature while comparative historical criticism makes all religions uncertain. This was Hume's line of thought, accentuated further by French radicalism and continued in positivism. Yet these are but the first stirrings of a new understanding. The main types of the modern scientific view of religion were not developed out of these movements until the nineteenth century. Broadly considered they can be understood under four headings.

(1) In the first place stands the philosophy of religion of *critical idealism*. This idealism is the final result of metaphysical theories which strove to combine the new mathematical and mechanistic philosophy of nature with an idealist and teleological view of the world. It abandons radically every metaphysics and every attempt to deduce a double realm of reality from a fundamental reality conceived in the mind, and believing such attempts to be fruitless, it limits itself to the analysis of the subjective human reason by which alone reality can be contained and on the basis of whose fundamental conditions it arises for us at all. At the same time the analysis is not essentially a psychological one which might categorise the contents of consciousness and examine their psychological origination, but rather it is an epistemological one which draws from the *de facto* psychological content the autonomous laws of validity which control our knowledge. Only through these laws of validity arises that knowledge of reality which is possible for the human reason. Among these laws of validity are found the laws of scientific, ethical, and aesthetic and teleological thought, but also the laws of the formation of religious ideas. For Kant and his nearest followers, among whom particular mention should be made of Fries with his doctrine of the religious sense of reason which finds expression in symbol and poetry, this law of the formation of religious ideas is most closely linked with the formation of ethical concepts, and it represents only the production of that religious world view which is logically pre-supposed with the moral consciousness. The essential religious idea that religion has to do with a contact with the ground of things is maintained, in spite of the strict limitation of attention to the subjective reason and its laws, by the fact that precisely in these laws it is not the arbitrary consciousness of the individual which is expressed but rather the inner necessity of consciousness in general and therefore a generally valid necessary reason which reigns above mere individuals. In concert with two other factors this concept of 'reason as such' reaches out towards the region of the metaphysical and the religious. The allied factors are, on the one hand, the net result of the theoretical formation of the ideas of natural philosophy, which because of the antinomic character of such concepts leaves open the possibility of the reality of an absolute ground to the world, and on the other hand, the formation of aesthetic and teleological concepts which entail an incomprehensible interplay between natural necessity and the freedom of intentionality. It would of course not be

permissible to attempt to interpret these trends in the other direction so as to reason deductively for consciousness and its contents as they in fact are on the basis of such an underlying metaphysical concept. Kant's theory of religion is thus unmistakably dependent upon the moralistic analysis of religion given by deism. Schleiermacher, by contrast, undertakes an epistemological analysis of religion on the same presuppositions but seeks the *a priori* and the law of validity of religion independently of ethics in a specifically religious category. With this law he offers the coping stone and epitome of all the *a priori* laws of consciousness. For him the law of validity lies in the sense of the unity of the finite and the infinite, a sense which flows from the nature and inner necessity of consciousness. This feeling bears in itself no conceptual or visualisable content, and it attains these only through the poetic symbolising of the unity which is sensed, with the general means of expression available in the world view of the time. Schleiermacher's solution of the problem clearly hangs together with the mystical and radically pietist analysis of religion. It still remains to find the way from this *a priori* and this law of validity to the psychological and historical reality of religion. Kant treated this task only in the most general and scanty outlines. Schleiermacher resolved it more centrally and more successfully though still with certain hesitations. From out of this second problem arises necessarily the third, namely the critical appraisal of the historico-psychological development of religion. For this it is natural to take as a criterion the view that the most fully developed religion is that in which the religious *a priori* comes to its clearest expression. Both Kant and Schleiermacher ascribed this position to Christianity, but of course in doing this they treated the Christian idea critically and emphasised within it those aspects which are homogeneous with the modern consciousness. At the same time it is unmistakable that, in spite of all the idiosyncrasies and the general orientation towards Christianity, the Kantian theory of religion is similar to the Stoic, and Schleiermacher's is similar to that of the mystics.

(2) The second major group is linked with the teaching of *Hegel*. In this case the Neo-Platonic theory of religion is renewed on a modern basis and the religious consciousness is identified with the desire for metaphysical knowledge. Thus there is advanced a reduction of the religious consciousness to the abstract content of speculative metaphysical knowledge, which is supposed to be popularly and visualisably disguised in the former. The starting point and the central point here is a scientific metaphysics, seen as a historically prevailing kernel of truth and the driving element in the development

of the religious consciousness. The essence of this metaphysics is that it applies in a full and determinedly metaphysical way the concept of 'reason as such' which Kant extracted from the analysis of consciousness purely as a concluding and delimiting concept. It deduces from reason itself the reality of nature and of the history of ideas as being a logically necessary explication of reason. To achieve this Hegel takes a new principle into the concept of 'reason as such', under the influence of modern historical thought, namely the principle of movement through contradiction to the resolution of the contradiction on a higher level. The concept of 'reason as such' is extracted for him, too, by epistemological and logical investigation, but it is a new logic which he thereby finds, namely one which includes both the necessity and the resolution of contradiction. In this way he wins for himself a principle of movement and development within reason which appears to human thought as progressive within time, but which in reality is only a timeless wealth and movement within reason itself. Such a concept of reason allows itself to be hypostasised, and from it can be constructed the becoming and the movement of reality, as governed at once by the law of reason and by a teleological ideal. Thus reality at any point is always nothing but necessary reason or the idea as such in a particular stage of its development. In particular the human mind is only the most developed stage of reason known to us, at which it is possible for it by subjective reflection to analyse and reconstruct the whole development leading up to and bringing about itself. Although religion is recognised as an essential *a priori* constituent of human reason, it does not need to stop at a mere statement of its *a priori* nature, but is able through self-reflection to analyse as logically necessary from within itself its appearance out of 'reason as such' and the stages of development which have been so far. As religion is the mystical belief in the unity of the world it can be understood without further ado in terms of reason grasping its own centre. For religion consists precisely in finite reason becoming conscious of its own necessary emergence from infinite cosmic reason, and thereby regaining for consciousness the unity of the finite which has come into being with the infinite from which it comes. Admittedly religion is only an imaginative form of this consciousness of the essential character and the developmental goal of the reason of the world. It brings to consciousness the darkly and surmisingly conceived sense of reason in the world by visualisable pictures and symbols, and it has need of the philosophy of religion which alone can translate the substance of this into conceptual knowledge. At the same time however for the sake of the popular strength of religion its imaginative character should be maintained, and it is only for the thinker that imaginative religion should be translated into the conceptual religion of philosophy. The popular religion should only be regulated on the basis of the philosophical understanding, and preserved from fanatical or superstitious byways. This Hegelian teaching had a tremendous influence, greater at first than that of Kant or Schleiermacher. It had the unmistakable advantage of doing more for the metaphysical need of religion for a relationship to ultimate reality, and it granted a firmer inner necessity to the sequence and direction of the history of the development of religion. The goal was seen as lying in the complete self-comprehension of reason, in a uniting of the divine and human reason which would emerge out of the developmentally engendered division between them. For this reason the goal of the development of religion and reason was seen in the Christian doctrine of the incarnation, this doctrine of course being conceived of as a mystico-religious unification brought about by the recognition of world reason, while the only connection with ecclesiastical christology is that it is an idea contained in but separated out from the imaginative dogmas of the church. Admittedly Hegel's radical followers soon drew the consequences of a radical progressivism out of this teaching. They declared Christianity to be a withering phase of religion, bound to anthropormorphically theistic conceptions, and they looked to a more or less aesthetic pantheism as the religion of the future. Since the latter has lost its aesthetic optimism it has now become instead a pessimistic monism.

(3) A stark contrast to the first two types is offered by the third major type, namely the *positivist* philosophy of religion stemming mainly from the school of *Comte*. This is at present the strongest and most influential and for this reason was already touched upon at the beginning in order to illustrate the presuppositions and fundamental standpoint of this whole discussion. Although different in important ways the two types described so far are both raised upon the fundamental thesis of idealism. Both are guided by a basic line of thought which seeks the ground of reality in what is supra-sensual and at the same time recognises autonomous ideal values of reason. For this reason they also both take up an affirmative standpoint towards religion. Positivism on the other hand is based on the opposite conviction and line of thought, on the presupposition that the only really firm element of thought, the real essence of scientific knowledge, is a continuum of physical reality governed by laws or at least regularities, and that only what is consistent with this can be reckoned to remain of the supra-sensual. This brings out clearly the inheritance

of the presuppositions of eighteenth-century French materialism, and even if positivism tries to avoid the weaknesses of the latter by deprecating every sort of metaphysics and recognises no metaphysics of the laws of nature, nevertheless its basic principle is a limitation to experience linked according to rules, and therefore the net result of this attitude of scepticism towards metaphysics is not very much different from that of materialism before it. It is also linked, across the intermediaries of eighteenth-century materialism, with the old Epicurean theory of religion, and its only new and important element lies in the psychological analyses of primitive religious thought. Dogmatic laws of nature are replaced by interconnections observed in experience, and the difference between mental reality and the physical world is recognised. But nevertheless the only firm content of scientific knowledge is thought to consist in the observed and systematised regularities of the natural process and of the formation of human society. The independence of mind lies only in its capability to put these recognised regularities to the service of the affirmation of life and of existence. Thus no room remains for religion as truth; it must be treated as an illusion. And so the major role which religion has played must be explained in some way other than the way in which religion understands itself, in terms of some function of which it was itself not conscious. This function is said to be that of the pre-scientific explanation of the world and of pre-scientific social ethics. On these presuppositions all the emphasis fell on the religions of the primitives and of pre-history. The task was to explain these in terms of the pre-scientific thought of primitive man. Analogies with Darwinist evolutionary teaching with its theory of survivals and revivals, adaptation and transformation, provided a wealth of methodological accessories. Thus by the side of the symbolic explanation of myth and of the history of religions found in the Hegelian school, which had everywhere interested itself only in the content of ideas borne by the religious conceptions, there came to be also an anthropological, ethnographical enquiry into myth, which illuminated the religious thought of primitive man and of the early stages of cultural history, in terms of the general patterns of thought among primitives and their accommodations to the environment. The Hegelian concept of progress and of the developmental drive of the idea was replaced by natural laws of mythical thought abstracted from masses of materials. Social dynamics were provided by the theory of the dying away of this mythical thought in the spiritualisings and philosophisings of the culture religions, and of the ultimate transition to the religionless social teaching of positive science. It must not be overlooked that by contrast with the Hegelian theories about the symbolic character of primitive religion this realistic conception of religion led to great advances in research into primitive religions. On the other hand it produced almost nothing of any value for the understanding of the higher, spiritualised and ethically developed religions. Only the mythical materials which they came across and used were understood more clearly. That Comte himself on such a basis ended up by recognising a supra-empirical metaphysical Being once again in the corporate intelligence of mankind, and founded upon it a new *religion de l'humanité* together with its own ritual, may simply be mentioned as a sign of the impossibility of escaping altogether from the religious. In itself it achieved neither religious nor scientific importance. Equally little importance was achieved by Herbert Spencer's attempt to graft an agnostic pantheism on to the idea of the universe conceived in terms of positivism and evolutionism. Real significance could only be ascribed to the pragmatism of William James, which was completely freed from all materialism. He gave the same value to religious experiences as to all other experience, but left us with the impossibility of getting beyond the chaos of the variety of religious experiences.

(4) It remains finally to consider how *the doctrine of revelation as a church dogma* has been shaped in connection with the upheavals of modern science. Thanks to its influence on theological and ecclesiastical circles it remains even today the most widespread form of a science of religion. Ecclesiastically influenced theology in general has recently drawn back altogether from the science of religion. It almost completely ignores the non-Christian religions and limits itself to the presentation of the Christian idea as the revealed truth. In the mode of exposition and validation of this revealed truth however it shows the influence of modern science. The concept of revelation is no longer validated by the evidence of miracle, by the inspirational character of the Bible, and by the direct intervention into nature by the miracles of salvation history. It is based instead on the psychological analysis of the Christian religious mood. This appears, by contrast with the experience of sin and the weakness of nature, as a divine inner miracle, and by the roundabout way of this inward miracle evidence is found also for the means of salvation which bring it about, that is the church, the Bible and salvation history, and above all the figure of Christ who sums up the Bible in his own person. These then are miracles too. Moreover, the revealed truth which effectively works in this inner miracle, giving evidence of its own divine quality, is no longer just a collection of authoritarian dogmas but a specific and coherent ethical and religious idea, taking shape around

the forgiveness of sins, and held in such a way as to give as little offence as possible to the knowledge secured by the contemporary historical and natural sciences. Elements of truth and analogies from the non-Christian religions are explained in terms of natural reason as the continuing rational disposition of primitive man, and dignified as preparatory grace. The whole scheme of ideas claims that a really powerful religion must stem from a definite and positive faith in revelation, and that only such a faith can provide the definite character needed to form a community. It also likes to claim the impossibility of being without presuppositions. Thus the science of religion, it is argued, can only have the task of demonstrating the concept of Christian revelation to be that of the uniquely real revelation, which overcomes original sin by an inner miracle. The explication of the experiential content of this revelation is then to be left over to a specifically Christian dogmatics. It is at once a theory of suprasensual experience and the theory that this supra-sensual Christian experience is absolutely unique and supernatural. A step forward in the elaboration of the general framework of the science of religion for theology is found in the teaching of the later Schelling, which provided the means for this and in fact contains very important ideas. It is a modification of the Hegelian doctrine which finds a place in the Hegelian concept of cosmic reason for the alogical and the irrational, for the Will which has no further ground but lies beyond the necessity of the Idea. Out of this nature within God arises dissension and opposition to God, thus giving the world its most immediate character and one which is correctly envisaged in the Christian idea of the fall. Yet while this will strives against reason and makes of itself a finite creature the divine reason once more operates against it in an ever increasing revelation. The non-Christian religions are the preparatory manifestations of reason, while the Israelite and Christian religion are its full revelation and thus a reconciliation and redemption which is to work itself out in the ethical organisation of humanity as a rational organism. Thus the Hegelian rationalism and optimism, and also the allegedly deterministic necessity of progress, receive a corrective, and at the same time the idea of redemption and reconciliation is metaphysically more firmly based and positive history more strongly evaluated. The religious development is no longer identified completely with the process of mind in general, but has a special position within that process and takes its start everywhere from foundations set by revelation. These are admittedly very bold theories which would by no means be countenanced by all the theologians of today, but whose historical influence is perhaps not yet exhausted. Others satisfy themselves with the mere assertion of the incomparability of Christian and non-Christian religion, rejecting every attempt to bring both groups under one concept. They construe the Christian revelation as a miracle proved by inner experience and not subject to any of the presuppositions of secular thought. What is true in the non-Christian religions is seen as a yearning for revelation and a presentiment of it. This approach of course almost always ignores the real difficulty of such regulation by the historical miracle of Christianity, it ignores the extension of the historical horizon brought about by the placing of man in the biological development of life, both the huge time-spans covered by human existence and by the alternation of ice-ages and cultural periods. The influences of the natural sciences which through biology, geology and prehistory touch directly upon our theme, are pushed away completely in the face of overwhelming momentary impressions of feeling. It is assumed that the challenge of documentary historical research, which daily presses further back into the distances of time, can be met by the doctrine that all spiritual and religious development is orientated towards Christianity, a view which, it must be said, considers only the Mediterranean peoples.

4. *The problems and the articulation of the science of religion on the basis of critical idealism*

The stark oppositions between these major theories leaves no room to speak of a common basis for the science of religion. There is no way of averaging out a general substance to it. The unprejudiced researcher will surely have much to learn from all of these groups, but to say that they were all somehow right and to stick together some kind of a compromise between them would be a most confused and cowardly eclecticism. It is necessary to adopt a position as between these various theories. One must have the courage of one's opinion and not be afraid of sharp polemics with contradictory doctrines, nor of the unavoidable reproaches that one is either irreligious or unscientific. Thus the following sketch of what, in the opinion of the present writer, the science of religion should be cannot be a neutral one. It represents a decision between the various available possibilities, and is a decision exposed to all the arguments. The possibility of seeking some further new basis is excluded by the discussion up to this point which has considered all the possible ways of posing the problem. One needs only to bear in mind that the modern theories referred to above have in principle only expanded and deepened the iniatives undertaken in Greek thought, to be convinced that all the major ways of posing the problem have been exhausted. The question is only which of these is the correct starting point. The present writer agrees essentially with the Kantian and Schleiermacherian method. This represents that critical idealism which in contrast with positivism was already characterised above as the only possible methodological presupposition. Only between these two philosophical foundations can the decision be taken. Compared with this opposition the other schools are secondary. The speculative theory of religion of the Hegelians contradicts the empirical nature both of the religious and of the intellectual processes. It is a drawing together of quite diverse interests in a metaphysical speculation which offers all at once a psychological analysis, an epistemological justification, a developmental theory for the philosophy of history and a proof for the existence of God. If these individual questions are separated out, and if each is allowed to be developed fully and freely, they no longer demand to be tied up in such a panlogical metaphysics but simply need to be arranged alongside each other in terms of a transcendental theory. Finally, exclusive supernaturalism, quite apart from other problems, has already been made impossible because Christian and non-Christian religious phenomena are similar in kind and interwoven with each other. This is incontrovertibly demonstrated by the sheer documents and facts of any unprejudiced history of the origins of Christianity.

The modern science of religion is usually said to be an enquiry into the *essence (Wesen) of religion.* The expression is correct and accurate, if it is intended to imply a methodological shift from the attempt at a metaphysical determination of religious objects or of the idea of God to an enquiry into religion as a phenomenon of consciousness. This is indeed the problem which all the metaphysical labours have left us with and which since Kant has taken this fundamental form. Otherwise however the expression 'essence of religion' has so many meanings that it can easily lead us astray. It gives the impression that it might be possible to answer the various problems tied up in it all by one and the same enquiry, at a stroke. It signifies for one thing the essential and characteristic traits by which religious phenomena can be psychologically recognised as being spiritual phenomena, thus a general generic concept which sums up the universal and particularly characteristic traits of the *psychological* phenomenon. It can also mean the real essence as opposed to a mere manifestation, or, that is, it can mean the truth content of religion. This latter is however by no means assured by any such psychological investigation. It would need its own enquiry pursued along quite different lines, which would be not psychological but *epistemological.* Even this does not exhaust the problem. Whatever such an epistemological enquiry might lead to with respect to the cognitive truth content of religion, it would still be related to the whole phenomenon of religion and to that which is contained in common by all its historical forms. But if the concept of essence is really directed towards the truth content of religion it cannot remain a mere generic concept of religion in general. Rather, just as the psychology of religion had to recognise an extraordinary historical variety of religious formations, so too must the concept of the essence or of the truth content of religion be critically applied to these various formations. It leads to a critical valuative grading of the historical religious formations, to the question of the religious ideal and the religion of the future. These are questions in which the specific character of individual religions lies in the foreground. Thus the concept of the essence leads to an enquiry in the *philosophy of history* which cannot rest content with a common general truth content. It has to strive to recognise the inner movement of this truth content through history towards a goal shaped in accordance with our own will. And finally the question about the essence is nothing other than the question about how we stand with respect to something, that is to say, what meaning and importance it has in the totality of our life. Thus it can never be resolved entirely from within the matter itself but must always take into account the environment and related or connected phenomena. So the question about the essence of religion can never be put without at the same time raising the question about its relationship to our other knowledge and consideration of the world. Thus necessarily bound up with it is the question about the attitude of our most general and fundamental knowledge of the world towards the realities asserted in religion. There is always a transition to the *metaphysical* question about the relationship between the idea of God to philosophy and to the summary outline of our knowledge in the most general concepts which the latter provides. However much the modern development of the science of religion has led to the aim of understanding religion in the first instance in its own terms, this is always a matter of 'in the first instance'. In the last analysis there quite rightly persist the questions of what is called the philosophy of religion in the narrower sense, namely questions about the validation of religious ideas or about the way in which they are related to knowledge as a whole.

Thus the apparently so coherent search for the 'essence of religion' dissolves into a number of very different but closely interrelated problems. It is only the answering of all of these that we can name, perhaps a little too proudly, 'the science of religion'. But the old view that we could characterise the essence of religion by means of a scientific definition of it, and that all of the problems raised above would be answered together in this definition, is misleading. The scholastics still carried on today with such definitions are all out of date.

The position is even worse with regard to another widespread approach, often linked with the concept of the essence or even identified with it, namely the concept of *the origin of religion*. If this means 'origin' in the proper sense of the word so that one would enquire into the manner of such an origin as well as into the cause of it, then it can only mean the origin of each separate individual case of religion known to us to exist whether today or in the past. But we never have before us a completely new origin. The individual religion always arises out of the tradition of religious ideas, however narrow this tradition may be and however massive its reconstitution. We are not vouchsafed to observe a completely new primary construction, and it is always possible to say in the first place that the cause of the religion arising lies in the continuation and power of the tradition. But whence this tradition itself first originated, how religion primarily arose at the beginning of the history of mankind and what its causes were, is something which is quite unknown to us. It is also something which will always remain unknown to us, just as in the analogous cases of ethics and logic. All attempts at the imaginative reconstruction of such an origination are based on analogies with contemporary cases, which however themselves already presuppose the main point, namely that religious conceptions are already present. If the question of origins is treated not as a question of the first appearance of religion but as a question about the inward causes and necessities of its production, then the ground of origination is already conceived of as lying in a disposition or inner necessity of the mind and it is only a question of the nature and validity of this disposition. In that case however we find ourselves before the epistemological problem which is not a question of origination but rather of validation. If finally one is not concerned to investigate the causes of the origination itself but rather the manner of its coming to be, contingent factors in its formulation and determinative influences in its elaboration, then we are raising a psychological-genetic question. This question, once granted that it is impossible for us to observe a primary origin of religion, has nothing to say about the real inner cause, but only clarifies the 'how' of the matter, and shows the reasons for the concrete forms of expression in their psychological context. Thus the concept of 'the origin of religion' is from each point of view unclear and worthless. Only under one condition does it have any meaning, namely if one is already certain on other grounds that religion is only a passing side-effect of other more fundamental psychological processes, and that it has no inner necessity of its own. In that case one can and has to investigate the 'origin of religion' as a passing and secondary psychological structure, and insofar as this origination can be successfully demonstrated the seal is set upon the already fundamentally assumed overall theory. This then is the theory of positivism, but the real starting point of this theory does not lie in the problem of the origin of religion but in a metaphysical perception into the impossibility of religion being true. Thus the concept of 'origin' really contains the whole problem of religion within itself and like that of the 'essence' it needs to be split up into its constituent problems. The matter cannot be dealt with in a simple formula, and it requires instead the individual investigations which are best named after the particular problems which characterise them. Here too the usual scholastics of the origin of religion in intellectual, volitional and ethical needs is out of date.

The task of the science of religion, or the question of the nature (*Wesen*) of religion, limits itself to the analysis of that mental phenomenon which we call religion, conceived of as purely and as objectively as possible, and treated from the four points of view mentioned above. These four, which emerge from the analysis of the usual but tangled and confused concepts 'essence and origin of religion', are psychology, epistemology, philosophy of history and religious metaphysics. The sum of these four investigations represents the attainable scientific understanding of religion and the contribution which science can make to the practical life and further development of religion. The special tasks of these four therefore need to be briefly sketched out.

(1) The *psychology of religion* is the basis and presupposition of all epistemological investigations. The phenomenon has to be seen in its factuality and in its objective individuality before we can ask about its validity. The neglect of this presupposition was one of the weaknesses of Kant's theory of religion, and even Schleiermacher for all his refined psychological observation introduced ontological and epistemological propositions much too quickly into it. Given the huge extension, the variety and the intimate character of the phenomenon, the task of psychology here is as rich in difficulties as it is in its possibilities of approach. The first task must be to grasp the phenomenon as far as possible in its naivety, to win from it the experience or outlook as yet uninfluenced by scientific interpretation. This was already marked out above as the starting point of a scientific treatment of religion. At this point of identification psychology begins. The first distinction then to be drawn is that between central and

peripheral phenomena, and here psychology has the task of describing both in terms of their characteristic qualities. Among the central ones is found everywhere faith in a presence of the divine which can be experienced under certain circumstances, the idea of the 'divine' itself being already presupposed, and with this faith the characteristic religious determination of feeling and of the will which it affects. Among the peripheral ones there appear everywhere the ethical and social elements of religion, and, above all, myth, which is not itself religion but is only very closely connected with it. The investigation can then pursue either the direction of group psychology or that of more individual psychology. In the first direction attention is paid more to regular mass phenomena and to the similarities and laws of the forms taken by ritual and by mythical thought. It is almost possible to establish here a morphology of religious thought. In the second direction it is a question of the inwardness of religious feeling, which also has everywhere something in common, but which nevertheless is always real only in its individual particularity. It can only be studied in the persons of some particular time, with regard to whom information and self-expressive accounts of the individual personal inner life are available. In all these cases it is necessary to enter into and to describe psychological states of affairs by means of one's own real or at least hypothetical religious feeling. But the attempt is also made to apply the methods of exact psychology and to build up a kind of statistics of the phenomena and the course which they take, by means of questionnaires and observations which are as objective as possible. Psychopathology is also called in so that conclusions can be drawn from pathological cases to normal ones. Since the discovery of the 'subliminal' consciousness is held by many psychologists to be the key to countless hitherto incomprehensible phenomena, this too will be applied in an important way. The result of all this will probably indicate that the primary phenomenon of all religion is mysticism, that is, belief in the presence and influence of supernatural powers and the possibility of an inner connection with them. It is in effect a confirmation of the mystical theory of religion, except in so far as it always sees naive religion as having a concrete conception of the nature and activity of the divine linked to revelation or tradition, whereas such a conception is evaporated away in the mystical theory and replaced by a metaphysics which is characteristically pantheist yet at the same time inclusive of the crudest dualism.

(2) The characterisation of the primary phenomenon in its various forms and levels of intensity is followed by the *epistemological*

investigation into the validity or truth value of these psychological events. The question as to how any judgments about validity can be gained from what is observed as psychological fact is a fundamental question which can only be answered in the context of epistemology in general. If this general question is answered then the further question arises as to what such an investigation into truth value can begin to achieve in the special field of religious life. In any case it cannot do more than indicate an *a priori* law of the formation of religious ideas existing in the nature of reason and standing in an organic relationship to the other *a priori* principles of reason. It can only undertake to deliver the proof for the necessity of the formation of religious ideas in reason, but not for the existence of the religious object in itself. Epistemology can only achieve a binding validity for the contents of consciousness which are present, and a subcategorisation of all others under those which are recognised as valid, but it does not produce evidences of existence as such. The only proof of existence which epistemology can mount is the demonstration of a valid necessity of reason attained according to various principles in all areas including the philosophical, historical, ethical, aesthetic and religious. In particular, proof of validity for the religious idea should not be confused with proof of the validity of knowledge of individual objects, because the latter rests only upon the demonstration of a relationship with other objects which can be expressed in terms of a law, whereas the religious object is in no way an object alongside other objects. The most important question is therefore that of the content and the nature of the religious *a priori*. It lies in the relationship to absolute substance effected by the nature of reason, by virtue of which everything real, and in particular all values, are brought into relationship with an absolute substance which is their starting point and criterion. This already implies that the religious *a priori* is dependent upon its relationship with the other *a prioris* and itself gives the firm substantial basis of their inner unity. Since the most important of these other *a prioris* is generally reckoned to be the ethical, with the logical and the aesthetic coming in second place, the harmonisation of religion first with ethics and then with logical and aesthetic aspects of life provides a further criterion of its validity or truth content in a given case. The validity of a religious idea may be greater or lesser according to whether it fits itself in to the harmony of consciousness or even takes the lead in this harmonisation. So from this point of view there arises an inner flexibility in the criterion of validity which can do justice to the varying degree of validity of various forms of religion. Finally it is necessary to find the way back from this concept of validity to the psychological-genetic reality of religion, and to show how this route to a valid truth content of religion is actualised in the psychological forms.

(3) Here the investigation returns to the historical and psychological reality and variety of the religious life, found everywhere in particular concrete or positive historical formations. But now however the task is to comprehend this variety as one which arises on the basis of an inner unity and which in its successive phases strives towards a normative goal. That is the task of *the philosophical history of religion*. The finest solution of this task so far lies in the teaching of Hegel. But since his teaching is based on a purely metaphysical construction of world reason which cannot be maintained in this form or with this argument, and on the logical law of the dialectics of reason immanent in world reason, Hegel's goal may be maintained but it must be reached by other logical and methodological paths. Without any metaphysics it is not possible at all, but it will have to be a metaphysics of *a posteriori* conclusions out of the facts and not a deductive metaphysics of the absolute. In particular a substitute for Hegel's dialectic must be found, a teleological law of development, this being under all circumstances the final and most important concept of all philosophy of history. The investigation moves here into the principle questions of the philosophy of history, which has to decide about the nature and meaning of the concept of development and to give an account of the distinction between the development of reason and the mere flow and course of consciousness. The specific problem arising here for the science of religion is then the question about the goal of religious development, whether this is to be found in a general historyless religion of reason, in a syncretistic summing up of all the elements of truth so far or in the development of the positive religions. There is also the question of the place and importance of the present major religions in the development of religion. Since, among these, Christianity is in any case the decisive religiosity of Western civilisation, the final question will be essentially that of the meaning and the future of Christianity and its relationship to the religions of the East.

(4) Religion is never however merely the psychological activity of the production and shaping of religious faith. It is with all that at the same time the assertion of a real object of faith, the idea of God. The idea of God is admittedly not directly accessible in any other way than by religious belief. Yet it asserts a substantial content which must stand in harmony with the other forms of scientific knowledge and also be in some way indicated by these, if indeed human reason

represents an inner unity. Thus we arrive at *the philosophical treatment of the idea of God*. This is admittedly not possible by way of a deductive metaphysics, but it must emerge somehow together with the metaphysical conclusions arising out of the examination of experience and the attempt to unify it in final terms. A strictly epistemologically directed philosophy also, if it does not get stranded in psychologism and scepticism, will always contain the initial points of such a metaphysics in its concepts of validity and of 'reason as such', the only question being how far this can lead. At this point the problems of the science of religion become those of philosophy or metaphysics in general. The science of religion becomes the philosophy of religion in the narrower sense of the word, that is, in the sense of the philosophical criticism of the idea of God and the location of its role in the overall context of our fundamental knowledge. The concept of God itself however is always the object of this philosophy of religion and is not produced by it. Only here do we reach the final justification of the starting point of the whole investigation with its initial rejection of positivism. In the present state of affairs the main responsibility is the assertion of an idealism which anchors the spiritual values of reason in the foundation of the world, over against the concepts of an all-consuming natural philosophy which would allow little to remain of idealism. It would leave only what is possible on the basis of its own metaphysical principles of the conservation of matter and of energy, and a consistent application of these would leave as good as nothing. Alongside this the second main problem is that of asserting the possibility of continuously new beginnings and new realities, in the context of the relationship of the foundations of the world or of absolute consciousness to its constituent parts or to finite minds. Without this possibility all religious language becomes either a mere jargon or a fruitless mysticism. It is the problem of pluralism or freedom over against monism, the latter knowing only necessary deployments of a substance which is always identical with itself. If this goal is achieved then this metaphysics of religion is not just an apologetics providing protection and coverage so that the idea of God can stand fast. Rather it represents at the same time a transformation of the religious idea of God which is able to conform with the modern scientific view of the world, a view which has had a deep effect on the traditional idea of God just as indeed science has always deeply influenced the world of religious ideas. An account of these influences however lies outside the scope of the science of religion itself and belongs rather to the exposition of a personal religious viewpoint based upon it.

The influence and the importance of such a science of religion which makes itself responsible for the whole area of religion is bound up with the loss .of influence of the old ecclesiastical doctrines of authority and with the spirit of tolerance and considered appraisal with which religious ideas are treated in the educated world. Nevertheless its positive unifying influence so far is still rather small. One might seek such influence first in the reconciliation and smoothing out of religious differences between the various cultures. So far, however, there is little to be seen of this at the international religious congresses and the congresses for the science of religion, apart from the fact that people have in fact met. It is also very improbable that these great struggles will be decided by means of science. We may expect more elemental forces to decide them. For the science of religion described above is after all a product of specifically European and American culture, and its effects above all so far over this cultural area. But even in this narrower circle its influence has so far been anything but reconciliatory and harmonising. It characterises the extremely difficult situation of religion in the modern world rather than offering a conquest of these difficulties. It does more to make us aware of the rivenness of the present state of affairs and our dependence upon positions of personal conviction than to work for religious unity and deepening. On the one hand it has given scientific title deeds and means of propaganda to the rejection of all religion by a large part of the modern world. On the other hand, to educated persons who have gone down with the crumbling ecclesiastical systems of Christianity or Judaism, it opens the perspective of a general, time-less and history-less religion of reason which of course varies very much between the various individuals and groups and cannot produce any strong religious current. Finally it has drawn Christian theology, in the various confessions but above all in protestantism, into the grip of its influence, and thereby gave a scientific basis to the progressive endeavours of protestantism. Precisely by so doing, however, it strengthened the gulf between the various directions of protestantism, and was hardly able to get a grip on the religiously quite exhausted world of modern culture. Nevertheless it has profoundly influenced modern Christianity so that it is necessary to speak of a new reformulation and transformation of Christianity on foundations other than the specifically ecclesiastical ones which have governed hitherto. Yet it is not possible to point to any discernible results in the anarchism of this modern religion of personal moods. If one accepts that religion only brings out its full power as positive religion, and that in the European and American world Christianity still remains the only real religious force, then the most important influence of the science of religion so far will have to be seen in its effect on the theology of the Christian confessions, that is on the free theology of catholic and protestant 'modernism'. It is precisely through being influenced in this way that free theology will remain in touch with intellectual life in general, the central movements of which have for a long time been outside the churches. It is in this way too that theology will share in the great religious movement of the present time which is growing up out of the depths of our society in opposition to soul-destroying naturalism and against the technological alienation of capitalism. What the future will develop out of this is still unknown to us. Yet the science of religion can at least make an important contribution in clarification and orientation if it surveys and appreciates what religion is and establishes the claim of the religious consciousness over against scepticism and naturalism. The essential work will be that of the religious life itself which, after the collapse of the old dogmatic churches in ruins and the rapid advance of secularisation, is slowly gathering itself for a new profundity.

Appendix: Troeltsch's bibliographical note

Literature on the history of religions. The complexity of its interests and the unlimited historical materials mean that the literature of the history of religions is inexhaustible. Its most important principle ideas were set out in the old literature of the great leading systems and present-day work is not very original or creative in this field. The only characteristic and important contributions of the present are antiquarian and anthropological-ethnographical studies of the primitive forms of religion. Central publications for these are the two journals: *Annales du Musée Guimet* and, coming from the same institution, *Revue de l'histoire des religions* (published by Réville, Paris), together with the German *Archiv für Religionsgeschichte* (published first by Dieterich and now by Wünsch, Leipzig, Teubner). Besides these some originality is shown in psychological researches, though German psychology plays a remarkably small part here and indeed like German philosophy in general has a very weak interest in religion. A claim to become the focus of such studies is presented by *The American Journal of Religious Psychology and Education* (published by G. Stanley Hall, Clark University Press, Worcester, Mass.), and the German *Zeitschrift für Religionspsychologie* sets itself similar tasks (published since 1907 by Runze and Bresler, Halle, Marhold). Two compendia of the study of religion, in which admittedly the philosophical side is not prominent, are: Morris Jastrow, *The Study of Religion* (London 1901), and C.P. Tiele, *Elements of the Science of Religion* (Edinburgh and London 1897/99, German edition Gotha 1899/1901), cf. also his *Grundzüge der Religionswissenschaft* (German edition by Gehrich, Tübingen and Leipzig 1904). In these books emphasis is put above all on the independence of the science of religion as consisting in the treatment of its own special empirical materials. Greater stress on the philosophical side of the problem is found in the Kantian-inclined textbook by H. Siebeck, *Lehrbuch der Religionsphilosophie* (Freiburg and Leipzig 1893) or the Hegelian-inclined introduction by John Caird, *Introduction to the Philosophy of Religion* (London 1889). A review of the state of research in the various fields is given by Troeltsch in 'Philosophy of Religion' contained in *Die Philosophie im Beginn des 20 Jahrhunderts. Festschrift für Kuno Fischer* (2nd ed. Heidelberg, 1907), and more critically in 'Die Selbstständigkeit der Religion' (*Zeitschrift fur Theologie und Kirche*, 1895/6). A detailed examination with all the main modern lines of thought is given by Emile Boutroux, *Science et religion dans la philosophie contemporaine* (Paris, 1908). Books on the sub-topics referred to above are as follows:

(i) Naive and scientific religion: Duhm, *Das Geheimnis in der Religion* (Freiburg, 1896); James, *Varieties of Religious Experience* (London, 1902), German by Wobbermin 1907; Heim, *Das Weltbild der Zukunft* (Berlin, 1904); Vierkandt, *Naturvölker und Kulturvölker* (Leipzig, 1896); A. Bonus, *Zur religiösen Krisis* (Jena, 1911 ff.).

(ii) Critical idealism: Kant, *Religion innerhalb der Grenzen der reinen Vernunft* (1793); Fichte, *Versuch einer Kritik aller Offenbarung* (1792), and *Anweisung zum seligen Leben* (1806, new edition in Deutsche Bibliothek, 1912); Schleiermacher, *Reden über die Religion an die Gebildeten unter ihren Verächtern* (1800), and *Der christliche Glaube* (1821); Fries, *Wissen Glauben Ahnung* (1805), *Handbuch der Religionsphilosophie* (1832); De Wette, *Vorlesungen über die Religion, ihr Wesen und ihre Erscheinungsformen* (1827); R. Otto, *Kantisch-Fries'sche Religionsphilosophie* (Tübingen, 1909); Rauwenhoff, *Wijsbegeerte van den Godsdienst* (Leiden, 1887), German by Hanne (Braunschweig, 1889); A. Sabatier, *Esquisse d'une philosophie de religion* (Paris, 1897), German by Baur 1900.

(iii) Hegelian teaching: Hegel, *Vorlesungen über die Philosophie der Religion*, edited by Marheineke (1832); the same shortened and annotated by Drews (Jena and Jeipzig, 1905); Pfleiderer, *Religionsphilosophie auf geschichtlicher Grundlage* (Berlin, 1896); Biedermann, *Christliche Dogmatik* (Zürich, 1869; 2nd edition Berlin, 1884/85). Pessimistically oriented: E. von Hartmann, *Religionsphilosophie* (1888); Drews, *Religion als Selbstbewußtsein Gottes* (Jena, 1906).

(iv) Positivist teaching: Hume, *The Natural History of Religion* (1755);

Comte, *Cours de philosophie positive* (1830-42); Herbert Spencer, *First Principles (System of Synthetic Philosophy*, vol.I, 1862), and *Principles of Sociology (System*, vols. VII and VIII, 1876-96); Goblet d'Alviella, *Introduction à l'histoire générale des religions* (1887), and *L'idée de Dieu* (1892); Feuerbach, *Wesen des Christentums* (1841); Tylor, *Primitive Culture* (1871); and *The Early History of Mankind* (1878); Andrew Lang, *Custom and Myth* (London, 1885) and 'Mythology' in *Encyclopaedia Britannica*, and *Myth, Ritual and Religion* (London, 1899).

(v) Theological doctrine of revelation: F.H.R. Frank, *Gesch. der neueren Theologie* (Erlangen, 1898); Schelling, *Philosophie und Religion* (1804) and *Philosophie der Mythologie* and *Philosophie der Offenbarung* (sämtl. Werke Abt. II, Bd. 1-4); C. Frantz, *Schellings positive Philosophie* (Cöthen, 1879-80); Portig, *Weltgesetz des kleinsten Kraftaufwandes* (Stuttgart, 1903/04); W. Herrmann, *Die Religion im Verhältnis zu Welterkennen und Sittlichkeit* (Halle, 1879); L. Ihmels, *Die christliche Wahrheitsgewissheit* (Leipzig, 1908); A. Hunzinger, *Probleme und Aufgaben der gegenwärtigen systematischen Theologie*, 1909.

(vi) Psychology of religion: James, *The Varieties of Religious Experience* (London, 1902, abbreviated German edition by Wobbermin, 1907); Starbuck, *The Psychology of Religion* (London 1901); A. George Coe, *The Spiritual Life, Studies in the Science of Religion* (New York, 1900), and *The Religion of the Mature Mind* (New York, 1903); Murisier, *Les Maladies du sentiment religieux* (Paris, 1901); Flournoy, *Les Principes de la psychologie religieuse (Archive de psychologie*, Genf, 1902 and 1903); Leuba, *Studies in the Psychology of Religious Phenomena (American Journal of Psychology* 1896); E. Kock, *Die Psychologie in der Religionswissenschaft* (Freiburg, 1896); W. Wundt, *Völkerpsychologie* (Leipzig II 1905 to 1909); v. Hügel, *The Mystical Element of Religion Studied in St. Catherine of Genoa and Her Friends* (London, 1908); Simmel, *Beiträge zur Erkenntnistheorie der Religion* (*Zeitschr. f. Philos. u. philos. Kritik*, 1902); A. Dieterich, *Mithrasliturgie* (Leipzig, 1904); Höffding, *Religionsphilosophie* (German by Bendixen, Leipzig, 1901); F.W.H. Myers, *Human Personality and Its Survivals of Bodily Death* (London, 1903); translated and abbreviated by Jankelevitsch, *La Personnalité humaine, sa survivance, ses manifestations supranormales* (Paris, 1905).

(vii) Epistemology of religion: Windelband, 'Das Heilige' (in *Präludien*, Tübingen, 1911); Fechner, *Die drei Motive und Gründe des Glaubens* (Leipzig, 1863); Eucken, *Der Wahrheitsgehalt der Religion* (Leipzig, 1912); Zeller, *Ursprung und Wesen der Religion* (Vorträge I [Leipzig, 1877]): Récéjac, *Essais sur les fondements de la connaissance mystique* (Paris, 1897); Troeltsch, *Psychologie und Erkenntnistheorie in der Religionswissenschaft* (Tübingen, 1905) and 'Das religiöse Apriori' in *Ges. Schriften* vol. II; James, *The Will to Believe* (London, 1897); Simmel,

'Die Religion' (in *Gesellschaft*, edited by Buber, Frankfurt 2nd ed. 1912).

(viii) Philosophy of history and religion: Jevons, *Introduction to the History of Religion* (London, 1896); Eucken, Siebeck, Tiele, Pfleiderer and Wundt as above; von Hartmann, *Religionsphilosophie* (Berlin, 1888); E. Caird, *The Evolution of Religion* (Edinburgh, 1893); Rickert, *Grenzen der naturwissenschaftlichen Begriffsbildung* (Freiburg, 1896/1902); Troeltsch, 'Moderne Geschichtsphilosophie' (*Theologische Rundschau* 1903 and *Ges. Schriften* II) and *Die Absolutheit des Christentums und die Religionsgeschichte* (Tübingen, 1912); Rickert, 'Geschichtsphilosophie' (in *Festschrift für Kuno Fischer*, 2nd ed., Heidelberg, 1907).

(ix) Religious metaphysics: Weisse, *Philosophische Dogmatik* (Leipzig, 1855-62); Teichmüller, *Religionsphilosophie* (Breslau, 1886); Lotze, *Mikrokosmus* (Leipzig, 1896), and *Grundlage der Religionsphilosophie* (Leipzig, 1884); Glogau, *Vorlesungen über Religionsphilosophie* Kiel, 1898); J.H. Fichte, *Die theistische Weltansicht und ihre Berechtigung* (Leipzig, 1878); Secrétan, *La Philosophie de la liberté* (Paris, 1879); Renouvier, *Essais de critique générale* (Paris, 1875-96); Volkert, *Kants Erkenntnistheorie nach ihren Grundprinzipien analysiert* (Leipzig, 1879); Wundt, *System der Philosophie* (Leipzig, 1907); James, *A Pluralistic Universe* (London, 1909); Eucken, *Der Kampf um einen geistigen Lebensinhalt* (Leipzig, 1896); Drews, *Die deutsche Spekulation seit Kant mit besonderer Rücksicht auf das Wesen des Absoluten* (Berlin, 1895); Rickert, *Fichte und der Atheismusstreit* (Berlin, 1901). Note especially Bergson's *Les Données immédiates de la conscience, mémoire et matière* and *L'Evolution créatrice*.

3

What Does 'Essence of Christianity' Mean?

1. *Harnack's work on the 'essence of Christianity'*

The expression 'essence of Christianity' has become widely known and used as a result of Harnack's well-known book *What is Christianity?*[1]. It can almost be said of many people that they believe in the 'essence of Christianity', and that they take Harnack's book, conceived in the context of very wide-ranging and successful historical study, to show them the correct interpretation of this essence. Harnack sees the problem as a purely historical one and he intends nothing other than simply 'to recognise the essential and permanent in its manifestations, even under the least amenable forms, to draw it out and to make it comprehensible'. One is dealing only with facts and realities, and out of a comprehensive view of these there emerges simply and overwhelmingly, at least at first sight, the permanent content of the Gospel and hence of Christianity. The essence of Christianity is not some dogma or other, nor church institutions, but the preaching of Jesus. First of all therefore the essence of the Gospel itself has to be clarified *vis-à-vis* its contemporary historical form, and then this essence of the Gospel has also be be shown to be the essence of Christian history, always firmly maintained and only variously adjusted as the general situation varied. At the same time it emerges as the critical criterion by which what is un-Christian or sub-Christian is excluded. Thus a purely historical account of what is essential is in itself the best account of the eternal content and the best apologetic against religious and anti-religious misinterpretation. All those apologetic arts and dogmatic subtleties which never fail to arouse suspicion become redundant, and only the subject-matter itself is allowed to work on the imagination and the heart. In place of dogmatics there appears, infinitely more simple, effective and convincing, the historical account of the Gospel and its impact as the essence of Christianity. Harnack's book is more or less symbolic of this historicising trend in theology.

Nevertheless, as is to be expected in the case of such an important

---

[1] *Das Wesen des Christentums*, 1900. By 1910 the number of copies printed, including numerous translations, had reached 100,000. See *Religion in Geschichte und Gegenwart*, von Harnack.

intellectual endeavour which stands in conflict with traditional viewpoints, the enterprise has attracted numerous objections. Disturbed dogmaticians object in principle to an attempt to perceive Christianity by means of critical investigations of a general historical sort, that is to say of a sort which makes use of the methods of secular history; they prefer to have it known purely out of the Bible as revelation and the Word of God. Others dispute that the by-passing of traditional ecclesiastical dogmas effected by Harnack's historical account really can or should be made possible through a historical investigation; the recognition and confirmation of these teachings through inner religious experience should, rather, precede historical work, and they should be understood in their own terms. Others again claim that a purely historical account itself results in an equation of Christianity with the main dogmas of the church, and clearly demonstrates how any Christianity which frees itself from them is a Christianity incomplete, disintegrating and degenerate. Such views have been collected and given their due in *Die Christliche Welt.*[2] The most interesting objections in this connection are those of Lepsius.[3]

Alongside these there has been no lack of sober critics, historically orientated like Harnack himself, who recognise the overall approach and the task as a whole, but who diverge not inconsiderably in their conception of the facts. Their judgment is based not on different presuppositions but on different consequences drawn from the same presuppositions. For them the account of the preaching of Jesus has been drawn too close to the ideals of an ethic applicable to modern circumstances, while there is too little recognition of the importance of the conception of the transcendence of God, the expectation of the kingdom and the ethics of indifference to the world which emerges from this viewpoint, or of asceticism in the broadest sense of the word. Yet that in turn is said to indicate a deeper difficulty and a more general problem. The 'essence' would have to be found in an 'idea' which is distinct from individual manifestations and also from the original form and which only finds expression in all of these together. Those who take this view see the relationship of original Christianity and the preaching of Jesus to the later development of Christianity differently from the way in which Harnack has seen it, and they tie the

[2] *Die Christliche Welt*, 1902. Rolfs, 'Das Wesen des Christentums in pietistischer Beleuchtung', pp. 653-60. See also in the same year the essay of J. Kaftan, 'Gehört Jesus selbst in das von ihm verkündigte Evangelium hinein?', pp. 295-8, and the further five essays which follow thereafter; also a series of articles by various authors in the 1901 volume.
[3] Lepsius, *Reden und Abhandlungen.* Also, Adolf Harnack's *Wesen des Christentums*, Berlin, Reich Christi-Verlag, 1902, 92 pages.

conception of the 'essence' less closely to the original historical form. Indeed many deny altogether that the development of the church has been essentially determined by the Gospel; significantly different ideas came into play even in Paul's thought, and the church has continually assimilated new elements since then without at all being orientated first and foremost towards the Gospel; under these circumstances the 'essence', it is said, is very difficult to determine at all. The importance of these objections has admittedly not always been fully spelled out and perhaps not everywhere fully realised. Nevertheless Jülicher referred to the problem very accurately in his Rectoral Address when he pointed out the difficulty of identifying the 'scientifically reconstructed original form' with 'Christianity in its pure form' and these two with the 'absolute and perfect religion'. The Hegelians Caird, Pfleiderer, Dorner and most recently Walther Köhler have pointed out these difficulties even more sharply. Fundamentally sceptical objections to the essence have been made by Wrede and Gerhard Löschke.[4]

Particularly instructive, however, is the reaction of a catholic critic.[5] Alfred Loisy, the leader of reforming French catholicism, a man trained in altogether free and exact historical method, has attacked what is in principle a protestant presupposition of Harnack's, namely that the essence is above all to be considered as a criterion to be drawn from *original Christianity* and used in the criticism of catholic-ecclesiastical development. Loisy is thereby attacking that one-sided protestant biblicism, which, he claims, when maintained from the standpoint of historical research into original Christianity, has an even more restricting effect than the old inspirational biblicism, or which leads to still more serious reinterpretations. Because Harnack cannot conceive of catholicism as the direct heir of the original Christian Gospel and does not wish to interpret the latter in terms of such a development; and because he takes the crucial point to lie in the protestant religiosity of the present, ignoring catholic-

---

[4] Jülicher, *Moderne Meinungsverschiedenheiten über Methode, Aufgaben und Ziele der Kirchengeschichte*, 1901. Dorner, 'Auf welche Weise ist das Wesen des Christentums zu erkennen?' *Preussischer Jahrbücher*, 1901. Köhler, *Idee und Persönlichkeit in der Kirchengeschichte*, 1910. Wrede, *Paulus*, 1905, and Gerhard Löschke, *Zwei kirchengeschichtliche Entwürfe*, 1913, and also my 'Social Teachings' show great caution with regard to achieving a purely historical definition of the concept, as also with regard to its Hegelian formulation. Wobbermin asks, by contrast, in an essay entitled 'Das Wesen des Christentums' (in *Beiträge zur Weiterentwicklung der christlichen Religion*, 1905), 'What can still be said on these themes after Harnack's excellent lectures, which would not be outdated and superseded in advance?'

[5] Alfred Loisy, *L'Evangile et l'Eglise*. Paris, Picard et fils, 1902. (Eng. Trans. *The Gospel and the Church*, Ed.)

ecclesiastical remnants within protestantism; for these reasons, it is said, he protestantises and modernises the Gospel. Because he does not recognise the essence of Christianity in the broadly unfolded reality of the church and cannot elucidate its meaning in the context of the latter, he has to seek the essence quite one-sidedly in the original form and this original form in turn in a new and coherent religious idea. In this way he ends up by taking for the essence of the Gospel something which was quite secondary for the altogether quite eschatologically orientated thought of Jesus; seeking the essence in what was new while for Jesus it largely lay precisely in what he held in common with Judaism; and considering the essence as the unchanging persistence and influence of this simple new idea, while in fact the development of the church never displays unchangeableness but consists of continuous reshaping and assimilation just as the preaching of Jesus had done before. The Gospel, says Loisy, was from the beginning a complex matter, and its expression in the church remained complex, lively and capable of change, indeed dependent on continual new constructions and adaptations. Harnack's conception is not the historical picture of the matter, but a stage in or rather a radical formulation of individualistic protestantism freeing itself from the collective unity of the church. In a purely historical view the Gospel would be rather the root of the church, while the church is the living and inexhaustible expression of the Gospel; the essence is the actual history which necessarily arose at every point out of the context of circumstances and which was a necessary condition of the assertion of the Gospel under just those circumstances. Gospel and church are fluid entities open on all sides. The unchangeable essence of Christianity can therefore never be constructed, but is available only in the totality of the living church and its activities.

All of this taken together shows that there remain difficult and by no means satisfactorily analysed problems about the 'essence of Christianity'. I do not intend to enter the debate about the substantial correctness or mistakenness of Harnack's conception of the essence. No doubt the work of the great historian will always speak for itself in this regard, and for the time being everything that can sensibly be said has been said. A truly different account would have to be based upon new steps in the whole conception of the history of Christianity and of dogma, which, at a time when Harnack's *History of Dogma* quite rightly commands the situation, cannot yet be taken. There would have to be a history of Christianity which placed its object much more firmly in the general history of culture and in intellectual history, but also in the history of the real and material presuppositions of thought. There can be no question of attempting this here. I wish rather, in view of the various appraisals which have been made, to raise the *methodological* question: What does the expression 'essence of Christianity' mean in the first place? What presuppositions are involved in a search for the essence of Christianity? What kinds of tools are taken for granted as being useful for the solution of this problem? Is the meaning and goal of this enterprise really so simple and straightforward? What does the task involve, if indeed it is necessary and feasible at all? How far is it really a purely historical problem? And if it is not, what importance is to be attached to the most important element in Harnack's so successful attempt, namely the historical-inductive starting point? These questions are by no means irrelevant side-issues of interest only to the expert. On the contrary, the possibility of taking up a position with respect to the problem as a whole depends upon understanding them. The way in which they are answered largely determines one's judgment with respect to the value of any work attempted in this field. The variety of reaction is largely the result of unconscious or confused differences with regard to these methodological presuppositions, and the various methodological presuppositions themselves often imply a position with regard to the substantial issue. With regard to these matters the immediate requirement is theoretical clarity, even though the importance of the purely historical, empirical questions is by no means to be under-estimated. Nevertheless only clarity about the presuppositions and their justification can bring stability, and the layman too will only perceive the importance of the matter by means of such clarity. I should like therefore to request the patience of the reader in the following sections in which he is invited to interest himself in a purely methodological question. When we are faced with tangled problems, self-examination with regard to the method of our thought is always the means of approaching the substance of the matter correctly.

2. *The presuppositions of the concept 'essence'*

The whole expression 'essence of Christianity' is linked to modern, critical and evolutionary history. Catholic theology would never have used it. It would have said 'the faith of the church' and would thereby merely have distinguished between the full knowledge to be demanded from the cleric and the relatively incomplete knowledge demanded of the laity and conveyed through belief in the church. Nor would orthodox protestantism have used it. It would have said 'the revelation of the Bible' and would thereby have distinguished between fundamental and non-fundamental items. Even for the Enlightenment the expression would have had no sense. The Enlightenment stands, with Locke, for the 'rationality of Christianity'. It rationalises the Bible by making the post-apostolic church responsible for all the untenable dogmas destroyed by modern criticism, and distinguishes the later distorting additions from the pure biblical kernel. Not until Chateaubriand's *Génie du Christianisme*, which is admittedly based on a very confused historico-empirical basis, does the 'essence of Christianity' really emerge. This shows its source in the historical way of looking at things and in the art of Romanticism, after Lessing and Herder had felt for similar concepts. Thus the problem itself is older and falls in the area of problems posed by Herder's philosophy of history. The term 'Christianity' was used by representatives of German Idealism and German Romanticism and thereafter more generally. It meant for them no longer the teaching of the New Testament or the teaching of Jesus or the teaching of the church or the creeds, but the totality of Christian life, to be understood in the fullness of the historical manifestations resulting from a driving idea. According to this conception an intellectual unity, of which the masses are unaware and which can only be grasped by historical abstraction, develops within the manifold detail of Christian history, and this unity is drawn up into consciousness as the essence of Christianity. Of course the empirical history, the factual material, is not assumed to be in the soft, motley condition in which Chateaubriand knew it. On the contrary, it is worked out, by methodical and critical research into sources and by the reconstruction and interrelation of facts, into a causally comprehensible historical picture altogether analogous to those produced by the study of other areas of culture. To grasp the decisive and driving religious idea and power out of this complex whole is the task of an account of the essence of Christianity. Thus the task has been taken up by all theologians whose work is based on the presupposition of modern historical thought. If the development of the scientific theology of the nineteenth century can be described in terms of the names of Schleiermacher, Baur, Ritschl and Harnack, it is also true to say that these names correspond with continually renewed attempts to determine the essence of Christianity. Schleiermacher's own definition is still very dependent upon dogmatics in so far as he selected the concept of redemption. Baur was the first to go fully into the historical material. Ritschl and Harnack go back more to the Bible again and stand by the picture of the historical Christ. In each case however the purpose of these definitions is to grasp the driving strength of Christian life as a whole, so that Christian doctrine can be provided with the proper materials for exposition.[6]

The expression therefore implies the application of a basic methodological idea and an extremely widely maintained presupposition of modern history in general; namely that large coherent complexes of historical events are the development of an idea, a value, or a line of thought or purpose, which gradually develops in detail and consequences, which assimilates and subordinates alien materials and which continually struggles against aberrations from its leading purpose and against contradictory principles threatening from without. The 'essence' of such a complex is the abstract idea, the *abstraction peculiar to history*, by means of which the whole known and precisely researched context of related formations is understood in terms of the basic driving and developing idea. The 'essence' can only be found in *a broad view over the totality of all the manifestations which are related to this idea,* and its discovery demands the exercise of historical abstraction, *the art of seeing the whole, both the details and the fullness of the various methodically studied materials, with a synoptic vision.* In this sense the concept was created by German Idealism, and in this sense, independently of the special philosophical presuppositions, it has been further developed by history as such, in so far as the latter does not attempt to do without such abstractions as being too complicated. In reality history cannot do without them, because such abstractions are the highest aims of history without which the latter would have no value. Only through them, and provided that they remain in close contact with the precise study of the details, can history be what it wishes to be, namely the extended experience of humanity, the orientation of the living within the overall life experience of the race, if indeed a picture of this can be achieved at all. Just as Jacob Burckhardt strove to establish the essence of the Renaissance and of Greek culture and Ihering the spirit of Roman law, so must the ever newly sought goal of the history of religions, applying and fructifying again and again the study of the details, be to search out the essence of primitive religion, the essence of Vedic religion, the essence of Buddhism, the essence of Islam, and so on. The search for the essence of Christianity is no different in meaning from these. In earlier times when the relationship between this

[6] On the history of definitions of the essence and their relationship with various theological attitudes in general, see Sell's Rectoral Address given in Bonn, 'Die Entwickelung der wissenschaftlichen Theologie in den letzten 50 Jahren', 1912, and the detailed book of W. Adams Brown, *The Essence of Christianity: A Study in the History of a Definition,* Edinburgh, 1904. Sell's own sophisticated definitions in 'Die wissenschaftlichen Aufgaben einer Geschichte der christlichen Religion' should also not be overlooked here (*Preussischer Jahrbücher* 1899).

historical way of thinking and the original philosophical impulses was still clearer and people were still content, especially in theology, to make use of Hegel's terminology, the phrases which were used were 'principle of Christianity' or 'principle of Catholicism and Protestantism'. The same meaning was intended, except that it was thought more strictly possible to deduce the historical reality quite necessarily out of a basic idea, once the essence was grasped as the principle. To wish to learn to recognise the essence of Christianity in the history of Christianity means to seek the organising and creative principle of the fullness of the living phenomena which we call Christianity, only more realistically and in a way not tied to the Hegelian dialectic of progress and logical categorisation of reality.

Insofar however as the method and idea of the definition of the essence is drawn from historical method in general and applied to Christianity it brings with it the general methodological presuppositions of modern historical thought. It arises out of the immeasurable totality of individual pieces of research, and includes in its presuppositions the methodical criticism of sources, the reconstruction of facts by analogy with events otherwise known to us or at least frequently attested, and finally the construction of a causal scheme which binds together all the phenomena. These presuppositions in turn are confirmed by the fruitfulness of the application of the idea. This means that a treatment of Christianity which seeks the essence of Christianity purely historically includes *a series of the most important and ultimately decisive presuppositions* which we affirm in connection with modern historical thought in general. It is in short the renunciation of the dogmatic method considered valid until the eighteenth century and the taking over of the historical method prepared by the Enlightenment and conceived in principle by German Idealism, or more precisely, the renunciation of a history possessing dogmatic, ready-made criteria and the assumption of a history which produces its basic concepts out of its own work. A firmly delimited normative truth, presented as available in the Bible or in the church, and both accredited and recognisable on the basis of divine authority, is dispensed with. The miraculous ceases to be a means for the separating out and definition of the essence. The factuality of the events described as miraculous can indeed under some circumstances, depending on the state of the sources, be maintained. But miracle, whether it be the inner miracle of the conversion and elevation of character or the outer miracle of interruptions in the course of nature, has ceased to count as a means of identifying the divine and essential in Christianity; and when miracle has once lost this function then its nerve has been cut; then the analogy of Christian and non-Christian miracle, the analogy between the various inner experiences, and the knowledge of the psychology of tradition and legend will increasingly restrict the area of miracle and hand it over to the principle of a psychological-causal view of the matter, which itself is in any case bound up with the whole idea of the historical definition of the essence. Just how far a rationalisation and reduction to causal laws could in fact be carried through here is a question we may leave unanswered; it is not relevant to the problem about the 'essence of Christianity' because the eventual frontiers of rationalisation valid for all other historical movements would be equally valid in this case. With this elimination of miracle as a means of knowledge of the Christian idea the normative authority of the tradition hitherto certified by miracle is also reduced, and it becomes possible to criticise freely all the ecclesiastical dogmas which are given with or which grow out of this tradition; or rather the criticism which has grown up from various quarters loses its most obvious opponent. In the search for the essence, these dogmas, which are no longer for any reason identified in principle with the essence, may be explained historically and psychologically in terms of intellectual processes. The criticism and dissolution of these dogmas can itself be considered as part of the movement of the essence, while new formations may be characterised as extensions of it; that is if on careful scrutiny this criticism and these new formations really seem to emerge from the impulse of the fundamental Christian idea itself. The abstracting of the concept of the essence is therefore as little tied to the church and the authority of the church as it is to miracle. Any attempt to clarify the essence by an alleged correspondence between the idea of Christianity and a natural religious truth, or a general conception of religion, or general ethical-religious postulates, must also fall by the wayside. History knows nothing of all these things, and even when it seems that it does the ongoing stream dissolves any attempt to establish such controls which, drawn from history, might seem to determine the way in which it is to be understood. The essential in Christianity is not that about it which corresponds to a general truth with a basis of its own elsewhere, such that everything which did not correspond with it would be the inessential. The essential is no more and no less than the epitome of fundamental religious ideas which makes itself clear from within its own manifestation in history, which determines consciously and unconsciously its own development, which stands at the centre of its own thinking and willing, and which is never complete and closed as long as it belongs to history in a living way. If however the definition of the essence is independent of Biblical Canon, miracle, church and dogma but related rather to the principle which reveals itself in the whole, and if further the normative principle is not to be sought in other than Christian, that is, in philosophical ideas, but only in the history of Christianity itself, this does not mean that the definition of the essence is independent of what is known of the world beyond Christianity and more specifically of religions other than the Christian. This perspective is again to be understood in a purely historical manner. The art of such historical abstraction must be practiced on a number of formations in order to achieve skill, sureness of touch and self-control. In particular it must be carried out in related areas in order to find the essential more easily through comparison, to characterise typical and persistent phenomena as forms which are everywhere repeated and inessential, and to sharpen the eye for the real spiritual driving forces and for the really essential expressions of these. Thus Schleiermacher attempted, in the introduction to his *Glaubenslehre* (*The Christian Faith*), to identify the 'characteristic mode of Christian states of mind'. And the Hegelians have gone even further in this, putting these analogies and distinctions into a genetic sequence leading up to Christianity, and so recognising the latter in its essence and in its truth at the same time. The process of abstraction which provides the essence of Christianity certainly has need therefore of the comparative history of religions and indeed requires the highest level of abstraction from the history of culture in general, in order to be able to proceed historically. The essence of Christianity can only be arrived at in so far as Christianity is thought of as a part of an overall religious and cultural development. For every peculiarity of a special area, every special essence, is after all only a particular form of the general development of spiritual life. In Schleiermacher's *Ethics* the main lines of such a procedure are worked out and justified in exemplary fashion.[7]

The definition of the essence is indeed a purely historical task. But 'purely historical' entails a whole world-view. It is not an arbitrary or individualistic world-view but rather the modern attitude of man to his memories and accounts of the past which has been achieved on the basis of thousands of penetrating reflections and justified by thousands of successes. The definition of the essence of Christianity, if the term is to have its natural sense, rests upon these presuppositions. Admittedly it is a world-view only in the sense that general basic concepts of history itself come into consideration. Questions of natural science and metaphysics and the influence of these on historical concepts have still not been taken into account. The idea of causality in terms of which the phenomena are linked is the purely historical

---

[7] Cf. Süskind, *Christentum und Geschichte bei Schleiermacher*, 1911.

one which never asks about the necessity of a phenomenon but only about its connection with previous phenomena, without denying newness and originality in each further case. It is no more than the drawing together of all that is historical into an overall view of human development, and the linking together and reconstruction of events according to the principles of probability based on analogy. The aim is to criticise all traditions in terms of these principles and to summarise the living stream of events in values which emerge from within them, values which thereby come to the attention of the races who produce them and which have nothing to do with the personal evaluations and attitudes of the historian or the reader from which they should at any rate be distinguished. These are the presuppositions of the concept of the essence.

If, however, the definition of the essence is a purely historical matter it is only so in the sense that it follows the general principles of critical history and applies the unavoidable process of abstraction with concerted energy to Christianity as a whole. At the same time however it already goes beyond the ordinary accounts of inductive-empirical history, which of course also uses general concepts of this sort but which nevertheless does not make their construction a task which overshadows all other interests. The definition of the essence grows out of the method and spirit of empirical-inductive historical writing but is nevertheless a higher order task. It lies at a point of transition from empirical-inductive history to philosophy of history. This is not so obvious as it should be in Harnack's work but is nevertheless in fact the case throughout. He considers the Gospel or Jesus' preaching of the kingdom of God as the essence of Christianity and works the details of the preaching of Jesus into a concept of Christianity which he then illuminates from the wider history of the church, partly by pointing out aberrations and partly by emphasising developments which are consonant with it. Loisy's objection against Harnack may be justified when he disputes what the latter in fact takes the essence to be or claims that it is too one-sidedly abstracted from the preaching of Jesus. Indeed he may find the essence to be precisely that Christianity is much too complex and diffuse for such abstraction to be possible. But he is wrong when he wishes to replace the concept of the essence by that of church. He displays here a remnant of unhistorical catholic-dogmatic thought. History demands the step from the detailed account to the concept of the essence to be taken, regardless of the extent to which the latter may in fact coherently emerge. If we really want to be clear about Christianity in historical terms we cannot avoid proceeding from detailed historical work to a concept of the essence, however this concept then turns out. Only with respect to such an essence can we then assume a religious attitude.

For these reasons those opponents are quite right who say that Harnack's essence is not a purely empirical-inductive piece of work, but that it includes and is deeply influenced by important presuppositions proper to the philosophy of history. They are only wrong when they fail to recognise the inner connection between what he is doing and the basic characteristics and concepts of the historical method in general. Instead of directing attention to the question as to *whether these themselves are justified and not rather some quite different presuppositions*, they imagine that they can counter the allegedly historically conceived 'essence' of Harnack with an even more historically conceived 'essence'. They believe that on account of its stricter historicity this could prove that church dogma or pietistic belief in the Saviour is the true and authoritative essence of Christianity. If this attempted demonstration were really a purely historical one, however, and if they were correct in it, they would only prove that the spirit of Christianity was consistently expressed in the forms of ecclesiastical world-view, dogmas and institutions and that it is itself being dissolved as the church is dismembered by a culture no longer dependent on antiquity and on the middle ages. They would show that only the church and the movements most closely connected with it come into consideration as a factual basis for the abstraction of the essence and that all later development by contrast is no longer to be conceived of as being Christianity, thus playing into the hands of radical opponents of Christianity such as David Friedrich Strauss in his later period or Eduard von Hartmann and his disciples today. If they show church dogma to be the essence which *counts* and yet at the same time wish to operate with history alone, even though dogma has to a great extent lost its power over the religion of the present, then they must on the contrary break in principle with the attempt to establish the essence by means of historical abstraction in the sense of historical method in general. The concept of the essence would have to be set upon a quite different basis and be arrived at not out of the totality of Christian intellectual development but out of fixed, delimited sources, separated from all other history by a definite characteristic, which would certify its unique claim to legislative authority. Such a characteristic however can only be *miracle*, whether it be the ecclesiastical-dogmatic miracle of biblical inspiration and of the church itself or the pietistic miracle of the conviction of the divinity of the Bible and the central teachings through conversion. A dogmatic history based on miracle, and of which the overall picture is constructed around a previously secured dogmatic centre, would have to be opposed to universal developmental history. Either one must move from history in general, and its methods, to a view of Christianity in its overall extent and to the question of its validity, or one begins from the ideas of the miraculously conceived normative value of the Bible and of dogma and works from there to history in general with its secular methods. The distinction is only obscured when the meaning of the word 'historical' is left inexact, and Christianity is defined for us in an allegedly historical manner as being summed up in its dogma and at the same time for this reason characterised as authoritative. Such a view claims that to find salvation in the Bible and therefore to believe in the Bible and in its fundamental ideas, or to become certain through conversion of the divinity of Christ and thus of the truth of the Bible, is the essence of Christianity. But this use of the word 'essence' is only misleading; it appears to accept the modern historical way of thought, and to pick out genuine characteristics of the real phenomena; but by making these into an authoritative norm because of their basis in a supernatural communication, it makes the whole work of historical abstraction redundant and becomes quite indifferent to the question as to how far the inductive material for the process of abstraction is supposed to extend. Anything which contradicts the doctrines fixed in this way as authoritative truth thus naturally no longer comes under the term Christianity and also cannot be used in the formulation of the latter. This is a use of the word 'essence' which twists it into its opposite. It is similar to the use of the word 'creation' when Häckel speaks of a 'natural history of creation'.

Our attitude to this great fundamental question will determine the way in which we react to Harnack's attempt. The person for whom the dogmas of the church have collapsed, and for whom the presuppositions of modern history are a matter of course, will find in such an approach the only way in which we can clarify our religious conviction and become certain of our Christianness. This is also the reason for the great success of Harnack's book. It addresses itself to modern man with the historical presuppositions which he takes for granted, and shows him on the basis of these presuppositions the coherent spirit of Christianity so that this can work on his conscience, imagination and feelings. If anyone wishes to dispute not merely Harnack's detailed account of the meeting of the Gospel but rather the handing over of Christianity to the fulness of its historical developments, then he must justify and defend the opposite principle, namely the dogmatic principle of miracle, with all its presuppositions and consequences, and not simply bring it into play with modern sounding phrases at a few key points in a quite alien world of ideas. If traditionalist theologians eagerly reproach progressives for using church terminology in an allegedly counterfeit manner, the modern thinker can always charge the traditionalist in turn with ascribing to modern terminology, conceived immanently and historically, a quite impossible ecclesiastical-supernaturalist meaning. For them, all modern, scientific words have a further meaning which takes away their significance again. What a dreadful sophistry of nonsense has been perpetrated with the word 'historical' in particular.

This is not the place to work out in detail which of the two principles is to be preferred. Indeed there is nothing new which could be contributed to the discussion. Rather, I presuppose that the historical method, which is most intimately connected with the whole modern world of ideas and which has established itself in thoroughly tested critical work, is in the right. This method, and this method above all, is what makes it impossible to give assent to the pietistic and ecclesiastical arguments, even though these often are emotionally attractive. If this is the case however, the essence must be sought with determination by way of modern historical thinking.

3. *The essence as criticism*

The enterprise of defining the essence thus involves presuppositions of a fundamental character. But it involves not only presuppositions but also *new problems and difficulties*. As every great idea is not exhausted by the introduction and consideration of its presuppositions but rather stands then only at the beginning of its work and raises new problems characteristic to itself, so is it too in the case of historically conceived theology and the definition of the essence of Christianity. About this its opponents too have made various quite correct observations. But to point to difficulties does not mean to refute. They only serve as a refutation when they are shown to be both insuperable and to stem from a mistaken method. But there is no question of this. They have been conceived miscellaneously and obscurely and pressed into service for a quick victory. Only those who are clear about the contradiction between the methods will understand the real meaning of these difficulties correctly, and those who seriously take the part of the historical method in this debate will consider them to be soluble. Otherwise nothing would remain but radical scepticism.

If the definition of the essence is an abstraction from the total extent of the historical manifestations down to the present day, and if the intention is to single out and formulate the driving forces, then the problem can only be solved easily under *one* condition. It has to be possible for us to think of all the manifestations as arising in series on the strength of a force or law of development inherent in the basic idea. We would then have a formula which would indeed be very different from a natural law which formulates the repeated regularity of consistently similar facts; but which would nevertheless control and explain the manifold variety, and precisely in this way give expression to the essence. This formula would admittedly not be the eternal and permanent in itself, in which we believe; but it would make it possible for us to give expression to the eternal and permanent in the necessary context of historical development, and to formulate it, as it has to be represented to us in our situation, as a result consistent with the development to date. One might take as the essence, for example, the idea of incarnation, which first appeared symbolically and vividly in the person of Jesus, then developed in the dogmatic religious philosophy of Trinitarian doctrine and christology, while still retaining its mythical form, and finally concluded by being stated in the modern doctrine of the unity of the divine and the finite Spirit realised in the development of the Spirit. The Hegelian school in fact understood Christianity in this way, Baur's school of church history is inspired by this great idea, and the modern descendants of the school state it as their doctrine of the essence of Christianity. Perhaps, if one considers the Biblical idea of the Kingdom of God more suited to give expression to the essence than the christology of the ancient church and of Paulinism, one could construct a similar dialectical developmental pattern with this idea, running from the eschatological teaching of Jesus through the doctrine of the church as the body of the Incarnate to the modern Christian social ethic. This is essentially the strategy of Harnack and of Ritschl, who after all do recognise a progressive development, namely in the area of ethics and of cosmology, in order to link reformation ethics to the Gospel and to exclude from the Bible metaphysical and dogmatic encumbrances arising from the world-view of antiquity.

But if the matter really were like this, then all the forms of Christianity, original Christianity, ancient, Byzantine and Roman catholicism, protestantism and the Baptist movement, the pietistic protestant sects, and modern Christian philosophy of religion, would have to be considered as being, each in its context, necessary, and indeed teleologically and not just causally necessary revelations of the essence. Moreover they would be such revelations not merely in the sense that the whole richness and driving force of the Christian idea finds expression precisely in the totality of such various formations taken together and side by side. In that case a necessary presupposition for the definition of the essence would be lost, namely that the essence is not fragmented into countless figurations each of which represents only a partial thought, or in a thousand miscellaneous individualisations of the idea, but rather that it progressively separated off unbalanced and alien elements which appear in all these formations, in order to arrive at the kernel, and only then is to be fully conceived as a complete and unified principle.

Against naive acceptance of all historical forms, if for the moment we ignore purely historical thinking, there protests immediately and above all our protestant conviction. We cannot consider the whole of catholicism as the teleologically necessary, organic development, and see in protestantism only a summary of Christian ideas achieved and deepened through the efforts of catholicism, ideas which then with the same organic necessity brought forth modern Christian humanism. Such a conception is not seriously possible for protestants. While allowing all historical fairness with regard to catholicism, and recognising the fact that the original Christian mission flowed directly out into catholicism, that catholicism is the presupposition of protestantism, and that early protestantism shares many important characteristics with catholicism, nevertheless there remains with protestantism the fact of a break with fundamental ideas of catholicism and the justification of this break by reference to the authority, even if only relative, of original Christianity. However else it may be viewed, protestantism remains a historical catastrophe and an attempt to take up again abandoned ideas of original Christianity. Those who share the protestant conception of Christianity cannot carry through the organic evolutionary theory unconditionally. In terms of this theory catholicism would indeed always retain the advantage. Catholicism alone disposes of a relatively unbroken continuity, is able to claim that its hierarchical, cultic and dogmatic structure represents the organic development of the essence, and can characterise protestantism as an outlying sideshoot of Christian development, even while admitting that the latter has a relative justification for its existence as a criticism of the faults of the church of the late middle ages. Ehrhård has construed the relationship in this way, and so too, even more clearly, has Loisy, who appealed to Caird's Hegelian conception of the development of Christianity. Anyone, however, who finds himself constrained to recognise in protestantism the purer and deeper understanding of Christianity can not share this theory of necessary development; on the contrary, just as he recognises in protestantism itself a catastrophe which invalidates this whole theory, so too must he see in catholicism, in spite of all its continuity with the apostolic mission and the foundation of the church, a similar break over against the pure, original Christian idea of the ethical Kingdom of God as proclaimed by Jesus without priests or sacraments. He is bound to consider catholicism largely as a divergence from the essence of Christianity, as a banalisation and weakening, as a vulgarisation and sensualisation, as an externalisation and contamination. The original idea is brought down in catholicism to the level of average human mediocrity, and displaced by alien elements from the folk religion of antiquity, from the sacramental cult of priests and sacrifice, the mysticism of the time and from the popular superstition which always persists in the background. Even if, as Loisy says, this was perhaps the necessary price which Christianity had to pay in order to develop a church and assert itself, catholicism nevertheless remains thereby a falling away from the essence and a composition of tendencies opposed to the essence, if indeed we are to be justified in conceiving the essence from a protestant point of view and are not forced to characterise protestantism itself as a falling away or a peripheral variety of the essence. To consider ourselves justified in this however would be to state directly our own conception and interpretation of Christianity. Thus it is clear that the essence cannot be simply abstracted from the overall sequence and the totality of the manifestations, but that it is necessary to distinguish here between manifestations which give expression to the essence and those which obscure it, or even distort it or which merely give it some individualistic nuance. There are not merely temporary, relative opposites which simply drive the development onwards; there exist also inner and absolute opposites which cannot be overcome by any formula of the essence and which cannot be organised into any formula of the essence.

Similar doubts about an easy solution to the problem arise when one sets oneself free from the one-sided ecclesiastical consideration of Christianity, which dominates catholic but also protestant historical writing, not least the church history of Baur and Harnack. For these latter the items in the developmental series are Jesus, Paul, the ancient church, catholicism, the churches of the Reformation, and modern, critical protestantism. One only needs to take an unprejudiced look at Gottfried Arnold's *Kirchen und Ketzerhistorie* (History of Heretics and the Church) however, to sense the extraordinary one-sidedness of this assumption. It is the point of view of the *beati possidentes*. In reality the sects and mysticism are also living forms of the Christian idea longside its expression in the church. They have their own meaning and independent relationship to the Gospel and to original Christianity, and they have in any case an extraordinary historical significance before which traditional ecclesiastical history simply closes its eyes. It is immediately obvious, however, to any unprejudiced observer that Saint Francis, Kierkegaard or Tolstoy certainly stand closer to the real preaching of

3. What Does 'Essence of Christianity' Mean?

Jesus than do ecclesiastical dogmatics, and that Meister Eckart and
Sebastian Franck understand certain basic elements of Christianity
more profoundly than does the mass Christianity of the church. From
this point of view the concept of the essence would have to become a
rejection in principle of the 'church' in all its forms, and the church
can by no means be reckoned as belonging to the essence. At the most
it could be construed, as by Richard Rothe, as a temporary resting
place which needs to be superseded. Conversely a historical view
based on the point of view of the church has to characterise the sects
and mysticism as being contrary to the essence, and to demonstrate
them so to be. This is indeed frequently done in traditional church
history, especially by that of the Ritschlian school, with a certain
degree of irritation.[8]

The protestant standpoint as opposed to the catholic, the
ecclesiastical as opposed to the individualistic, the sectarian as
opposed to the ecclesiastical, the synthesis which views church, sect
and mysticism together: all of these are, as conceptions of the essence,
at the same time critical points of view which exclude what is
inessential or contrary to the essence from what is essential. It is
always criticism from a particular standpoint; but the statement in
general is however also at the same time a result of purely historical
considerations. It cannot be otherwise even for the most impartial
approach, if one considers it possible to achieve a concept of the
essence at all. The unified idea of the essence only exists after all in the
thought of the historian summarising the material. Reality nowhere
displays the essence as the absolutely clear, complete and convincing
result of the process. It displays instead great, divided churches, in
none of which the essence can be perceived to be realised, and which
do not even realise the essence all together. It displays moreover all
kinds of sects and groups and also completely individual conceptions
of Christianity. In all of these is to be found not merely the
imperfection of an essence which is not yet fully clear about itself, but
at the same time, sometimes more and sometimes less, a variety of
positive perversions and distortions of the essence. With respect to all
of these the conception of the essence is at the same time a criticism. It
is *not merely an abstraction from the manifestations, but at the same time a
criticism of the manifestations*, and this criticism is *not merely an evaluation of
that which is not yet complete in terms of the driving ideal, but a discrimination
between that which corresponds to the essence and that which is contrary to it.*

[8] An example of the judgement of the essence on the assumption of the
individualistic standpoint may be found in the writings of Johannes Müller, while an
example based on the ecclesiastical presupposition may be found in Wernle's
criticism of my 'Social Teachings' in *ZThK*, 1913.

Alongside the idea that some things may be contrary to the essence, it must also be remembered that others may be fortuitous. Real history contains not only distortions which degrade, exaggerate or counterfeit an idea, but also pure coincidences, a whole variety of phenomena which for their own part arise from quite different contexts, and under given circumstances become involved with the development of an idea which they may influence deeply or with which, for various reasons, they may become firmly enmeshed. Thus there are many fortuitous elements which arose out of the contact with antiquity and out of the conditions of the middle ages and which seem to have flowed together along with the essence, and which, through a recognition of the essence, have to be separated out again. In such cases one must seek only to discern the mastery of the various specific situations by the Christian idea, and not to confuse the latter with those special individual forms which it took at the time. We must be able not only to exclude what is contrary to the essence and what is inessential, but also to detach the inner drive of the essence from its temporary individualisation conditioned by other factors. Thus in this respect also the definition of the essence involves criticism.

According to what criterion, however, is this criticism to be carried out? It is a criticism of historical formations in terms of the ideal which lies within their main driving force. It is what is commonly called an immanent criticism. To this extent it is in fact conceived purely historically; for the historical is measured by the historical, the individual formation is measured against the spirit of the whole conceived intuitively and imaginatively. In this way the influence of intangible personal considerations, which was already a factor in the very thought of such a far-ranging historical abstraction, is further increased. But it is still not for this reason an impossible task. When partisan spirit and personal wishes are left in the background, and if one simply gives oneself over to the impression made by the material and attempts to distinguish the specific within the whole and to judge the distortions and the accidental additions and insertions in terms of the whole, then such a problem is soluble, at least to the extent that unprejudiced persons ready to learn may be brought to a sympathetic understanding or at least inducted into the main direction of the conception and evaluation of the essence. Admittedly it is a task which demands for its fulfilment important scientific and spiritual resources, a personality at one and the same time trained in the exactness of history and disciplined in religion and ethics. It is also a task which cannot be demanded of or forced on anybody. There is too much which is personal and subjective contained both in the problem and in the solution, for just anybody necessarily to be brought to it, not to speak of those among whom prejudice or passion make such a dispassionate analysis impossible. But at bottom it is the same task as the immanent criticism which is applied in an account of any development in politics or law, or of any economic organism, and indeed no different from the immanent criticism of any book. Such problems are in fact posed by the reality of life, and the more important and comprehensive a set of historical data is, the more difficult such an immanent criticism becomes. An account of ethical and religious developments which attempts to be at all comprehensive and coherent cannot dispense with it, and such accounts are themselves indispensable if history is to show us what has been, so that its significance and meaning for human life as a whole can be evaluated. For the historian really to touch upon the main trait, and to recognise really sharply the distortions and the matters of chance, depends only upon his immersion in the facts and upon the maturity of his judgment, and is therefore a matter of historical competence. Various competent historians are in a position to correct each other, and by so doing to further perfect the analysis. The amateurs, the doctrinaire, the fanatics, the narrow-minded, beginners and specialists, on the other hand, should leave the matter alone.

With all this nothing is said about the essence of Christianity which does not apply just as much to every historical definition of an essence. The problem must be posed not only in the sense of pure abstraction but also in the sense of an immanent criticism. Every idea, every item of value, arouses opposing formations of value which from that standpoint seem to be negative ones; and these formations of negative value are often themselves principles with far-reaching consequences, the development of which becomes involved in the development of the positive value, forces the latter to a continuous struggle, limits it by qualification or even under some circumstances suffocates it altogether.

This means that one cannot ultimately be satisfied with such a neutral, objective conception. If history is ceaselessly striving to realise values which have an objective, inner necessity, then these formations of negative value ultimately have to be understood as objectively inimical to the value and goal of history. As soon as one goes beyond purely empirical-inductive history and dares such high things as the definition of essences, the ethically indifferent standpoint of a mere grasping of relationships or mere appraisal in terms of an immanent developmental drive can no longer be maintained. It must be recognised that in our experience every value produced out of a sense of its own necessity is met everywhere by negation, individualising, fragmenting selfishness, crude animal and sensual drives, dullness and complacency refusing to see beyond its own limits, an apathy which diminishes and degrades everything, or at least a mediocrity which coarsens and sensualises. Anybody who combines with the idea of the essence in history the idea of a value and a purpose arising out of an ideal necessity must also admit at the same time the radically evil. It is at any rate not possible to avoid this in any account of the great ethical and religious systems of life. Without that any attempt to define the essence in these fields would become a possibly splendid but infinitely deluded glossing over of reality. That monism, sometimes more materialistic, sometimes more spiritualistic, which is questionable enough in all other fields of thought, is an incomprehensible self-deception in the field of history. It contradicts any straightforward impression of what actually happens and can be refuted directly out of that piece of history known to each of us, because each lives it himself, namely our own experience of life.

The more that theology is convinced that it has to do in Christianity with the highest ethical-religious values of humanity, the less it will be able to avoid the necessity of delimiting in the history of Christianity those phenomena which emerge out of the pure impulse of the essence by contrast with those phenomena which appear out of radical evil or out of a compromise between good and evil. The definition of the essence will have to be a criticism of everything which is produced out of apathy and banality, passion and short-sightedness, stupidity and malice, indifference and mere worldly cleverness. It will not be able to shy away from the reproach of being a moralising conception of history. However much such a conception is to be held back in the study of detail, when it has to give way to the causal explanation of relationships between things, it is equally impossible to avoid it when considering the whole. Indeed, a comprehensive view of the essence is only sought at all in order to make possible an evaluation of what is essential, on the basis of which the inessential can be ignored and that which is contrary to the essence can be condemned.

From this position there finally falls some light on a concept which frequently confuses the definition of the essence, namely the concept of the 'necessary'. The double meaning of the word 'necessary' is all too easily forgotten. Necessity in a psychological-causal sense is something different from necessity in the teleological and ethical sense. Empirical-inductive history has to do with psychological-causal necessity, and necessity here never means more than the linking of an event to the preceding influences sought out in the investigation; the connection between the cause and the effect is not considered otherwise than as a factual link confirmed by other analogous, known cases. The investigation sees everything from the stand-point of the completed event and only seeks to link the latter with a motive. The various possibilities with which the subject of the action had himself reckoned, and the, for him, matter-of-course consideration of things in the light of what is possible, become irrelevant. The result which in fact took place is linked to the motives which brought it about, in so far as these showed themselves, by the result, to have been the strongest. But this psychological-causal, explanatory necessity is not to be identified with the teleological-ethical deciding necessity of one who is thinking and acting in terms of what he believes the inwardly demanded consequence of a particular idea ought to be. It is to this latter however that we refer when we speak of the necessary working out and manifestation of a principle. And for the judgment of necessity in this sense only personal decision and inner conviction is determinative. It is therefore of no importance whatever for the essence if the development from the original Christian mission to catholicism and from catholicism to protestantism and so on is perceived to be necessary in a psychological-causal sense and so described. That only shows that there were in each case motives available which in fact suggested such a development. It proves nothing about what ought to have been, in correspondence with the essence, what really would have come about if the essence had been fully sensed and appreciated, or what would have been the consistent and therefore teleologically necessary development from the point of view of the essence. The conception of the essence is however only concerned with this latter and therefore it is bound up with a personal, ethical judgment with respect to the correspondence of a given manifestation in history with the idea and driving force of Christianity. For this very reason Loisy's views about the necessity of catholicism are interesting and largely correct as an exercise in historically induction; but they have nothing to do with the essence. The definition of the essence does not only involve an imaginative abstraction, but also with it and as part of it a criticism grounded in personal, ethical judgement, which measures the manifestations against the essence. For this reason it is only possible for protestantism, which is based precisely upon the principle that personal insight into what is essential in Christianity is able to evaluate selectively the mass of actual historical manifestations.

4. *The essence as a developmental principle*

If a definition of the essence is required to make distinctions of principle within the material of the historical manifestations, and if it needs above all a criterion for making such distinctions, then there arises *the further problem about where the pre-eminently important revelation of the essence is to be found,* in terms of which the basic idea can be sought which forms the guiding principle of judgment and the starting point for development consistent with the idea.

At first the answer to this seems very simple. The classical revelation is to be found in the origins, where the whole set of ideas is still in its first new, juicy growth, in the purity, unsullied by compromise, of the ideal challenge. It lies in original Christianity, and behind original Christianity in the person and preaching of Jesus. All are agreed on this. Catholicism recognises this in theory and emphasises above all the authority of factual continuity; protestantism bases its whole practical position upon this and from that standpoint criticises a merely factual continuity.

This answer is however really a new and difficult problem. The reason why original Christianity and the preaching of Jesus are above all to be taken into account is, for a definition of the essence, not the formal dogmatic reason of an absolute authority recognisable and confirmed by means of miracle, which might be ascribed to original Christianity itself and also to the sacred writings, that is to say to the ancient Christian writings assembled in the New Testament. Such an approach leads to no definition of the essence but rather to the setting up of a supernatural authority. No difference is made to this even when those with 'positivist' views in the approach to Biblical research do without the doctrine of inspiration and see in the Bible a purely human account of superhuman facts and truths. This is because care is always taken to see that the humanisation or historicisation of the Bible does not extend to the historicisation of the content. It does not really make any difference for our present purposes whether belief in the inspiration of the Bible is proved first in order to demonstrate the divinity of the history to which it refers, or whether we are first assured of the supernatural character of the sacred history in order to establish a certain supernatural divinity of the Bible. For the purely historical way of thinking which is the presupposition of a definition of the essence, the earliest history of Christianity is on the contrary to be studied according to the normal methods of history; and the New Testament is a creation of the church, which by the selection and sanctification of apostolic writings, or writings considered to be apostolic, and by fixing an absolute gulf between the original time and the time which followed, attempted to create for itself precisely that authority which would not have been possible given a purely human-historical view of the beginnings. But this artificial authority, which is only possible on the presuppositions of popular, traditional supernaturalism, has been destroyed by the discovery of the events which led to the formation of the New Testament, and the authority which the original time really has for a definition of the essence must therefore be a quite different one from that which is founded dogmatically on miracle, that is to say, on the basis of the suspension of ordinary history.

It is a question then of a purely historically grounded importance of original Christianity for the definition of the essence. Such a significance is indeed now in fact available in the fullest sense, and easy to demonstrate. The original meaning of a historical phenomenon is contained most powerfully and purely in its origins; and if this is only partially true for complex cultural formations such as the Renaissance, it is altogether true for the prophetic, ethical religions, which draw their whole life out of the founding personality, which call upon their believers again and again to revivify themselves at the original source, and therefore connect their name and their essence most intimately with the relevant personality. In particular it is altogether true of Christianity, which refers its believers more strictly than any other religion to the constant nourishment of their religious life by means of contact with the founder, and which in its Christ-mysticism has given rise to a unique phenomenon which gives expression to this state of affairs particularly clearly. It is admittedly true that while Jesus maintains the central position each age interprets him really quite differently and puts its own ideas under his protection. It is just the same with Paul and with original Christianity. But nevertheless the original time really is recognised as crucial, and out of this recognition its real and genuine meaning always has some effect on the Christianity of the time. This original history laid down in the New Testament remains the criterion among all confessions, sects and groups, and it is never applied without its real meaning having some inner effects. For this reason the definition of the essence must of course hold fast to the original time and consider it as the classical period. The expression 'classical', which is of course also used in other cases to indicate phenomena which are particularly important for the definition of the essence of a given culture, is perhaps the most appropriate word available to us in the vocabulary of history.

But in so far as we consider the original time in this way to be classical we are immediately led on to further questions. The original time is not the New Testament and certainly cannot be conceived without further ado as a completely unified complex. We have to ask: *What is it about the original time which contains the truly classical element?* Furthermore the original time is after all only the seminal form of which the further development is the outgrowth, and if no absolute miraculous gulf exists between the original time and the further development, then in accordance with ordinary historical principles the *further development* is also of fundamental importance for the definition of the essence.

It was not pure Christianity but catholicism which emerged from the original Christian missionary proclamation whose permanent monument is the writings of the New Testament. In those writings themselves may be found already the beginning of the catholic substitution of dogma for history. A definition of the essence must therefore go behind them, and in particular has to reconstruct out of them the historical proclamation and personality of Jesus. That alone is the finally decisive point within the original time. It is for this reason that the problem of the preaching of Jesus has taken on the importance which it has for modern historical theology. Almost half of Harnack's book is given over to this theme. The well-known author of the *Grundlagen des neunzehnten Jahrhunderts* ('Foundations of the Nineteenth Century') collected together the words of Jesus as a basis for the understanding of Christianity. The historical work of modern Bible research is geared to the Gospels and to the historical picture of Jesus which is to be extracted from them. And this work has also not been without great value for our present task. The simple greatness of the fundamental Christian ideas is available more freely, more unselfconsciously and more powerfully in the words of the Lord than in all the apostolic literature, and out of this research into the Gospels a more manly, strong and free spirit has poured into our whole conception of Christianity. However, that which we have perceived through all the uncertainties of the tradition is still the essence of the preaching of Jesus about the Kingdom of God and of his prophetic and messianic self-consciousness rather than that of the Christianity which emerged as a result of his activity.

The very gaps and difficulties in research into the Gospels indicate that the problem is by no means exhausted. The picture of Jesus is not directly available in the sources, but is transmitted and influenced by the faith of the community and above all by the faith of the great apostle, whom he himself did not call and prepare, but who in a struggle with his own heart worked his way to the risen one and who, like the original community, provided the picture of the risen Messiah with the most sublime divine predicates, as a result of which the latter came to replace the coming Kingdom of God as the object of faith and redeemer of the community who honoured him in the cult. This leads to a new picture of the Christ. It can probably be argued that even if much in this image of faith is certainly unhistorical nevertheless the spirit and meaning of Jesus's preaching and the consistency and force of his personality find expression in it. This elaboration no doubt illuminates in many respects what the historical personality in reality was; we cannot dispense with the apostolic and above all the Pauline proclamation in trying to understand Jesus and thus the essence of Christianity. But herewith there is immediately introduced yet another aspect of the matter, and one which does not stand in a perfectly clear relationship to the historical Jesus but can only be connected with him mysteriously in the manner of the fourth Evangelist. It is no longer the historical Christ, the Christ according to the flesh, who is the basis, but the spirit of Christ which is released when the earthly manifestation is shattered in death. He takes everything away from the historical Christ, but he opens the spiritual eye and leads into all truth. If one looks more closely however, that which is new in the apostolic faith, namely in the Gospel of Paul, cannot be understood in this way alone. Linked with the devotion to Christ and the joyful sense of salvation there grows up here the idea of a church for humanity and of free, non-legal grace providing all that is good, that cannot be derived from Jesus' preaching of the Kingdom alone. The latter is essentially individualistically and heroically, ethically oriented, living in the salvation of the future and preparing for it by challenge and promise. The preaching of Paul by contrast lives in the consciousness of present salvation, builds up the community as the body of Christ, and transfers all that is essential into an idea of grace which is admittedly supposed to lead to sinless sanctity but which is not dependent upon its achievement. This is a religious element which is new in content and of the highest importance. In the preaching of Jesus ethical challenge and promise are paramount, while in the preaching of Paul present salvation and the certainty of grace come to the fore. Thus there are already in the two main areas of original Christianity different basic trends which, even though they may be patent of harmonisation, have also had a distinctive influence through the whole history of Christianity. The essence of Christianity has had from the beginning two distinct accents, if not indeed two altogether distinct elements. The Gospel of Jesus leads on here already not only to the elaboration of its own inner consequences but also takes to itself new elements.[9]

This observation however brings us on to further ideas about the matter which severely limit the appraisal of the original time as being above all the authoritative period. 'Christianity' is already in the apostolic faith not the 'words of Christ', but faith in Christ and in the

[9] In the meantime Harnack himself has expressly recognised and treated this problem in his lecture to the World Congress in 1910: 'Das doppelte Evangelium im Neuen Testament.'

Spirit which, in this faith, is given to the community and which works through the community. This Spirit however did not exhaust its influence in the Pauline and Johannine Gospel. It has continued to work in various ways through all the changes of the times, of circumstances and problems, through changing conditions of scientific and practical knowledge, and it has produced magnificent new formulations and reformulations. It has taken possession of new and alien elements. Arising out of a class which was not at all interested in literature and knowledge it penetrated the higher classes of education and culture and developed, on contract with classical thought, an attitude to the world and a system of thought regarding the world, which in spite of all the changes of speculative thought have come to form an inalienable aspect of its essence. The truths of Platonism and of Stoicism have so grown together with it that Christianity can no longer be conceived of as a cultural power without them, while they can no longer be practically influential without Christianity. When Christianity, during the emergence of new states in the medieval world, was called upon to provide intellectual and social direction in an ecclesiastically defined culture, it continued to formulate the idea of a culture which embraced the whole of life and which was shot through with the Christian spirit. This culture was far from the eschatological character of original Christianity and was demanded by the elimination of the immediate expectation of the end and by the educational needs of newly formed and immature peoples. The Byzantine world continued the ancient culture undisturbed and did not produce this kind of idea of a Christian state and culture. As the reformers reconsidered the Christianity of this culture, there came about an alliance between the first awakenings of modern individualism and the genuinely Christian spirit of inwardness and personality, which offered a liberation from the external ethical dualism of catholicism and enabled Christianity to be sought within the shape of ordinary life itself. Reforming protestantism has inextricably interlaced world and church, this-worldly, natural culture and the supernatural ethic of conversion, and thereby laid the basis of a conflict within Christian spirituality itself which can hardly be solved. Then again modern Christian humanism, that is to say, the conception of Christianity created by the Enlightenment and by German Idealism, has emphasised the idea of ethical and religious immanence, perceiving here ideas and forces which signify a present salvation through the transformation of the inner life in the knowledge of God, and in which with an inner necessity the Kingdom of God is realised as it matures towards its perfection. In every case this involves the drawing out of elements which were already hinted at in the original form and which were considered to have been contained within it from the point of view of the later development, but which only emerged later under special circumstances and which in any case have taken on their own independent accent. We must recognise these as being contained within the essence of Christianity as it has come to be and as influencing the definition of the essence; but in the original form considered by itself we cannot find them expressed and indeed we cannot even interpret them directly into it.

Thus it must be unavoidably concluded that the recognition of the essence cannot be exclusively based on the original time and on the preaching of Jesus. Such a view would only be a late reflection of the protestant scriptural principle, and one which would maintain not its blessings but its limitations. On the contrary, the original form and the revelations of the essence which emerge in the further developments have to be understood together. If we are to speak of the essence at all it cannot be an unchangeable idea given once for all in the teaching of Jesus. Rationalism has indeed conceived of it in this way as a result of its being dogmatically accustomed to unchangeable truths of reason and to the protestant scriptural principle. In reality however the essence has to be an entity with an inner, living flexibility, and a productive power for new creation and assimilation. It cannot be characterised at all by one word or one doctrine, but only by a concept which includes from the start both flexibility and richness; *it must be a developing spiritual principle*, a 'germinative principle' as Caird calls it, a historical idea in Ranke's sense, that is to say, not a metaphysical or dogmatic idea, but a driving spiritual force which contains within itself purposes and values and which elaborates these both consistently and accommodatingly.

This has rightly been emphasised again and again by Hegelians and by free Catholics and they assert thereby an important and indispensable element of the concept of the essence. Admittedly however this does still not yet solve the problem, but rather itself again raises *new problems*, which are usually not adequately considered by proponents of the developmental character of the essence.

It would be a simple matter if the presupposition of the proponents of this view, which is usually made in very summary fashion and which has already been touched on earlier in another connection, were correct, namely that the development of such an idea takes place in accordance with definite general laws of the movement of the human or divine Spirit, in other words that the line of development can be constructed in advance with logical necessity and only needs to be illustrated by the factual experience of history. In reality however such a law is not to be found and by every attempt at demonstration it shrinks down to the general proposition, which by no means exhausts the reality of historical development, that the development moves through opposites to new syntheses or at least has the tendency to move in this way. By this means however nothing is said to confirm a really necessary historical view of the elaboration of later formations of Christianity out of the original form, and an objective way of relating all the named elements in the essence is not achieved. The connection between objective historical considerations and subjective personal evaluations and decisions is better maintained when we recognise the original Christian belief in Christ, the Pauline idea of grace and of the church, the idealist teleological belief in the relatedness of the soul to God, the catholic conception of culture, the protestant emphasis on autonomy, and modern Christian humanism all as expressions of the essence, and ourselves inwardly feel these to grow out of the original form, out of the preaching and personality of Jesus. We have to have a sense for what is still Christian, and be able to show the threads through which a formation which apparently is far removed from the original form, but which we nevertheless sense to be Christian, is linked with the latter. Our sense for this is corrected by history and yet at the same time our sense for it plays a leading part in our grouping of the historical facts. According to our own inward working through of the Christian idea and according to the conscientiousness of our grasp of the historical material, we will arrive at various conceptions of the line of development, and in accordance with the points of view thereby achieved we will conceive of the seminal potential of the original form in various ways. That which for one person belongs in the development of the essence is for another a disruption of the continuity. These are difficulties which will always remain with us as long as the creative power of the Christian idea continues to belong to modern history. On the other hand real historical mastery, delicacy in the discernment of transitions and perspicacity in the discovery of changes can display a continuity which is not visible to the crude observer, and in this way history can seriously advance our insight into the essence of Christianity. How much we owe to Herder, Schleiermacher and Hegel, Baur, Wellhausen and Harnack! There is no logically necessary dialectical law which can be constructed for the step by step emergence of the essence, but only a continuum which spreads through everything and which contains within itself rich possibilities for development.

One of the main difficulties is therefore the definition of this continuum itself, the connecting unity in this multiplicy of formations developing out of the original form. This continuum can of course neither simply be taken from the preaching of Jesus as being that major part of it which persists through all times, nor can it lie in the generic character of that which all the formations of Christianity have in common. Then again this continuum by no means consists in an idea which can be briefly formulated, in a simple main idea, but in a spiritual power which involves from the beginning several ideas and nowhere lies directly available in a simple formulation. Thus the essence as a continuum is nowhere simply to be grasped. In the preaching of Jesus precisely that is after all essential for us which for the preaching itself was not directly essential; not the approaching end of the world and the coming Kingdom, but the conditions for the reception of the kingdom and the community which grows up in the fulfilment of these conditions is the essential for us. Catholicism, protestantism and Christian humanism are all quite similar in this respect. For each of these forms of consciousness it is not that which stands in the foreground which is the essence and its continuum, but the seminal element capable of growth which is enclosed within it. From this aspect of the matter too therefore we have confirmation of how difficult the definition of the essence is and how strongly it is influenced by personal and subjective factors. A formula to cover the developing whole will have to include the principle of reformulations within itself and go back far behind the pattern of any particular reformulation to an under-lying basis which itself is conceived of as being in motion. This problem can only be approached with the most delicate historical skill and even then it will always find various solutions.

But the problem of the continuum in the development of the essence of Christianity is still not finished with. The various formations of the Christian spirit display extraordinarily divergent orientations. There are quite extraordinary oppositions between Jesus' indifference to the world, his expectation of the end and proclamation of salvation, and the world-shaping ecclesiastical culture of the middle ages, the individualistic autonomy of protestantism and Christian humanism. If all of these are to fall under the notion of the essence of Christianity, then this essence, as an abstraction for bringing the continuum into focus, cannot be a simple concept, but must go so far as to bear opposites and tensions within itself. It must contain within itself an oscillation between several basic ideas. That is obvious enough in an unprejudiced historical consideration of the matter. A historical phenomenon as powerful and as infinitely rich in consequences as Christianity draws the contents of its thought from various elements of the preceding development and simply reorganises them around a new spiritual centre. A development encompassing such a rich and numerous area of culture is, further, only possible if Christianity bore strong inner tensions within itself and was in a position to emphasise various ideas in accordance with the intellectual and spiritual situation. And it is precisely that which historical research is confirming more and more almost with every day that passes. The ethical monotheism of Israel with the optimism of its belief in creation and the eschatology of late Judaism with the pessimism of belief in redemption, but also religious and ethical individualism with the seeds of humanitarian thought, all flow into the preaching of Jesus. All of these different elements develop with multiple tensions and oppositions; but they also involve further appropriations of related and conciliatory elements. Thus the formula for the essence of Christianity can by no means be a simple concept such as sonship of God, spiritual religion, personal religion, belief in God as Father, or similar. It can only be a complex idea which determines the specifically Christian form of the basic ideas of God, world, man and salvation which are linked together in all religion. On the other hand it is necessary while admitting the complication of the formula to indicate the tension between the elements summarised here which above all is the cause of their living motive strength. It is clear that the original form of Christianity, while neither monkish or ascetic, was indifferent to the world and heroic, and that it was completely ruled by thoughts of the coming Kingdom and the conditions for the reception of the Kingdom. It is also equally clear, however, that with the first steps it took in the world Christianity began to develop an immanent ethic out of its belief in God and in creation, and that as the expectation of the end receded a whole profusion of ethical and cultural formations emerged which then remained in continuous inner tension with the religiously transcendental and eschatological ideas. Thus the essence of Christianity contains a polarity within itself and a statement of it must be dualistic. To take over an image which Ritschl used in a rather different sense, it is like an ellipse which does not have one centre like a circle but which has two focal points. Christianity is an ethic of redemption whose world-view combines optimism and pessimism, transcendence and immanence, an abrupt polarisation of the world and God and the inward linking of these two, a dualism, in principle, which is abrogated again and again in faith and action. It is a purely religious ethic which refers man brusquely and onesidedly to the values of the inner life, and yet again it is a humane ethic which forms and transfigures nature, overcoming the struggle with her through love. Sometimes the one is more apparent and sometimes the other, but neither may be completely lacking if the Christian idea is to be preserved. This inner differentiation finds expression especially in the sociological and cultic formations. As a comprehensive church and medium of grace for mankind it attempts to unify the two sides by setting up graded demands for the believers while the possession of salvation remains of fundamental importance. In the sects which always make themselves felt alongside, the heroic, future-believing, ascetic indifference to the world is emphasised as a demand made on all believers equally, while ready-made salvation and the cult are left in the background. Religious humanism settled for a mere community of thought and attitude. As mystical union with God, Christianity became an altogether individual matter of inwardness coming to terms with God and the world.

The dualism of this formulation finally leads again however to the problem, already touched on, about the relationship between the classical original time and the further development. After all that has been said, and considering the facts of history, this relationship cannot be that of a simple elaboration from the germ. This germ always remains the onesided and abruptly transcendent ethic and it can never simply move over and be transformed into an immanent ethic. There remains within it an orientation towards the coming perfect Kingdom, towards that which is beyond history, an overplus which is never given up with all the development which takes place, and the loss of which really would represent an abrogation of continuity with Christianity. The Gospel always remains precisely and clearly a promise of redemption, which leads from the world, nature and sin, from suffering and error, to God, and which does not find the last word of God to have been said in ordinary life. However strong may be the impulses of reconciliation which spring from the Gospel, the latter is never exhausted in them, and the importance of the classical, original time always remains in that it calls human hearts again and again out of all culture and immanence to that which is above them both. The ethic of original Christianity is neither the formula for the essence of Christianity nor the complete original manifestation of it, but it is a sharply onesided imprint of the Christian idea as is quite understandable in a situation of spiritual revolution and missionary propaganda ready to sacrifice everything and aware only of the opposition. For this reason the essence of Christianity can never be abstracted from original Christianity alone. But the basic orientation is nevertheless so clearly indicated that all further elaboration of the essence, all its cultural and humanitarian impact, must be called on again and again to link up with the original idea of redemption. On the other hand all these accommodations and appropriations themselves belong to the essence, as it has now become, in the only condition in which it is able to bear a general culture. Without the identification with Platonism it is untenable scientifically and in terms of the philosophy of religion. Without the human, social ethic, and without the concern for the needs of society, it is socially unfruitful and alien to the world. Without the elaboration of an art which in its own way takes nature and sensuality as a means of expression, it is dead for the imagination and helpless against the artistic forces of a complex differentiated culture. Thus the statement of the essence is not merely dualistic, but this dualism contains a characteristic circle within itself, in terms of which the original time must always be considered in the light of the later development and this latter from the point of view of the original time. Now the one is more important and now the other, but the essence is only to be found in their interrelationship, and in their interrelationship the preaching of Jesus is the stronger.

5. *The concept of the essence as an ideal concept*

If the considerations given above have shown that the definition of the essence is not only an operation which is rooted in historical empirical science, but one which is at the same time in principle a matter for the philosophy of history, there is a further circumstance which leads us still deeper into this latter area. At the same time this circumstance belongs inseparably to the question about the essence of Christianity. It consists in the fact that the answer emerges very differently according to whether one takes Christianity to be a religious force which is not yet exhausted and which will persist indefinitely to influence the future, or a transient formation of the religious life already gripped by the beginnings of its dissolution. One's own personal attitude to the Christianity of the present and the concomitant appraisal of Christianity as a whole influences the definition of the essence decisively. One appeals from past and present understanding to the future understanding which will be produced through correct knowledge and meditation, and one includes the future seen as an ideal as part of the material out of which the inductive definition of the developing essence is constructed. But whoever fails in this undertaking and is unable any longer to find an inner connection between what he takes to be the religion of the present and the future, and historical Christianity up to the present time, will be inclined to emphasise especially the strange or out-of-date elements and to see in present-day forms not continued development but dissolution.

This too is part of the very nature of that type of abstraction which the concept of the essence is. The estimation of the future is admittedly not one of the tasks of history. Nevertheless, when it is a question of summarising a large and important area under unified concepts, history can never altogether avoid thinking of the future, drawing out existing lines into the future and illuminating the present and the past by means of this projected continuation. Depending upon how one judges the value and thus the present significance of a living phenomenon, for example of classical culture, of the Renaissance or of Buddhism and Islam, the historical appraisal of the whole will vary. A positive evaluation will mean confidence in the ability of the ideas included in them to persist, to be purified and to be strengthened, which means that the phenomena themselves are regarded in the light of the future. A negative appraisal will mean holding to the externally available characteristics of the past and excluding any possibility of idealising them in terms of the image of a purified future. The purpose of history is indeed never simply to reflect a past world in the memory. Quite apart from the fact that this is impossible it would also be empty and superfluous. The understanding of the present out of how it came to be, a view of the experience of the race, or at least of our own people and cultural area, insofar as this is still attainable and can be understood in its total context, the consequent historical disciplining of our thought and the guiding lines for the future which can thereby be achieved: these are the purpose of history. For this reason even the most distant and self-contained developments are not altogether free of indirect relevance to the present and to the future. Only when we sense in them the pulse of our historical life which links everything together do they become history; apart from that they are antiquarian curiosities. This is why the conceptions which we have of all cultural areas reaching down to the present time are so diverse; sometimes they are modernising and idealising, when we count along with them the future development as we think it ought to be and as we think we should shape it; sometimes they are sober and realistic, emphasising the contrast with everything belonging to our times, because we wish to serve historical accuracy and impartiality by renouncing all thoughts about the future, and in order to do this we set aside that which gives rise to such idealisations, namely our personal attitude towards the areas which are described and studied.

Thus the conception of Christianity is also very strongly conditioned by personal attitudes to it in the present and by the consequent conception of its future. This conditioning is only partial and thus the claim of objectivity in historical research is maintained. But it does mean that in coming to a conception of the essence on the basis of history the personal attitude and the evaluation of the future shape of Christianity have something to contribute. For him who believes the validity of Christianity to count no more for the majority of his contemporaries or even only for himself, there is no longer any motive to ascribe to the essence a maturer or purer idea still to be worked out in the future, because he has no confidence that an idea which has had its day is capable of such further influence. On the other hand, he who affirms Christianity and who strives to work out the ideas in it which have a living power for the future, in his own work and in the work of his colleagues, will at the same time see the essence in the light of these ideas and emphasise that in the past which is amenable to the possibilities of the future. One of the preconditions of a definition of the essence is therefore above all the identification of one's personal position with regard to the value and truth of Christianity. If this position turns out to be negative or mainly negative, one of the methods of the definition of the essence will be to contrast it with present and future developments. If it turns out to be affirmative or on the whole affirmative, the definition of the essence will take up within itself the future form which is to be effected by our work, or our ideal of Christianity as we understand it as living human beings of the present day. The future development will have to be counted in with the developing essence, and, since the future development is controlled by our insight into how it ought to be according to the essence and driving force of the Christian idea, *the essence changes quite automatically from being an abstracted concept to being an ideal concept.*

In a similar way almost all essence concepts have the tendency to be transmuted into ideal concepts, when past, unalterable history is linked in the concept of the development of the essence with that which lies in the future and is to be formed by us. Precisely out of this transition arise the fundamentally different conceptions of the essence of classical antiquity, of the middle ages, of Islam, of Buddhism, and so on. Relative agreement is after all possible about the facts; but the coefficient of the future facts which still have to be added on in thought, and the relationship of these future additional facts with an ideal, make the interpretation of the essence a procedure of considerable logical complication. Not only the creative imagination used in the process of abstraction but also the imagination which attempts to foresee a further unfolding of the basic ideas meet together in the concept of the essence. In a matter as important as Christianity it is merely the case to a quite special degree, and every definition of the essence must know that it cannot escape the pressure of this aspect of the problem. The most difficult problems in the definition of Christianity arise out of this unavoidable transition from an abstracted concept to an ideal concept, whereas in the case of less important and drastic or perhaps completely exhausted and redundant phenomena the ideal concept can be more easily eliminated or at least held back.

The position taken towards Christianity however, in spite of all the accompanying objective considerations of a historico-philosophical or metaphysical and speculative kind, is in the last analysis a thoroughly personal matter conditioned by personal religious acceptance and appropriation of the Christian idea in the living context of the present. Of course I do not intend to give here a concrete justification for this position. Rather, I presuppose that in the struggle of intellectual currents and ideals about life we in fact take a decision for Christianity, and that the personal decision for Christianity, in comparison with the various ideals and religions of mankind, suggests or confirms that no physics and no biology, no psychology and no theory of evolution can take from us our belief in the living, creative purpose of God, and that no anti-teleology, no brutality and no fortuitousness of nature, no contradiction between the ideal and the real, can take from us our belief in redemption as the destination of the whole world. I am only pointing out that on this presupposition the definition of the essence, however strictly historical it is, will turn out quite differently, and must do so, than it would on the contrary presuppositions. None of the possible decisions about the problem can be absolutely presuppositionless and impartial. It must merely be made clear that a negative decision must by its very nature give an impression of stricter historicity, because it only looks at the past without taking the future into account, and because when it looks at the past it only emphasises that which is concrete, strange and unfamiliar to modern man; but then a picture is drawn which is perhaps quite onesided and which at the very least is influenced by the rejection of all the ideas out of this historical whole which have a forward influence in the present and in the future. It must equally be made clear that a positive decision, even accompanied by the strictest possible conscientiousness with regard to history, will nevertheless emphasise above all what the past has in common with the present and the future, and place the definition of the essence strongly under the influence of the ideal which, achieved through abstraction from the historical essence, critically refined and capable of unlimited development, is supposed to shape the future.

Thus it is evident that precisely with a positive decision for the truth of Christianity, the definition of the essence stands well and truly under the influence of personal presuppositions, and in view of this the question becomes even more pressing than heretofore, as to how the starting point of a purely historical approach, chosen precisely with a view to an objective clarification, is related to this recognition of the strongly subjective factors which contribute to the result. *Here indeed is to be found the real knot of the whole problem.* But this knot – to give the answer at once – cannot be undone at all. It contains, and here we may simply continue the metaphor, the two main threads which we always have to spin, and which seek to be knotted together, not divided. The knotting, however, can never be achieved by theory, but only by the living act, which here as always combines the objective and the subjective in spite of their theoretical incompatibility, and has the right, with sovereign self-confidence, to point to a combination formed out of a rich objective survey as well as out of a deep inwardness, as being the only possible solution. The only thing that matters is that the two threads to be united should be spun with the fullest conscientiousness and care. The combination itself is then a *creative act*, which can only be refuted or completed and amended by a more convincing and more deeply liberating act.

The concept of the essence seeks, and in the first place indeed has, an objective, historical foundation. It arises indeed precisely in a submission to the breadth and depth of history, out of the need to come to understand an imposing intellectual force in its full range, in its origin and in what it has become. The purpose and meaning of historical thought is, by pursuing the matter to its roots, by taking a comprehensive view of all the relevant phenomena, and by making comparisons with other historical formations, to remove the onesidedness, prejudices and superficialities which attend one's first image of partial or fleeting impressions and effects of the moment, and to press forward to a much more profound and substantial knowledge of the inner spiritual driving power of the whole complex. In this way we are able either to draw new sap from the roots of our existence or to get rid of dying roots, in order to direct our attention to the healthy, growing roots of our future existence. This already involves saying that while we seek out what was essential for people in the past we do so only in order to appropriate the essential for ourselves, in such a way that it may be a principle with on-going effect for the future. Whether we settle for a permanent or for a temporary appraisal of what was essential for the past, we nevertheless only conceive of it in a way in which we intend it to direct both our own will and that of the generation to come. We are seeking not merely an abstract unity of what has been, but a unity of what has been and what is to be; and the abstract unity should not merely be a scientific proposition stating a factual relationship conceived with as little ado as possible, but also at one and the same time a rule for our wills and via these a driving spring of future history. Since it is not a mere copy of the interplay of the purposive values of others which is sought, but since the judgment which gives expression to the essence also determines our own will, it takes on a share of the purposive character of all history, that is, it becomes an act. Only the courage of an act combines the past and the future, by so emphasising the historically grasped essence of a cultural complex for the present, that the future arises out of the essence in a manner demanded by the present and yet at the same time exhausting the depth of the historical impulse. But if in this sense the definition of the essence is an act, then it is no longer merely a judgement about history but it is itself a piece of history. In such a definition progress is made in so far as the historical is newly formed and available for the future; and the definition of the essence is itself a constituent element of the continuing historical development and indeed one of the most important and crucial means by which it takes place. If the development is not to take place by means of unconscious or semiconscious elaborations of the consequences of the past, through wild passions and fanaticisms, through struggles between short-term opinions of the day and the pressure of external circumstances, if rather it takes place as a result of mature and conscientious consideration on the part of the intellectual leaders of a people or a community, and their creative use of the intellectual heritage, then the definition of the essence is precisely the most appropriate means. Just as politics and sociology have influenced modern development as a result of this kind of immersion in history on the part of intellectuals, leaving popular passions on one side, so scientific work on the essence of Christianity is the contribution which theology has to offer alongside the day-to-day opinions and passions of ecclesiastical controversy. In this case however it follows that this definition of the essence is itself above all an act, a faith for the future based on a history which has been historically and scientifically researched. This is the case and cannot be otherwise however much some might wish to conceal it. After a long and careful consideration of the past, present and future, after extending one's view over as much detail as possible, after taking into account all available cases which might further understanding through comparison; there then remains one final act, in which the purely historical which belongs to the past and the normative which belongs to the future are combined in the judgement of the present. This act involves an overcoming of space and time in the judgement itself and an immediate reinsertion of the judgement into space and time as a means of the further development of the whole based on the idea conceived with intuitive insight and freed from space and time. And when such a definition of the essence is carried through in a clear, scientific consciousness, then it is, in so far as it is correct, after all no more than the emergence into consciousness of an inner process which really does drive forward the forces of the future out of those of the past. Only when the scientific judgement succeeds in raising such an instinct into consciousness does it give expression to a real historical movement and formulate the great act of its time. The scientific consciousness contributes clarity and care in the appraisal of the past, and a broad view of the demands of the present, but it regulates, clarifies and establishes only a preliminary step which is completed in the dark depths of the general consciousness. This is true of every definition of the essence which does not analyse a dead past for scholars but which attempts to bring a living historical power to the victorious expression of its 'permanent content'. Almost all definitions of the essence which are undertaken today strive to achieve this. That too is the character of Harnack's work and that is the basis of his success.

Insofar as the essence plays a part like this in the forward development, however, it does not in the end remain an abstracted concept. It is at one and the same time an abstraction and a new combination, a combination of the essence sought in the history with the concrete ideas of the present, with the latter's view of the world and of history and with its ethical and aesthetic ideas. It is not a naked essence, for the essence only casts off the clothes of incidental historical formations to put on immediately the new ones of the present and the future. The essence is an ideal thought which at the same time provides the possibility of new combinations with the concrete life of the present; it is itself a living, individual historical formation which joins the series of those which lie in the past. It is nothing other than a formulation of the Christian idea in a manner corresponding to the present, associated with earlier formulations in laying bare the force for growth, but immediately allowing this latter to shoot up into new leaves and blossoms.

To define the essence is to shape it afresh. It is the elucidation of the essential idea of Christianity in history in the way in which it ought to be a light for the future, and at the same time it is a living view of the present and future world together in this light. The definition of the essence for a given time is the new historical formulation of Christianity for that time. Nobody can abstain from this who both seeks the essence of Christianity in a purely historical manner and believes in the ongoing power of this essence. A different course is open only to one who considers it to be an exhausted and superseded historical formation or who understands Christianity only as an exclusive supernatural announcement in the Bible.

The definition of the essence includes the living religious production of the present, and moreover not of a present which is a mere naive continuation but one which is shaped on the basis of historical insight. The Reformers too acted with an instinctive appreciation of what was historically essential and what was demanded of the present. For this reason they appealed fundamentally to the 'Spirit' which spoke out of the Scriptures. Today this instinctive approach is less feasible, although conversely there is less danger that the 'Spirit' will be bound again so quickly to the letter of the Bible as it was then. The situation itself was the same then as it is today, demanding a rejuvenation out of the historical past and an organic combination with the present. There is within the definition of the essence a living new creation, related afresh to new circumstances, and since it is a question of the re-creation of the highest religious revelation it is a new vouchsafing of revelation in the present. This implies nothing other than the 'Spirit' of the Reformers and of the Pneumatists of the Reformation period. The ties with the past, naive traditionalism and conventional Christian piety are loosened to make way for new movement and growth. We then want to clarify the continuity felt to obtain with Christianity and therefore we search for the essence which is incorporated in the historical manifestations. We also wish to shape the living reality for ourselves and therefore the essence cannot simply be identified with any of its past forms. In the whole concept of the essence there is an element of religious subjectivism which is conscious of maintaining the continuity but which itself shapes the continuum afresh.

6. *Subjectivity and objectivity in the definition of the essence*

It will by now be clear that to raise the question of methodology is not just complicated and pointless scholasticism, but that to understand and answer it is just as decisive for the problem as a really exact source-critical knowledge of the history of Christianity. There are those who reproach Harnack's book and similar attempts on the grounds that they are unhistorical, that they do not stick by a mere affirmation of earlier historical forms of Christianity but project the Christianity of the present and of the future. But such critics fail to see the wood for the trees, overlooking the rich and profound historical world of Harnack's book by picking out the essence which it shapes on the basis of the history. For it is in fact quite clear that all these studies are born out of a real inner debate with the history and that the spirit of such theology is shot through with a concern for learning out of the historical object. The exclusion of personal opinions and desires, the whole submission to the characteristic, concrete object is indeed the real contribution of our historical theology; and the purpose of this submission is simply to grasp the spirit of the matter itself, to let it work fully upon one and to broaden one's own religious understanding precisely by means of what is objectively given and grasped, to deepen this understanding and to free it from the prejudices and limitations of fortuitous education and inclination. This is a leading characteristic of the historical studies of all of us, and we can all say from experience that our view of what is permanent and essential in Christianity has been quite inwardly and fundamentally conditioned and in fact extremely stimulated by this immersion in history, through this extension from selfconsciousness to the common consciousness, from individual experience to the general experience of Christianity and of religious humanity. On the other hand, however, it is also quite evident that the question about the use to which the historical results are to be put must be taken in the context of the more general question about the value and meaning of Christianity for the present and for the future, and that the definition of the essence which is to be given in this process will give expression above all to that from among the past which is of importance for the present and the future. A definition of the essence which is convinced of the lasting power of Christianity and which nevertheless avoided this question would be quite senseless.

It is indeed true to say that the definition of the essence is an extremely complicated undertaking which is conditioned by many points of reference. The essence is an intuitive abstraction, a religious and ethical critique, a flexible developmental concept and the ideal to be applied in the work of shaping and recombining for the future. It partakes of everything and yet is itself fundamentally an independent religious idea. The definition of the essence is the crown and at the same time the self-abrogation of historical theology, it is the unification of the historical element of theology with the normative element or at least the element which shapes the future; and this not least is the fascination of Harnack's book, that it combines the work of this extraordinarily successful historian with a lively Christian analysis of the various tendencies of religious and irreligious modern thought. He has thereby characterised the problem correctly and given an instructive contribution to its solution, instructive, that is to say, even if one has a somewhat different view of what the essence actually is.

We should not be put off by the complicated character of the problem. The problem with which we have to do is after all none other than the major, general problem of the relationship between history and normative thought. Where custom and tradition have brought a single idea to supremacy, as in the markedly national or polytheistic cultures, the problem is as good as non-existent, or else it is solved with a few minor rationalising corrections to the tradition. In international cultures and in those based on a propagandist world religion it is certain to appear. As soon as the first conflicts appear in these cases the main attempts at a solution are worked out. Firstly there is the rationalistic solution which assumes a self-evident, universally agreed judgement on the part of thinking individuals about how things ought to be, and considers history as the more or less sullied execution of this ideal. Secondly there is the supranaturalistic solution which recognised normative truth to reside in an authority itself recognisable by its manner of being, that is to say by miracle, by divine revelations and institutions, a truth which history may keep pace with as best it can, and which the worldly, sinful understanding of proud men is content to ignore. Thirdly there is the most modern solution, evolutionary historical idealism, which is based on history and which draws its norms from history, but which does so by seeing within history the traces of an objective reason, of higher status than individuals and revealing itself step by step in the history of the race, and which is to be read out from within history by a process of abstraction. All these attempts to solve the problem contain of course a grain of truth. The rationalistic solution is correct to demand that only a present inner conviction of the truth of an idea can be decisive; but it fails to perceive the historical conditioning of all the truths which we confront and the historical conditioning of the needs and spiritual conditions by which we ourselves feel led to give assent to an idea. The supranaturalistic solution is correct to recognise the dependence of the average weak, confused and shortsighted person on the authority of great, original creations; but it is not able to carry through by means of miracle an external delimitation of this authority from the rest of human life, nor to assert in life the unchangeability which would be appropriate to such a divine, miraculous truth. Finally, evolutionary historical idealism consciously strives for what is in fact needed, namely an inner identification of the historical and factual with the rational and necessary; but its assertion that this lies within the reason of reality and can be read off from this reason by a process of abstraction is a panlogical prejudice which reckons neither with the folly, sin and apathy of men nor with the irrational, creative factuality and intricacy of history. The untenability of these solutions has been demonstrated again and again in critiques through the centuries. There remains no other solution than that which lies at the basis of observations made above; the doctrine of an ever renewed, purely factual and irrational combination of that which is recognised to be necessary and true with historical tradition and experience. Every great formulation of ideas and values is an individual, creative act which arises out of the possession and appropriation of previous acts, but which conscientiously shapes the development of what is possessed in such a way that in the new formation of values the acquisition of the past coincides with personal conviction, and the necessity of a driving idea within the development is united with the personal grasp of this idea. This new idea within the development is united with the personal grasp of this idea. This new unity is influential until it in turn at some time is also transformed in a new combination. It is always a question of submitting to that which has already been acquired and of newly creating the value for the future from within a personal appropriation of what has been acquired. The objective is not available to be simply picked up each time, but *every time it is newly created, and it becomes binding through the meshing together of what is possessed historically with a personal, conscientious, shaping and transforming activity.* That which is objective demands of us the courage to believe in its objectivity, and it exists in this continually renewed act. 'In the beginning was the act', as Faust said. It is also the 'courage to think' of which Hegel speaks, and which fundamentally means nothing other than the confidence of the well-considered act of personally seizing the necessary, rational content of reality and of the historical process in its present form, and to align oneself through correct intuition with the creative course of world teleology. Such acts of commanding influence are however rare, as rare as the great heroic spirits, and for the great majority of mankind there remains only a belief in authority tempered with the sincerity of inner devotion and gentle individual adjustments. This is because in the last analysis a belief in authority remains in countless cases the method of linking on to any new formulation of the essence of Christianity.

Is that not in reality however a very dangerous kind of subjectivism? Does this not give the essence of Christianity in hostage to quite individual and various interpretations which on the basis of a doctrine such as this could all claim to be correct? And does not the pernicious effect of such a subjectivism find expression in the dissolution of the Christian community which is given up in favour of utterly individual accounts of what Christianity is? Can there be any reassurance at all that in defining the essence one is maintaining the ideas of Christianity and not in fact merely proclaiming a philosophy of religion or a new religion vaguely influenced by Christianity? It is necessary, in conclusion, to give an answer to these questions.

As far as subjectivism in general is concerned it cannot be denied that such a theory in principle opens the door wide to it. At the same time it is difficult to find this objectionable. The fact that the conception of the essence varies with the individual, that is to say its basis in subjective conviction, is in fact always present even when it is thought in theory to have been most carefully excluded. All attempts to establish unchangeable norms fail to alter the fact that in reality everybody conceives of the norm in a different way. This cannot be otherwise if one accepts the presupposition, which has flourished in protestant soil, that there is a right to criticise the historical development. If it is an unavoidable matter of fact however, it is better not to try to deny it but rather to recognise it freely and openly. The less effort one spends in self-deceit, trying to find a theoretical escape from subjectivism, the freer one's hands are to set practical limits to it and defuse the danger. It is after all not a matter of a sheer, arbitrary subjectivism, which could consider anything to be the essence which just happened to suggest itself. It is rather a question of forming a judgment which arises from the most conscientious and comprehensive historical study, and from the will to learn from the reality of history. This historical work is located within a coherent view of modern historical science which is always correcting contraries within itself and pressing towards a consistent conception of history. Thus there are guarantees that the judgement will have coherent and consistent presuppositions, and that the serious scientific intention to find out the truth which emerges for the present will also lead to consistent results. To this may be added the consideration that, as has already been emphasised, the definition of the essence is not something to be done by just anybody. Most people have nowhere near sufficient materials to do it. There can always only be a few leading ideas which are thrown into the general consciousness by lively religious interpreters of history, and which then force others along the same tracks. The more conscientiously and penetratingly someone attempts to arrive at his judgment, the more he will be able to hope that he has given expression to a perception which will prove itself to others. For this reason too the difference between the conceptions of the essence which in fact compete with each other is by no means so very great. Really the most important difference remains whether one wishes to recognise the essence on the basis of authority and miracle, or as the leading spiritual force in the overall historical development. This opposition can, it must be admitted, not be resolved, although there are many middle positions between the two which belong to the many arts of contemporary theology. As between cases of the second group however agreement about the main phenomena is not too distant. Insofar as there admittedly still remains a final remnant of quite personal subjectivism, because the definition of the essence always at the same time involves a shaping of the essence, this is not only not a defect but it is a prerequisite for religion itself. Religion is not the appropriation of doctrines about things which lie in the past, but it is the present awareness of the redemptive presence and holy rule of God, all through the mediation of history but still a new reality, the rising up of a new life, a creation in the present. We must learn to find the authority more within us than without us, and to entrust ourselves more to the creative power of religion to give a living answer to the questions of the present. Of course this is not meant to imply that the mere thoughts of a shortsighted and sinful man might bring forth new truth, but it means that we should trust the Christ who comes to us through history to have the power to create new life even in us. The prophetic element in religion belongs not only to the past but also to the present, as Bonus has correctly explained several times. When we are certain that the spirit of Christ, through history, is speaking a new *word* to us, we do not need to be ashamed to admit that it is a *new* word.

Such a subjectivism equally does not abrogate the religious community and the church. Admittedly it excludes one thing, and that is the church in the sense of a community of belief in legally obligatory and unchangeable dogmas. The church in this sense however was not dissolved by the subjectivism in question; on the contrary the dissolution of compulsory belief took place for other reasons and in turn led to the attempts to define the essence. The definition of the essence itself attempts precisely to bring about that inner unity and understanding which is the only possible sort after the destruction of the authority of dogma. It builds up in a new form that which has become impossible in the old form. Moreover it seeks to build it up in such a way that while the essence, the substance of the matter, is recognised, there is room for quite different views about details and for quite different attitudes towards dogma. For the truly pious person an approach to the piety and the deeds of the Fathers, participation in the common prayer of the congregation and the stimulus of a strong community spirit remain a deep need. It is precisely a deep and broadminded conception of the essence which enables him to sense what is common even in very alien dogmatic and institutional manifestations, to subordinate the doctrinal incompatibility behind the unity of feeling and atmosphere, and to reap edification and strengthening even from that which at first appears foreign and repellent. Harnack correctly characterises his book as a work of peace and unification. Even if it had no influence on the official church in this sense, nevertheless it has united thousands of Christians who were confused and distrustful of official theology and brought them closer again to the Christian community. It is also true to say that churches are not founded on the basis of such a scientific view. In founding a church a simple and energetic authoritative belief is required. But the foundations grow into times of reflection and scientific debate and then they can no longer survive without steady scientific work. The work by which their existence is served consists then precisely in the recognition of the essence, in the free flexibility of which very different attitudes are possible and all can be unified in a common tolerance and in common progress. Precisely the relative subjectivism of the definition of the essence can have a unifying effect, and the existing historical community in turn will always lead this subjectivism in search of a concrete contact to the historical forces. A subjectivisation of ecclesiasticism and its means of unity is admittedly the necessary consequence of such a conception of the essence. But this is already in existence among the laity and even allowed for the lay person by the church. Spiritual and religious development takes little account, on the other hand, of official theological circles.

The last question mark is whether any guarantee for the maintenance of the continuity of Christian thought is given with such a subjectivism, or whether such a definition of the essence does not lead unnoticed away from Christianity and issue in a new religion only loosely related to Christianity. Admittedly no means can be offered to prevent this in advance. Death is possible in a situation of danger. This danger is not light-heartedly sought however; we are driven into the struggle by the religious crisis of the present. Whoever enters this struggle of the spirits with a deep, inner impression in his experience of the strength of the Christian confidence in redemption and of the purity of Christian morality, will also hope to confirm and clarify his possession in the struggle. One thing is certain here, namely that anyone who includes a religious ideal for the future in his definition of the essence which has an inner incompatibility with the basic ideas of historical Christianity will sooner or later become aware of this and then delimit his new conception over against Christianity and withdraw from the Christian congregation. The people who are concerned with these things are after all, for all the mistakes which they make, really people who are concerned with the truth, and such an inner incompatibility would not long remain concealed from them. However, just as insight into the disruption of continuity can only come from thinking it through inwardly in experience, so too can certainty with regard to the assertion of continuity only be based on a conscientious, inward, personal conviction that one has taken up the genuine and real ideas of Christianity in one's conception of the essence and appropriated them and shaped them for the present time.

He who finds this certainty confirmed in a continued more or less close relationship to the congregation, in his own religious life, in prayer and in moral activity, may be assured of the maintenance of continuity. A criterion for the maintenance of continuity in advance does not exist. It is precisely the living and creative characteristic of religion that its continuity asserts itself only in this continuous new formative process. Christianity is affirmed when one has the Father of Jesus Christ present in one's daily struggles and labours, hopes and sufferings, when one is armed with the strength of the Christian Spirit for the great decision to be taken in the world and for the victory of all the eternal, personal values of the soul; whether and how these are present however is decided only by one's own experience and inward certainty, and the extent to which one independently shapes continuity with the tradition or limits one's independence out of devotion to the tradition.

The above sentences also indicate our attitude towards one of the severest recent attacks on the Christian character of the essence of Christianity as understood by Harnack and his friends and pupils, and as it was in the last analysis also rather similarly understood by Schleiermacher and Baur. The attack is really directed towards the whole of neo-protestantism which transfers the essence from the authoritative dogma of the old catholic or protestant orthodoxy to a conception of the Christian spirit which has to be newly shaped. Eduard von Hartmann,[10] who has already characterised so-called

[10] See E. von Hartmann, *Die Selbstzersetzung des Christentums und die Religion der Zukunft*, 1874, *Das Christentum des Neuen Testamentes*, 1905, and *Die Religion des Geistes*, 1882. For an essence of Christianity constructed in this manner Jesus naturally is of no importance, because the value of christology for von Hartmann lies in a world-metaphysic and not in a redeeming personality. For this reason he characterised Jesus as a grossly overestimated, narrowminded fanatic. As is well known, his pupil A. Drews followed this up in his *Christusmythe* by denying the very existence of Jesus. This sensational thesis has to be seen against the background of Hartmann's theory of the essence in order to be understood in its full sense. In this way the essence is well and truly transferred to the divine humanity of the world process and purified of all connection with the person, while on the other hand the opponents and representatives of a free Christianity linking itself to Jesus by means of a new interpretation are left completely in the wrong. The Hartmannian attack is here continued and outdone. The denial of the existence of Jesus and the explanation as to why he was invented and linked to an essence or principle which had no need of him is admittedly as fantastic as the accompanying theory of the essence. This background has thereafter often been forgotten in the debate between the various opinions. For Drews it is fundamentally only a matter of stabilising the monistic, pantheistic religion of the future and of finally disarming 'liberal theology' which in his opinion is the one thing which stands in the way of the rise of this religion of the future. The real issue is about the religious idea of Drews himself, and it is merely enlivened by Drews' acceptance of that queer theory of the essence of Christianity,

liberal theology as the self-induced disintegration of Protestantism, desires not to allow the 'left-Ritschlians', that is above all Harnack and like-minded persons, to count any longer as Christians. Their essence of Christianity, he claims, is an abandonment of Christianity, and their Christian spirituality is a self-deception based on education and on emotional needs. What they claim to be Christianity is their own modern religious conviction which is now only loosely connected with the real spirit of Christianity, and which therefore clings all the more anxiously to a few fortuitous pieces of historical evidence, and especially to the proclamation and personality of Jesus which is really quite strange to us.

Thus an important thinker is here putting forward the thesis that this whole neo-protestantism has developed beyond real Christianity and is now only apparently and externally related to the latter, a thesis with regard to which Hartmann counts on the support of catholic, traditional protestant and pietist believers. Such a judgment is however by no means a purely historical, objective proposition, but in Hartmann's case too is closely connected with his own doctrine of religion, with his attempt to lead the development of Christianity over to the pessimistic, evolutionary pantheism of his own philosophical religion of the future, and at the same time to cut the ground away from beneath the religious development of neo-protestantism. He too makes use of the concept of the essence, but in such a way as to link it to a new religion of the future which displaces Christianity and on the other hand to exclude the neo-protestant Christian consciousness from any influence on the orientation of the future. It is evident that he too conditions his conception of the historical essence in terms of future orientations, which, on the strength of his personal, religious intuition and philosophical view of the world, he takes to be springing forth and asserting themselves from within the historical essence. For him the true historical essence of Christianity is ecclesiastical orthodoxy; his own, von Hartmann's, doctrine of religion is the correct evolutionary historical continuation of what is relatively true in Christianity; critical theology is an unstable *entr'acte*. Thus on the one hand his account and those of his followers are an instructive confirmation of the character of the concept of the essence as developed above, while on the other hand his exclusion of neo-

---

which he finds rather attractive, and by his uprooting of liberal theology. The debate has however been drawn away from its real object, and as the Drews sensation was taken much too seriously, there arose among ourselves a renewed discussion about the relationship between faith and history. Such a discussion can only be useful, but it would do better not to take its point of departure from Drews' fanciful ideas. There was sufficient need for such a discussion in any case.

protestantism turns out to be conditioned by the desire to attach what is in the last analysis an anti-Christian religion of the future to the expired Christian period and to dispute the right to life of free Christianity. It is an attempt to make an anti-Christian religion spring from Christianity as the next stage in its development, while characterising neo-protestantism, which really feels itself to be Christian, as a futureless disintegration and rootless self-deception. The whole attack of the Hartmannians amounts to characterising themselves as the only legitimate continuation and heirs of a superseded Christianity, and with this end in mind, to withdrawing the right to existence of the other possibility of development, namely, neo-protestantism. All of this moves along precisely the lines of thought described above, except that the result is an opposite one: the essence of Christianity is exhausted, but at least it displays the possibility of being developed into pessimistic pantheism, while free protestantism offers no possibility for the future but only the appearance of one. It is clear that before this conclusion can be evaluated it must first be asked whether von Hartmann's construction of the essence for its own part corresponds to the historical facts, whether it has an objective justification in the facts or whether it is not an altogether subjective arrangement and interpretation of history. Only then can the question about the Christian character of the neo-protestant essence of Christianity be raised impartially and without alien, distorting, side interests. For von Hartmann the question is quite openly raised in the service of his own doctrine of religion, and not impartiality.

There is no doubt at all that the section of Hartmann's thought in which he states his own account of the essence, and the connection between this and his own anti-Christian doctrine of religion, is an extremely violent construction which distorts all real history. He seeks the 'essence' in the most important historical dogma, namely in the doctrine of the incarnation, that is to say in christology and in the doctrine of the Trinity. But he interprets this dogma in a completely new alien sense. For him it is the doctrine of a continuous unity between the finite and the infinite Spirit, a short formulation of pantheism expressed mythically in the doctrine of the God-man. The person of Jesus himself is a completely irrelevant matter and he might just as well never have existed at all. The essence of Christianity is for him the mythical expression given in christology to the sameness of God and man, that is, to the sameness of God and the world. It is supposed to be a special contribution of Christianity that this sameness is conceived of pessimistically and tragically as the destruction of the finite in God through suffering, and that the incarnate God is consequently represented in the myth as suffering. Christology, and that is to say christology interpreted as a mythical symbol of pessimistic pantheism, is for him the essence of Christianity; and everything else, its whole theism and the idea of personality, its belief in salvation and the beyond, its forgiveness of sins and its trust in God, are for him inessential anthropomorphic limitations. On account of these inseparable limitations Christianity is finished, the argument goes, but the pessimistic pantheism of future religion can link itself to the myth of the suffering incarnate God, while free protestantism discards precisely that which is great in Christianity, namely the christological myth, and holds fast to the limitations, or clings to the personality of Jesus, which, when free from the christological myth, is grossly inadequate. By so doing, free protestantism is supposed to have lost precisely what is essential and to remain attached to what is inessential; therefore it is no longer Christianity.

There can be no doubt however for anybody with a knowledge of real history that this construction of the essence is pure fantasy. The importance of christology never really lay in a particular metaphysic, but in the consolidation and justification of Jesus' authority and his position as an object of devotion in the cult, which in turn was and is only the presupposition and means of what is really essential, namely the recognition of the living, sin-forgiving and sanctifying Father in Christ. There was never any question in this of pantheism, of the unity of man or indeed of the world in itself with God, but only of the unity of the redeemer with God. Equally, the suffering of the incarnate does not at all have the meaning of a suffering God and a painful world process, but rather the meaning of the sacrifice of the one for the many, and of salvation for eternity in the face of world judgement. This Hartmannian definition of the essence is therefore violently subjective and breaks down altogether when confronted with real history. Its true historical connections are with Brahmanism and Buddhism, and not with Christianity.

Therewith, however, disappears any possible basis for the assertion of the non-Christian character of free protestantism. If this latter, according to Hartmann, is attached to the limitations and husks, it is certain on the basis of objective history that precisely these limitations and husks, that is, the personalist Christian belief in God and salvation, are themselves the essentials. The problem is only that for the newer protestantism the relationship of the belief in God to history has changed, and that the unworldliness or asceticism of Christianity, which is still maintained, has to be set in a new and different relationship to cultural values. The relationship between faith and history can no longer be interpreted in the forms of incarnational christology, and that which can be experienced in the present has to be set above history. It is only for this reason that the old christology falls away and that the attempt is made to formulate the relationship to history anew. (We do not need to consider here the various particular solutions to the problem.) Similarly, the ultramundane depth of personality cannot be expounded after the manner of cultureless original Christianity, nor again in the hierarchical style of medieval culture, nor yet again in the bourgeois vocational ethic of early protestantism, but a new solution of this fundamental problem of all religious ethics must be sought. The task here is to differentiate the inner-worldly and ultramundane values in their full polarity and to span the tension between them with a superior religious idea. With all this however one may be confident of standing in the continuity of the Christian spirit and that one is only restating the essence in a new way which corresponds to the total situation. There is not the slightest need to be confused by the Hartmannian construction of the essence, which, taking its cue from the pantheistically orientated interpretation of Christianity of Schelling and Strauss and adding for its own part the element of pessimism, is quite obviously dictated by the wish to accommodate to essentially non-Christian and indeed anti-Christian religious doctrines. This construction of history is utterly impossible, indescribably onesidedly selective, and interprets what is selected completely inappropriately. It has in reality no connection whatever with Christianity but is a Europeanisation of Hinduism such as was already found in Schopenhauer. By contrast it is crystal-clear that whatever faults may be attributed to free theology this latter has a real link with the genuine history of Christianity and represents with its definition of the essence the genuine and essential fundamental traits of the prophetic, Christian idea of God. This is confirmed by the way in which the Hartmannians scorn it as banal theism and anthropomorphism.

Admittedly this continuity cannot be proved in an exact historical sense. It lives in feeling and in the will and it can only appeal to that which is homogeneous with itself in history. It is a living, religious subjectivity which is aware of its inner rapport with the great basic drives of the Christian approach to life and which finds this feeling confirmed in conscientious historical research, even if it cannot be denied that the interpretation and comprehensive view of this history are themselves partially conditioned by the fundamental conviction in question. It would admittedly be possible to conceive of a limit beyond which this confirmation is no longer possible, which would mean that the present subjectivity is a further development going beyond

Christianity. This could however only really be established from the point of view of a much later stage of development. Our own feeling is completely justified in considering our positions to be Christian and we can leave it to the future to decide whether we are producing a movement which moves away beyond Christianity or one which remains in continuity within it. These are problems which lie in the future, but in any case it is not possible to conceive of a pessimistic monism ever being the future result of a religious development springing from Christianity. That would indeed only represent a loss of the differentiation and profundity already achieved, a swallowing up of the greatest gain of history, of the idea of personality, by the Moloch of dull isolationism. Whatever elements of modern natural science and aestheticism may be favourable to such a monism, it cannot for ever hold up and obscure the urge towards freedom, conquest of the world and a union with God which takes place precisely in the most personal forms of life, as driven on by prophetic religion and Christianity. It is in this direction that the conjectural future is to be seen, and such a future will always in fact assert, probably consciously, its connection with prophetic religion and Christianity. In any case we remain thus in closest contact with the one living religious power of our world, and we remain within that which the historical moment shows us to be the true within Christianity. In the last analysis we are concerned not with Christianity but with the truth, and we are without doubt not yet at a point where there might be a religious truth beyond Christianity. The abstract possibility of such developments in the future does not need to confuse us. We seek God as he turns towards us in the present, and in this respect that which he says to us in Christ and in the prophets is by no means superseded, but rather remains yet the only power which provides among us simple health and living profundity, true reverence and beatifying trust. This may suffice, regardless of whether it is 'no longer Christianity' or 'still Christianity'. Wherever the further path may lead we are certain that no higher truth lies in pessimistic pantheism, but that any such lies in the direction of religious personalism which has to overcome suffering and sin through a higher life and not merely succumb to it. We are therefore certainly not on a false path with Christianity but remain with it in the line of the true development of the revelation of God, and thus need to be concerned neither about whether or not we are Christian nor about the future. This remains in the hand of the same God who turns towards us in our present-day Christianity and allows himself here to be found.

We also do not need to be perplexed about the fact that free

Christianity with its acceptance of the whole universal historical way of thinking, as compared with the older protestantism, does indeed involve something new, and for this reason finds it necessary to define the essence differently in many points while making a living scrutiny of the historical powers of the present day. If one does not take the view that catholicism is the 'essence' of Christianity and that protestantism is merely the beginning of its dissolution, but if one sees rather in the latter a new formation of the essence which corresponds to the overall historical situation and is nourished out of the Bible, then one will be able to see these new, modern formations not as shocking distortions of the essence but, so to speak, as the second act of protestantism, which corresponds to the completely changed overall situation. We do not thus fall apart from the essence, but do only what the older protestantism itself did, that is, we formulate a new expression of the essence. From our overall point of view we need have no second thoughts about this. For to deduce the essence from the Bible alone is indeed a quite impossible expedient. Where there have been so many breaks and new formations a further such is by all means possible, and by no means needs to lead us away out of the matter itself. It is after all not a matter of isolated individual theologians, but of a search for a new conception of the essence which began with the eighteenth century and continues with this formulation of the question down to the present day. If this whole development is named neo-protestantism, as has been done above several times, it is because this is indeed nothing other than the attempt to formulate anew the essence of Christianity. And there is no reason to doubt that it will succeed.

Here we find ourselves admittedly once again faced by the fact that the definition of the essence is not something which is purely historical but is indeed that synthesis of history and the future which has to be created at all the great, crucial junctions, and which in the last analysis can only be fully sure of continuity in personal, subjective certainty because it is conscious of having grown out of living and deeply comprehended history itself.

There is a fine saying of Zinzendorf, which I admit is only in my memory as I remember it from Ritschl's lectures, namely: 'Belief needs daring and much loyalty.' This is true of belief in general, and it is particularly true of the definition of the essence of Christianity. Much loyalty in meditation on and devotion to history and above all to Jesus, but also the daring to bring a living idea forward out of history for the present time, and, with the courage of a conscience grounded in God, to set it within the intellectual world of the present: this is what is involved in the work on the essence of Christianity. In the one there is perhaps more loyalty and in the other there is more daring, but the ideal is the closest possible linking of the two.

7. *The conclusion*

With the above the meaning and purpose of the concept of the essence is clarified and the knot of interests which it represents is loosened. It is by nature not a purely historical, empirical concept, but the highest contribution of historical abstraction or, that is, the formation of general historical concepts. The formation of this general concept is not possible, even with the strictest historical concern for facts, without contrasting it as a critical, evaluatory criterion with a portion of the facts, and without linking the various formations by means of a developmental concept which does justice to its ability to change and accommodate. The real interest in the concept of the essence however only appears clearly when that which is historically felt to be essential at the same time emerges as the decisive developmental impulse for the future, and is handed over to a systematic, philosophically religious treatment for the presentation of the Christian faith of the present. Harnack's book attempts to satisfy all these interests at once, seeking thereby to give a basis and object of faith from a historical starting point. It is already of course for this reason no longer purely historical, but it develops the future out of pure history.

Harnack's whole historical work, especially his great history of dogma, which is really a history of Christianity, is to be seen against this background. It is this that gives his history its compelling tempo and human significance. It is this too which gives his standpoint of faith a concrete, living, historical fullness. It is a historical enterprise which links history to the working out of a normative religious position, and its dominant significance lies precisely in that point.

If, however, one considers the very delicate linking of interests which has been indicated above, one cannot avoid thinking whether perhaps alongside this great achievement, which incidentally may worthily be placed side by side with Karl Müller's history of the Church, it may not be possible to justify a stronger separation of tasks. It is perhaps good to separate more clearly what is the properly historical and what the philosophically historical, normative element. At any rate this would seem to be desirable for the present situation. In the meantime, in comparison with Harnack's account, the historical material has grown enormously. The linking and grouping of facts has to some extent come to be seen from new points of view. In particular, an account which is no longer essentially ideological, that is to say, interested only in the development of the ideas of belief, but sociological, that is to say, seeing the ethical and religious ideas in their close relationship with the various Christian social formations and in their interaction with the secular forces of society, will no longer be able to formulate the essence as simply as Harnack did. The concept of the essence, which is necessary for empirical history, will have to recognise far richer possibilities of development and sifting in the history of the Christian idea, if it wishes to recognise the phenomena as falling within a common area. The concept of the various possibilities for development inherent within the Christian idea will be more important, for the purely historical attainment of a general concept, than the demonstration of a simple continuum or even of a dialectical necessity in the sequence of ideas. Harnack's mature and delicate realism has countered the Tübingen theory by already giving up the second of these. However, the simple continuity of the Gospel of Jesus, centralised in its essence and released from its contemporary conditioning, also fails to satisfy the need which now obtains. Thus it will also be necessary, for a purely empirical, historical account, to seek a concept of essence and development which includes within itself the possibilities and complications.[11]

Under these circumstances, on the other hand, the systematic, normative task of defining the essence as a basis for future development and as material for the teaching of the faith is also seen to be clearly distinct from the purely historical task. This task reckons with various possibilities in terms of which the essence may vary and link itself with other forces of history giving special effects. These possibilities are then thought of as lying within the principle, but they contain the ramifications and interconnections of the latter. They strive to separate rather than to come together. They are understood in an essentially causal way, but not teleologically as if towards the

[11] It is in this way that I understood and characterised the essence of Christianity in my 'Social Teachings', especially in the concluding treatise. Precisely for this reason they consciously have no direct connection to doctrine or ethics and may seem to many to be over-realistic or sceptical. But all my other work shows that I separate from these the dogmatic and ethical concept of the essence, and that I really make no concessions to historical scepticism here. On the idea of 'value-free teleology', which is related to the historical concept of the essence, see now the second edition of Rickert's *Kulturwissenschaft und Naturwissenschaft*, 1910. The whole line of thought of this present study is based considerably on what I have learnt from Rickert. Under this influence I have also turned away from the more Hegelian definitions of the essence which I earlier set out in the essay 'Geschichte und Metaphysik' (*ZThK* 1896), which is for this reason not taken up again here. I may refer also to my criticism of this concept of development in my notices of A. Dorner's *Grundriß der Dogmengeschichte* (Göbl. Gel. Anr., 1910), the same author's *Grundriß der Religionsphilosophie* (ditto, 1905), and of W. Köhler's *Idee und Persönlichkeit* (H.Z., 1913); and also to my article 'History' in Hastings' *Dictionary*.

realisation of the pure concept. For this reason it is not possible on the basis of this concept of the essence to achieve the coherent objective of shaping the future, but only to gain a historical understanding of the facts. The dogmatic, normative concept of the essence by contrast aims at a rejuvenating synthesis, at the selection and extraction of that which corresponds to the present and future and at a new connection between that which is so extracted and the practical and intellectual world of the present. It does not seize a dialectically necessary, one and only goal of development, but itself realises one of the possibilities, the one which is demanded by the present and the immediate future. Everything which has been said above about the relationship between the historical and the creative must stand. But the dogmatic concept of the essence is nevertheless somewhat different from the historical concept, because it concentrates on a coherent Christian spirituality to be affirmed only in an act of will.

This is admittedly a somewhat sober and realistic appraisal of the way things stand. But it corresponds to the fact that the historical is coming to be taken everywhere for granted, and is demanding ever more insistently a method of its own, distinct from the establishment of personal convictions and evaluations proper to the philosophy of history. This is a real gain for the impartial understanding of history and thus for the understanding of real life. The idea of a 'value-free teleology', that is, an understanding of historical ideological forces without the intrusion of our own evaluations is decisive here. On the other hand the systematic, normative formation of the idea of the essence thereby becomes more free of historical details, and more energetically and sharply thrown back on the treatment of the whole and on the recognition of its richly responsible, creative character. The historical ballast which sometimes weighs heavily upon theological work nowadays may be discarded, and the spirit of history may declare itself more clearly and powerfully; more enthusiastically and comprehensively, as real spirit, and as a living act.

However much we may distinguish and discriminate here, all such distinctions are admittedly only provisional and hypothetical. The unity of life and of knowledge will always bring together again what is divided. Just as history and the philosophy of history can only be separated artificially and methodologically, while in reality the first of these always contains an element of the second while the second can only be built up on the first, so too the historical essence and the essence of faith will have to seek and find each other again and again. The task of theology consists in their unity, whether the two tasks are carefully shared out and solved as far as possible independently, or whether they are brought together again in a great, comprehensive account of Christianity which is at once both history and faith.

Note by S. W. Sykes

Troeltsch made in all about seventy alterations to the text of 'Was heißt "Wesen des Christentums"?' when it was printed in the second volume of his collected works. The period 1903-1913 covered by the interval between the two versions was one in which important intellectual developments took place, and some of these are mirrored in the changes to the text. The largest alteration consists in the substantial expansion of the discussion of Eduard von Hartmann. In 1903 Troeltsch had contented himself with a bland paragraph pointing out the similarity of the method of their respective arguments despite the diversity of their conclusions. Although claiming greater historical backing for his own position, Troeltsch recognised the reciprocal effect of personal convictions and historical study, and doubted whether any neutral tribunal could arbitrate between their different claims. Sensing that this had given away too much of the case, by 1913 Troeltsch felt moved to launch a slashing attack on von Hartmann's *historical* right to construe Christianity as giving birth to his form of 'pessimistic pantheism'.

Weber's development of the notion of an 'ideal type' and his strict separation between a value-related and a value judgment also had a marked effect on Troeltsch. This can be seen in the theme of Section 7, 'The Conclusion', which is wholly new in the 1913 edition. Here Troeltsch inclines more markedly than in the rest of the essay to the separation between 'the historical essence' and 'the essence of faith'.

Another shift of view has taken place in his handling of the New Testament. A paragraph maintaining a substantial continuity between the preaching and personality of the historical Jesus and the belief of the early church has been heavily altered to include the references to the radical novelty of Paul's picture of Jesus. The idea that Christianity 'has two distinct accents, if not indeed two altogether distinct elements' (p.149) is used in the 1913 edition to justify a much greater degree of innovation in the development of Christianity. Thus only in the later edition does he add the suggestion that the changes and assimilations which have occurred in the history of Christianity 'themselves belong to the essence' (p.155). This thought, which does not cohere with the main drift of his 1903 position, is expressed in its plainest form in another essay of 1913, 'The Dogmatics of the "religionsgeschichtliche Schule" ', where Troeltsch bluntly asserts that the essence of Christianity differs in different epochs. No such thought is envisaged in the 1903 version, which contents itself with affirming the complexity of the perpetual oscillation between an immanental and an other-worldly, redemptive view of the world (Jesus' own view). The possibility of real novelty in Christianity (for example, the novelty of the influences from Platonism and Stoicism) is the theme of a number of insertions. Troeltsch may have felt that such examples strengthened the right of the neo-protestants to offer their innovations as the next stage of Christianity's development; but the same argument might be used for other novelties (like those of von Hartmann). Hence, by 1913, Troeltsch feels constrained to add that in the final analysis he is more concerned with truth than with Christianity, and that it really matters little whether neo-protestantism is 'still' or 'no longer' Christianity (p.175). The increased scepticism of this remark is reflected in a number of other additions, for example where the relationship to the Christian community of the theologian searching for a sense of the continuity of Christianity is reduced from being 'close' to being 'more or less close' (p.170).

The work which Troeltsch had undertaken on the social teachings of the Christian churches had given him a clear insight into the narrowness of Harnack's, *History of Dogma*, which a number of additional sentences reflect. He also dropped from the footnotes references to his earlier essays in the philosophy of history and religion, which now gave a too Hegelian view for his present convictions. There are a number of attempts to incorporate Rickert's 'value-free teleology' more explicitly into the argument, by the addition of clauses emphasising the emergence from within the living stream of events of a sense of their goal (e.g. p.134, where these 'values' are sharply distinguished from the personal values of the historian). The essay remains in conception an expansion of Schleiermacher's work, and a few additions make the indebtedness still clearer. Otherwise the changes comprise various amplifications and expansions of minor significance.

4

The Significance of the Historical
Existence of Jesus for Faith

1. *The effect of historical criticism upon faith in Christ*

Christian dogma, as constructed by the early church, has finally
disintegrated; there is no longer a unitary christian culture; and
historical criticism of the Bible is now a reality. One of the main
questions for Christian religious thought today is therefore the effect
of historical criticism upon faith in Christ. What can a picture of Jesus
subject to and shaped by historical criticism mean for a faith that is by
its very nature concerned with the eternal, timeless, unconditioned
and supra-historical? When it first formed its religious ideas the
primitive Christian community had already taken Jesus out of history
and made him Logos and God, the eternal Christ appearing to us in
historical form, one who is related in essence to the eternal Godhead
and so not unnaturally the object of faith. But historical criticism,
grown up in a world no longer dominated by the church, has returned
him to history where all is finite and conditioned.

Is it still possible to speak of any inner, essential significance of
Jesus for faith? The crisis began when criticism and historical and
psychological methods were introduced into research on the gospels.
It has today found its sharpest expression in the silly question that is
just now occupying many people, whether Jesus ever existed,[1] and in
the more justifiable concern whether we possess enough certain
knowledge about him to understand historically the emergence of
Christianity, let alone justify attaching religious faith and conviction
to the historical fact.

The development leading to this radical form of the question is
clear. To begin with people still believed in sound historical research
into the life and personality of Jesus through critical treatment of the
sources. The result was that the picture of Jesus' human life was
brought closer and made more powerful. But at the same time the

[1] Cf. for example A. Drews, *Die Christusmythe,* Jena, 1909; Eng.tr. London, 1910. On
this, E. Troeltsch: 'Aus der religiösen Bewegung der Gegenwart', 1910. (*G.S.* II, pp.22-
44, esp. pp.36f.). [Notes and sub-titles in this essay are those of the Siebenstern edition,
ed. T. Rendtorff, with English references added by the translator.]

painful pressure of particular critical questions upon faith's
convictions made itself felt. From the Deists and Reimarus[2] on,
devastating answers to these were not excluded and a growing
historical critical apologetics was necessary which very soon showed
the difficulties in tying religious convictions to the facts of history that
were to be established by criticism. A further advance of criticism
discovered how very foreign was the religious and ethical stance of the
early church and even of Jesus himself. They were tied to the popular
world picture of antiquity, to Jewish and oriental notions and to
apocalyptic eschatological ideals. The 'Christianity of Christ' was
something entirely different from the Christianity of a church which
had settled for compromise with science and the indispensable secular
morality of political, legal and economic life. Here Platonic, Stoic and
modern scientific influence seemed to be present and, above all, the
radical break between the world and the kingdom of God, this world
and the beyond was greatly toned down. So the question arose
whether the historical Christ, his view of God and the world, above all
his ethos could 'still' be ours today. Affirmative answers needed such a
'correct' understanding of Jesus (as opposed to the simple meaning of
the text) and such enormous departures from temporally conditioned
traits to the 'abiding significance' that a simple religious relationship
to him seemed scarcely possible any longer. Finally, as source
criticism grew more complicated and semitists and classicists joined
in, biblical criticism became so radical as apparently to threaten or
even make impossible any certain historical knowledge. Since *The Life
of Jesus* by D.F. Strauss[3] this criticism has on the whole become
steadily sharper; the radical views of today are well-known. Linguists
cast aside the anxiety and religious constraints which acted as a brake
upon even the most critical theologians, and asserted that the gospel
history was almost completely unknowable. The whole problem of a
life of Jesus was abandoned as insoluble and accounts were restricted
to his teaching. Finally, even this was considered doubtful; the
material could not be purified of what had been subsequently read
into it by the faith of the community. The ground for any connexion
between religion and historical facts had been completely taken
away.[4]

[2] Reimarus *Fragments* (published by Lessing 1774-8). Eng.tr. ed. C.H. Talbert,
Philadelphia and London, 1970.
[3] D.F. Strauss, *The Life of Jesus*, 1835. Eng.tr. of 4th ed., by George Eliot, 1846. Rp.
ed. P.C. Hodgson, Philadelphia and London, 1972.
[4] On all this cf. A Schweitzer, *Von Reimarus zu Wrede*, 1906, since 1913 called *Geschichte
der Leben Jesu Forschung*, Siebenstern Taschenbuch, 1966. Eng.tr. W. Montgomery, *The
Quest of the Historical Jesus*, London, 1910. Troeltsch's lecture is evaluated critically on
pp.521f. of the later German editions.

It is not necessary to criticise here the most radical assertions. To say that Jesus never existed is clearly ludicrous and even to say that the main lines of his teaching cannot be known is a great exaggeration. But conclusions like these do stem from critical historical research, and the possibility, or rather the necessity of posing such questions at all does at least indicate very clearly what the problem is. If objectivity is maintained, and these kinds of questions are not and cannot be excluded, is it possible to speak of an inner and essential significance of the primal New Testament history for Christian life and thought? Must these not rather be made internally independent of all necessary connexion with historical elements which are always subject to science and which present to scientific research a picture that diverges considerably from contemporary religious life? That is in fact the question which arises for Christians today.

2. *The modern conception of faith and the historical factuality of Jesus*

This question makes sense only if one presupposition is granted. It would be pointless if one assumed the Christianity of the early church with its dogma of the God-man, its church and sacraments established by Christ and the redeeming effects of his saving work of reconciling God. For all this stands and falls with the conviction of the reality of the historical person Christ and a church and salvation which are only effective at all on the basis of his work. From this standpoint the whole question would be simply to issue the death-certificate for all Christianity. The question only makes sense on the assumption that Christianity is not belief in a work of salvation which reconciles God and so frees men from the results of contamination by original sin, nor in this saving work being established in the church as an institution of salvation. It assumes that Christianity is understood in the first place as a living faith in God that is new in every moment; it sees redemption as an ever new work of God upon the soul resulting from this faith. Or to put it another way, it assumes that Christianity is a particular faith in God, a special knowledge of God with a corresponding practical attitude of life. In other words, it is, as we say, a religious 'idea' or a religious 'principle'.

That does not have to be understood intellectualistically and philosophically, neither need it be derived from a general idea of the world. It can be understood in a purely practical way as faith's idea of God and of his relation to the world and man, as an ethical and religious orientation of life, and it may be based purely on sense, feeling and inner experience. But this does mean a complete transformation of the idea of redemption. In this view God redeems us by effecting in us faith in him as a holy will that forgives sins. Redemption is not something achieved once for all in the work of Christ and then appropriated by individuals. It is something always new which takes place through knowledge of God in the operation of God upon the soul. No historical work of salvation is then necessary. The church is no longer an institution possessing Bible and sacraments for communicating objectively the power of Christ's saving work to the believer as a result of some miraculous arrangement of Christ, the God-man, by which the miracle of the God-man is extended in the divine humanity of the Bible and of the church as the institution of salvation. The Church here is rather a fellowship of faith or Christian knowledge of God which for the practice and extension of this faith may take any form and organisation it pleases. It is thus conceived simply in terms of purely human organisations with all their variety and differences, or it may dispense with these altogether. Then no historical Christ is necessary as founder of the church and the one who vouchsafes to the church and sacraments the miraculous powers which they possess. Finally, this knowledge of God is based upon personal experience and certainty in which a transmitted religious knowledge is transformed into one's own sense of divine revelation. The mission and teaching of Jesus does not here have to be made credible by the historical miracles of his life. External authority and facts which guarantee it are unnecessary. In all this the assumption is that Christianity is reformulated. Instead of being the redemption of sinful humanity by a miracle which makes God change his mind and gives the church the power to neutralise the contamination, we have a redemption through practical knowledge of God's true and innermost essence as will. Granted this transformation there is no inner necessity for the appeal to a historical fact. The historical personality of Jesus and his saving work are not absolutely necessary. On this view the question we have raised can be posed without being at once meaningless.

As a matter of fact this presupposition is now a reality for many Christians today. It reflects the great transformation which Christianity has undergone since its crisis of world-historical dimensions in the seventeenth century.[5] There were hints of this even in the ancient church and middle ages, wherever people tried to give inner grounds for Christian belief in God and not just factual ones. It was formulated clearly and sharply by sectarian protestantism and is today the secret religion of the modern educated man in so far as he asserts an inner relationship to Christianity. How far modern

[5] Cf. 'Religion and the Science of Religion', 1906, in this volume, especially pp.101f.

Germany really wants and maintains any such relationship is not at issue here. But there are wide circles who want to assert it and yet are fully removed from the church's dogma. What follows is meant for them alone. They continue the development to a Christian belief in redemption which like that of Meister Eckart or Sebastian Franck is a real religious faith but has severed its connexion with the old belief in redemption that divinised history.

Here too the stages by which this transformation progressed to a clear formulation of principle are clearly recognisable. Ever since the humanists, Socinians and the radicals of the Reformation, the beginnings of modern criticism took offence at the realistic doctrine of redemption, the miraculous purifying of our contaminated world by a particular historical event, and reverted to the Christian idea of God and its ethical consequences. History was only considered necessary in that the historical miracles of Jesus had to communicate and verify the truth of this doctrine. This view was current from Erasmus and the Socinians down to Locke and Leibniz. Then people objected to the external way in which this was established and instead saw in Jesus and Christian history only the means by which the Christian idea was launched into history. Once launched the idea itself was expected to be maintained and advanced by virtue of its own inner power. It was called for by the clarity of ethical consciousness and neither needed nor could tolerate any additional scientific proof from a theism which had been simplified to what produces the power of the good. This was the view of Lessing and Kant who were leaders of German culture and of those idealists who stood for a moderate progress in ethics and religion. Historical facts were only useful 'for illustration, not demonstration' and so could be surrendered to scientific criticism.

This idea reached its sharpest formulation in the thoroughly historical thinking of the Hegelian school. Here both the idea and history properly understood were said to require that religious faith should arise from history but without its inner truth and validity being based on history. The most famous account of this conception was that of D.F. Strauss during his Christian period. He distinguished between the principle of Christianity (i.e. knowledge of the unity of God and man) and the person of Christ (i.e. the historical point at which this principle began to assert itself).[6] It is possible to understand the content of the Christian principle differently from Strauss. We can abandon his certainly unhistorical derivation of the God-man dogma, according to which an ideal of divine humanity that applies to mankind was subsequently referred to the individual person

---

[6] *The Life of Jesus Critically Examined*, 1970 edition, p.780.

of the founder. But the form of the problem remains the same. It is perfectly clear in A.E. Biedermann, the Tübingen school and O. Pfleiderer.[7] It is supported today by Kantians, neo-Friesians and neo-Hegelians. In addition, a mass of popular religious literature proves that people who know nothing about religious philosophy and theology find it easiest to think along these lines.

There are of course also half-way houses in which this separation of person and principle, personality and idea is not carried out so consistently but moderated somewhat. At least a relative necessity for the historical person and a relationship to him is said to be required for the Christian belief in God that brings redemption. These views also share in the fundamental change that Christianity has undergone in the modern world. A real miracle of redemption effected by a historical act is transformed into a redemption that is continually new and achieved by the knowledge of God in faith. But they connect this redeeming knowledge of faith to an awareness and making present of the historical personality of Jesus who is considered here in his total effect as a religious personality, not with respect to his miracles or individual sayings. This view was established by the later ecclesiastical[8] Schleiermacher and has been continued most emphatically today by A. Ritschl and W. Herrmann. For Schleiermacher it is the suggestive power of the personality which, effectively mediated by his community and visible in the picture provided by the gospels, overcomes the insurmountable religious impotence found everywhere outside·the sphere of Jesus' influence, and creates the power, the certainty, the joyfulness and the perseverance which go with knowledge of God. What without the impression of Christ which creates faith remains a mere idea and divination becomes, through this personal impression continued in the community, a victorious and effective power. Ritschl relates the same idea less to the suggestive power of the personality than to the authority of Jesus which creates a certainty of the forgiveness of sins. By this authority Christ is made Lord and King of the kingdom of God, the kingdom of life, based on trust in God. The community's message about him makes him the source of certainty without which sinful men did not and should not dare believe in God's forgiving grace.[9]

[7] Cf. E. Hirsch, *Geschichte der neuern evangelischen Theologie V*, pp.491f.

[8] Troeltsch here employs the widespread distinction between the Schleiermacher of *The Christian Faith* and the Schleiermacher of the *Speeches*. But cp. the modification of his judgment below, p.203.

[9] Cp. *The Christian Doctrine of Justification and Reconciliation*, vol. III, 1874, Eng.tr. pp.1f.

For Herrmann the humbling and exalting ·fact of Christ's personality is a historical reality which only an evil and unrepentant will can deny, and which only a believing will that thirsts for God and is tormented by sin will see. It is this fact which gives courage to believe in God as a grace which forgives and so gives bright joy and power to achieve whatever is good and in accordance with conscience. Those who cannot find certainty in this fact of God, on the other hand, founder in despair or settle down in scepticism and wean themselves of their religious needs.[10] In all these cases it is clear that Christianity is the idea of God, an idea or faith's knowledge of how things really are. There is nothing about a unique historical miracle of redemption and the establishment of an institution dispensing its grace. Yet the power of the idea is still tied to the historical personality of Christ. This is what gives it force and certainty in the first place and makes the potent idea the possession of a fellowship united in the sense of the presence of Christ. Apart from the tacit assumption that the religious personality of Jesus can be known and its power felt by mediation of the tradition through the community, the presupposition of this view is that a man who does not know Christ cannot come to a joyful faith in God. 'Were it not for Christ I would be an atheist.' That is the expressed or silent assumption made here about those who do not know Christ. Christianity is here set in absolute opposition to the rest of humanity. It follows that the kingdom of God or the Christian community, the church as object of faith or context of redemption proceeding from Christ – this is the sole sphere of redemption, the necessary, everlasting consummation of the redeemed in the kingdom of Christ. It will last till the end of humanity and beyond into eternity as the gathering up of humanity into a religious fellowship of absolute salvation and absolute truth made possible in and through Christ.

However, both presupposition and consequence are anything but obvious to modern man. Even in Schleiermacher they stood in perceptible contradiction to his overall view as this was developed in his greatest and most authentic intellectual achievement, the *Ethik*.[11] It has become even more intolerable in the harsh formulations of Ritschl and in Herrmann's intangible form. It is anything but obvious that the religious personality of the historical Jesus can be fully and clearly known and made directly and personally effective, just like the immediately operative influence of one man upon another. Even if this way of grasping Jesus ever was a possibility it has in fact certainly

[10] W. Herrmann, *Der Verkehr des Christen mit Gott*, 1886, Eng.tr. 1900 and 1906 *Communion with God*. Rp. Philadelphia and London, 1972.

[11] *Grundriss der philosophischen Ethik. Schleiermachers sämtliche Werke*, Abt. III Bd.5, Berlin 1835.

been rendered impossible by modern criticism. If instead one stresses the mediation through the community and the living effect by means of subsequent Christian personalities, one is then dealing not with the historical fact but with its infinitely modified and enriched continuing effects, and it is impossible to say for certain what comes from Jesus and what from the later period and the present. Even if one considers the main lines of Jesus' preaching to be fully knowable, that still does not give direct contact between one man and another. There is a good deal of alien matter to be overcome. Neither is it legitimate to say that only the recognition of Jesus as divine authority and source of certainty gives the confidence and joy of faith. These have existed and still exist without any knowledge of or specially emphasised relationship to Jesus. In fact the burden of the historical Jesus problem is as a matter of experience more likely to shatter faith than protect it. It is rather that our souls are overcome by the grandeur of prophetic Christian faith in God and that this leads to acknowledgment of Jesus, than vice versa.

With every advance in history of religions research into the origins of Christianity we see so many related yet originally independent religious and ethical forces flowing together, that it is quite impossible to treat Christian faith as something absolutely separate. Christianity is by no means the product of Jesus alone. Plato, the Stoa and immeasurable popular religious forces from the ancient world are involved in it. This also seems to make the consequence impossible – calling the Christian community the eternal absolute centre of salvation for the whole span of humanity. Of course nothing certain can be said here; but it is not probable. Man's age upon earth amounts to several hundred thousand years or more. His future may come to still more. It is hard to imagine a single point of history along this line, and that the centre-point of our own religious history, as the sole centre of all humanity. That looks far too much like the absolutising our own contingent area of life. That is in religion what geocentricism and anthropocentricism are in cosmology and metaphysics. The whole logic of Christocentricism places it with these other centricisms. We have only to think of past ice-ages which will presumably recur, the effects of the minutest polar variations and the rise and fall of great cultural systems, to judge this absolute and eternal position improbable. It goes with the idyllic small and narrow world picture of the ancients and the middle ages, with their few thousand years of human history and the expectation of Christ's return as the conclusion of world history. To modern man it is alien and incomprehensible because it does not fit in with his general instinctively held presuppositions.

There has therefore been, especially amongst lay theologians and non-theologians, a growing rejection of this half-way house. The history-of-religions placing of Christianity in the process of emerging religious life in Europe and the extension of our view to the measureless spans of human history past and future, a disinclination to concentrate the measureless totality of life at this single point when everywhere else it flows through the whole breadth of things – all that has now brought about a reaction against this half-way house. Today people turn back to the ideas of the early mystics and spiritualists who found Christianity in the inner eternally advancing operation of God upon the soul, and who did not tie it with intrinsic necessity to a knowledge and acknowledgment of the historical personality of Jesus. There is no need to illustrate that in any more detail by reference to current trends. Even the sensational assertions that Jesus never existed are essentially only intended to aid this struggle against connecting the idea to historical facts which are always uncertain and at the same time hinder the development. There are several people who do not want to burden faith with historical research and so surrender questions concerning Jesus' life and preaching entirely to science and make their faith in the living God independent of any internally necessary relation to Jesus. For them Jesus is then the historical starting-point of Christian life and culture, his picture is pedagogically significant or a symbol of Christianity, but an inner conceptually necessary connexion of the Christian idea to the personality of Jesus is no longer there for countless people. Further, unless appearances are deceptive, the number of those who think in this way is – outside properly theological circles – on the increase in German culture.

3. *A restatement of the central position of Jesus based on the needs of the religious community*

This brings us to the actual formulation and meaning of the problem. It has no meaning for those who maintain Christ's supra-humanity and who see their task simply as defending this against those blinded by pride of reason, or as securing the removal of clergymen who are heterodox on this matter.[12] Neither has it any meaning for those who see Christianity as a real pardon and liberation of humanity from the curse of sin, suffering and death by means of an act of reconciliation by Christ directed at God. The problem only makes sense for those

---

[12] The reference is to the Prussian heresy law of 1910 and the Jatho case. On this see Troeltsch's essay 'Gewissensfreiheit' in *Die Christliche Welt*, 1911, reprinted in *G.S.* II, pp.134-45.

who accept the whole-hearted historical criticism of and research into the gospel narratives, and at the same time wish to preserve Christianity as redemption through faith's constantly renewed personal knowledge of God. These two presuppositions do not necessarily coincide even though they originated together and originally conditioned each other. They only apply for people who in all the confusion of modern thought consider the prophetic and Christian knowledge of God the only source of both profound and healthily active knowledge of God and who at the same time are not closed to the legitimacy of a completely historical critical view of human things. In a word, they apply only for those who recognise modern thought and at the same time see in Christianity religious powers which should not be given up. The writer of these lines gladly and resolutely includes himself in this group.

The question of course arises more and more clearly, how is modern thought to relate the Christian belief in God to the person of Jesus? Is this connexion something contingent, purely historical and factual, for pedagogical and symbolic purposes not easily dispensed with, but nevertheless not required by the idea itself? Or is it something unchangeably and eternally inherent in the essence of the christian idea? In the first case we are essentially independent of historical criticism, in the second essentially dependent upon it.

It must here be said quite definitely and with total clarity that only on the basis of the ancient church's orthodox ideas of redemption, authority and church is there a real inner necessity for the historical person of Christ for salvation. The historical existence of the person of Christ is of course absolutely necessary, given a view of redemption as Christ's effect on God for the liberation of a creation trapped in suffering and death as a result of the fall; or given an authority in matters of faith, that rests infallibly upon the superhuman divine dignity of Jesus; or given a Christian dispensation of salvation in which the primal historical miracle is continued in the miraculous effects of the church and divine word of scripture. Only then is historicity absolutely necessary, and then acceptance of it does not depend upon historical research but upon bowing to the supernatural authority of church and Bible. Everything is perfectly clear here.

The position is less clear in the mediating type of theology represented by Schleiermacher, Ritschl and Herrmann. As already observed this type cannot be protected from the effects of historical criticism because here an external appeal to biblical authority is dropped and inner experience is not used as in modern orthodoxy to establish such an authority of the Bible together with its doctrine of salvation and its world picture. It is basically only appealed to for creating certainty about God as loving will who forgives sins and sanctifies us amidst the pains and struggles of life and especially conscience. Schleiermacher's *Life of Jesus*[13] and the relationship between his historical criticism and the faith in Jesus of his *Christian Faith* were subjected to an unforgettable and precisely for that reason generally ignored criticism by D.F. Strauss.[14]

A perfect analogy to this criticism of Schleiermacher by Strauss is to be found in the development of the Ritschlian school. The so-called history of religions school sprang from the Ritschlian school and explained its birth by reference to the harsh tension in which Ritschl's picture of Christ stood to the historical critical research which he himself acknowledged. It is the natural reaction against the violence of Ritschl's procedure. Herrmann's talk about 'the fact of Christ' which, however, cannot be established like other facts but only seen by faith, is an obscure and mystical expression of the same violence and is almost incomprehensible to people who think historically and critically. The whole position is untenable in the face of historical criticism. It plays virtually no role in the development of biblical research but remains in the preserve of dogmatics. But that is a science which today exists only in the narrowest theological circles and even there is scarcely really to be found.

But once we give up this dogmatics or systematics base we soon realise that the inner necessity for the connexion is here a very relative matter. It is limited to the Christian life and culture being launched into history or set in motion by Jesus, and this would not exclude the possibility of its continuing by its own inner power. Then comes the second point, where the Christian life and culture provides the decisive power or authorisation, something which would not be possible for men who on their own are impotent and in despair without the elevating or suggestive impression of the person of Jesus. But this is clearly a remnant of the ancient doctrine of original sin. Ever since Paul the function of this doctrine in the church's system has been to extinguish all lights other than faith in Christ and to deny all powers other than his, in order to make simple and radically obvious as the sole power of redemption the Christian community's miracle of God's reconciliation. But such a doctrine of original sin needs the courage of its convictions – the presupposition of an original perfection prior to the contamination of the world by the sin of the first couple. It must also develop its necessary consequence, a real redemption and

---

[13] Schleiermacher's *Das Leben Jesu* appeared posthumously in 1864. Eng.tr. ed. J.C. Verheyden, Philadelphia, 1975.

[14] *Der Christus des Glaubens und der Jesus der Geschichte*, Berlin, 1865. E.T. Tr. forthcoming, 1977, Philadelphia, *The Christ of Faith and the Jesus of History*.

decontamination. The doctrine that human development in and outside Christ is unable to find power and certainty, and is raised to a higher stage of development in which the consciousness of God is strengthened or all doubt overcome, only through Christ, is, however, simply a weaker form of the old idea of original sin and redemption. Its motive is clearly simply to preserve the old position of Christ as redeemer and object of faith while at the same time establishing the new idea of redemption as the heart of the matter. The reason for its influence in theology is this capacity for getting relatively close to the old doctrine. But it has had no influence upon modern thought in general on account of the inner contradiction between the two interests which are united here. It contradicts the idea which lies at the foundation of all modern thinking – a development of spirit which emerges at different nodal points from the depth of the divine life, and a possibility of future developments which can never be circumscribed in advance. The attempt to encompass all future developments of religious life by this remnant of the doctrine of original sin is intolerable to the whole of modern thought, as is the assertion based on this that religious power and certainty can never be obtained except by subjecting oneself to what Christ has effected. It only needed the addition of historical research on the gospels to these religious and philosophical reservations to scatter the whole theory to the winds, despite the enormous intellectual and religious significance of its originators.

So there remained nothing but a purely historical factual and a pedagogical and symbolical significance of the person of Jesus for the Christian idea! We were back with Lessing's saying about a third Gospel[15] or Ibsen's third kingdom[16] in which religious faith is asserted and propagated by its own purifying and redeeming power without the support of history. It was to develop freely within the total context of life by its own inner depths!

That seems in fact to be what follows from all this. But it cannot be denied that there is not much of this kind of development to be seen. Quite frankly it does not seem to have much future. The truth is that almost all forms of contemporary religiosity are variations of what was nurtured in the churches; only here are the treasures of religion strongly alive. When one thinks of those other developments one cannot help a slight shudder. There must be some reason for all this in the character of the thing itself. And so there is. Continuing the Christian idea of the sole basis of its inner power to convince can

[15] *The Education of the Human Race*, 1780, § 85f. See H. Chadwick, *Lessing's Theological Writings*, London, 1956, pp.82-98.

[16] *Caesar and Galilean*, 1873, Part I, Act. 3. etc.

ignore all notions of a religious community and all thought of a cult. It can ignore anything which connects all believers to historical archetypes and authorities, and so can rid itself of the whole problem of history, and live simply in what is present and personal. But in doing this it renounces whether consciously or unconsciously *all* forms of community. In spiritual and ethical religion this cannot consist in rites and magic, but only in actualising a spiritual possession. That cannot take place without its being presented in a personal and living way in a normative archetype. This solution therefore renounces all cult or worship and adoration of God together with the effect this has on the believing community itself, because for Christianity a cult in the sense of magic or a mystery of redemption is not possible, and because all that remains as cult – gathering round the head of the community and being nourished by his spirit and life, worshipping God in a community that is determined by God and is actualised in a concrete way – is removed by the elimination of any historical element. Personal solitary devotion and meditation, the anarchy and chance expressions of personal enthusiasms, or more or less intellectual specimens of religious instruction take the place of cult and of a community gathered together for worshipping and actualising God in the infinitely concrete and yet infinitely variegated image of Christ. This lack of community and cult is the real sickness of modern Christianity and contemporary religious practice generally. It is what makes it so impermanent and chaotic, so dependent on who happens to be there, so much an amateur thing for enthusiasts, so much a matter of world-view and the intellect. It has no dominant centre from which it can be nourished, but just as many centres as there are sensitive individual seekers. But it is not just that modern religion has become chaotic and indefinite. It is also feeble and insipid because it lacks the effect which a total spirit and fellowship has upon the individual, with its power to encourage and sustain, intensify and diversify, and above all to set practical goals for the like-minded group.

Now one perfectly clear result of the history and psychology of religion is that in all religion what really counts is not dogma and idea but cult and community. Living communion with the deity is a communion of the totality which has the roots of its life in religion generally and its ultimate power for uniting individuals in a belief in God. Even where this communion is exercised through representatives by a priesthood it always has a backwash on to the totality. That is obvious in the case of nature religions. But it is also true of religions of spirit where the communion is achieved not by sacrifice and rites but by prayer and edification. That is why Platonism and Stoicism were absorbed by Christianity even though the religion of spirit had begun to stir in them. And that is why as soon as it broke with Judaism Christianity became a Christ cult. It is not the worship of a new God but the worship of the old God of Israel and of all reason, in his living and concrete highest revelation. The Christian believers' faith in God had at first no dogma and no doctrine but only the concentration of all religious content in a Jesus transfigured by belief in the resurrection. It had no sacrifice and rites, no magic or mysteries but only the adoration of God in Christ and living union with Christ in the Lord's Supper. No matter what emerged later from this earliest form of the Christian community as a Christ cult, the original motive is clear. The need for community and the need for cult had no other means than the gathering to worship Christ as the revelation of God. The dogma concerning Christ which emerged from this Christ cult was only meant to show and give access to the one eternal God in Christ in order to create a new community. It could only establish itself by having its own cult. Regardless of what mythology and mysteries, pagan and gnostic analogies may have contributed, they have only clothed and made comprehensible to ancient consciousness a process which lay in the inner logic of the matter.

The original motive responsible for the emergence of faith in Christ and for linking the new belief in God to the Christ cult is still operative under different forms and conditions today. It is a law of social psychology that individuals with merely parallel thoughts and experiences (which is how a refined and individualised culture initially produces them) can never simply co-exist for long without affecting each other and joining forces. Out of the myriad connexions community groups with higher and lower strata are everywhere produced and taken together these need a concrete focus. This law holds for religious life too. Here too, therefore, these kinds of circles emerge with definite hierarchies, firm centres, means of extension and centres of strength from which religious thought can continually renew its power.

In nature religions the structures are provided by nature or society. Here the old cultic tradition provides the focal point. In the religions of spirit it is the prophets and founder personalities who serve as archetypes, authorities, sources of power and rallying-points. As images of personal concrete life they can be interpreted with a versatility and flexibility possessed by no mere doctrine or dogma. They also possess a vividness and plasticity never found in theory and understanding but only in imagination and feeling. That is why all the great religions of spirit consist in reverence of their founders and prophets. This was the case with the religious philosophy schools of Platonism and the Stoa, and then later with Christian monastic orders and sects. Present recollection of one's prophets, even to the extent of giving them divine reverence, not as enlargement of a pantheon but as the expression of the common religious truth, is everywhere fundamental for community and cult. It is moreover extremely improbable that this will ever be otherwise. A really new religion would certainly not be a purely individual further development of personal religious convictions. It would be a new religion based on prophets and like the old it would remain an effective power capable of development only for as long as it could maintain its basis alive in a shared cult. The third kingdom in which everyone is to be independent as regards religion, and the spirit fully free to develop in each individual in isolation, will probably never arrive. It is no more likely to come than a state and economy that rest simply on the natural and necessary concurrence of individual interests and reason.

The Christian idea, therefore, will never become a powerful reality without community and cult. Whether the existing churches can be awakened to this life is a question of its own. It is possible that they will be forced by a change in our general political situation to return to the circles which still maintain the dogma of the early church. It is, however, also possible that faced with such a development they will be able to become broad national churches in which the variety of contemporary protestant religious thought is allowed to find expression. But whatever emerges, there is no possibility of a sure and powerful redeeming knowledge of God without community and cult.A cult illuminated by the Christian idea must therefore always centre upon gathering the congregation around its head, nourishing and strengthening it by immersion in the revelation of God contained in the image of Christ, spreading it not by dogmas, doctrines and philosophies but by handing on and keeping alive the image of Christ, the adoration of God in Christ. So long as Christianity survives in any form it will always be connected with the central position of Christ in the cult. It will either exist in this form or not at all. That rests on social-psychological laws which have produced exactly the same phenomena in other religious areas and recur a thousand times over on a smaller scale up to the present. They render utopian the whole idea of a piety that simply springs from every man's heart and nevertheless forms a harmony, that does not need reciprocity and yet remains a living power.

Social psychology therefore provides the main aspect under which our problem must be seen. The connexion of the Christian idea with Christ's central position in cult and doctrine is not a conceptual necessity inherent in the notion of salvation. Even if we are right to point out the need which ordinary piety has for support and strengthening, it does not absolutely require the person of Jesus. In fact a real personal relationship with him is not possible. But neither is this person a purely historical fact, simply clarifying the origins and then no longer essential. For social psychological reasons he is indispensable for cult, power, efficacy and expansion, and that should be sufficient to justify and assert the connexion. Without it a further development of the Christian idea is unthinkable. A new religion would have to be a new cult of a historical prophet. All hope of a non-cultic purely personal and individual religion of conviction and knowledge is mere illusion. If on the other hand we need a cult and community then we need Christ as the head and rallying-point of the congregation too. The Christian knowledge of God has no other mode of union and visibility. Lectures on religious philosophy will never produce or replace a real religion.

If this is how things stand it is of course not possible to be really and completely indifferent to historical critical questions either. Admittedly Jesus is here the symbol of Christian faith generally. But those who think that it does not matter whether such a symbol is rooted in historical factuality and that the great achievement of religion in history is precisely the embodiment of ideas in myth, are themselves not in the least inclined to enter a religious group. They personally do not wish to surrender themselves enthusiastically and through practical work to a group whose idea is embodied in this mythical symbol. They only expect that believers can tighten their belts and be fully satisfied with a mythical symbol. Examples of this like Samuel Lublinski[17] are merely cases of that aesthetic playing with realities which is so common today. The aesthete expects believers to satisfy their existential hunger on a mythical symbol because he himself never thinks of stilling a real hunger for certainty and conviction but only the unreal needs of imagination. Someone who really belongs in his heart to the world of Christian experience will never be able to see in the centre and head of the congregation, the focal point for all cult and vision of God, a mere myth – no matter how beautiful. For him, God is not an idea or possibility but a holy reality. He will therefore insist upon standing with this symbol of his on the solid ground of real life. It is for him a truly significant fact that a real man thus lived, struggled, believed and conquered, and that from this real life a stream of strength and certainty flows down to him. The symbol is only a real symbol for him in that behind it stands the greatness of a superior and real religious prophet. Not only is God

---

[17] *Die Entstehung des Christentums aus der antiken Kultur*, Jena, 1910; *Das werdende Dogma vom Leben Jesu*, Jena, 1910.

made visible by reference to this; he can also find here support and strength in his own uncertainty, just as elsewhere he needs to hold on to superior personal religious authority, and experiences it in life in many ways. This much is legitimate in Herrmann's talk about 'the fact of Christ'. It is not just that the individual's certainty of salvation can only be gained by becoming certain of Jesus, but rather that the Christian spirit can find no context for supporting and strengthening life without this gathering around Jesus. This in turn must go back to real, vivid life if it is to have inner power and veracity.

Granted these circumstances it is of course impossible to ignore historical critical research. The 'fact', like all other historical facts, given first only in the form of reports, can only be established by historical research. Faith can interpret facts; it cannot establish them. There should be no need to waste time arguing about this, though even here theology frequently works with most confused methods. It is not a question of individual details but of the factuality of the total historical phenomenon of Jesus and the basic outline of his teaching and his religious personality. This must be capable of being established by means of historical criticism as historical reality if the 'symbol of Christ' is to have a firm and strong inner basis in the 'fact' of Jesus. This was of course unnecessary for a world that did not think historically, so the problem did not arise until the eighteenth century. But given a fundamentally historical mode of thought like that of the present then faith cannot escape this admixture of the historical and scientific way of thinking. It must face this and secure the historical basis of its community and cult as far as the historical questions have any significance for these. There is no ducking or ignoring this. The struggle must be fought out and if it were decided against the historicity of Jesus or against any possibility of knowing about him, that would in fact be the beginning of the end of the Christ symbol amongst scientifically educated people. From there doubt and dissolution would soon percolate down to the lower classes, so far as it had not reached there already as a result of their social reforms and anti-ecclesiastical inclinations. It is a mere playing with words to hold on to the Christian principle and yet want to leave the historical questions on one side. That is a practical way out for individuals in difficulties and confusion; it is impossible for a religious and cultic community.

But it is just as much mere playing with words to say that simple faith may not be made dependent upon scholars and professors. That too is correct for the individual case where guided by a strong instinct someone breaks loose from the throttle-hold of the whole academic business. But it is impossible to want to withdraw historical facts in general and in principle from scientific criticism. There does remain in this respect a dependence upon scholars and professors, if one wants to put it that way; or better, a dependence upon the general feeling of historical reliability produced by the impression of scientific research.

This should not be matter for complaint. It is not a difficulty that is limited to the historical problems of faith. In a scientifically educated world faith has never been independent of the effects of learning. It was for centuries influenced by ancient philosophy. Then it had to measure itself by and reconcile itself to natural science which utterly transformed ancient and Christian philosophy. Today the historicising and psychologising of our whole view of man and his earthly existence must be added. It is an illusion to suppose that faith can avoid debate, accommodation and opposition to the views on offer as the scientific knowledge of the day. It cannot withdraw into itself while absorbing all positions which bring it into opposition. It can do that in its enthusiastic first beginnings and in its practical and social dominance over the strata in society which are indifferent to science, but not in a world filled with scientific education and modes of thought. To escape by abandoning all those elements which science lays claim to means to renounce content, definiteness, power and the formation of a community.

This is of course what Kant began to do. He therefore explained Christ too as an allegory of the Christian principle. Only by a remarkable piece of violence has he been made the patron of a faith in redemption that is not bothered with metaphysics and natural science but rests on the 'fact of Christ'. Those concrete Christian elements which remain in Kant's idealist theological view of history, his dualist moral philosophy and his belief in immortality have in fact come in for criticism from subsequent science. Struggle and accommodation only cease when philosophy of religion withdraws fully to the mere factuality and actuality of religious moods which colour and permeate the life of the soul. But it is only illusion that makes them into concrete contents and intimations of a deity who brings about the moods and is distinct from the mere data of a religious condition in the soul.

This solution does admittedly avoid any conflict with science but it also excludes religion from any practical achievement and community formation, not to mention the total abandonment of all Christian content. That is the capitulation of faith to the intellect, a renunciation of all practical significance and community. These depend on having a view of the idea of God which involves concrete obligations and determines the practical life of the community. This again depends in its concreteness upon recognising the great prophetic personalities as leaders and guarantors. So a belief that wants to get free of that strangle-hold of mediating is bound to engage in the debate with modern knowledge, which includes getting clear about the factuality of its historical basis. Opposition to this is fruitless. No matter how many people are unaffected by all this and just want to follow their religious impulse and feeling, nevertheless an atmosphere and mood of security about the reliability of the historical basis is necessary for their purely practical existence to be natural and possible. And in the modern world of thought only scientific research can produce this. All the difficulties, distress and uncertainty connected with this, even the dependence on scholarship, must be taken into the bargain. They cannot be avoided and it is no use moaning. Neither can one boast of not being bothered. That is in truth impossible.

The most one can say is that a part of historical research is admittedly irrelevant so far as religion is concerned. That does limit somewhat the religious significance of scientific research. Not all the minor details of historical research in theology are at issue here, but the basic facts – the decisive significance of Jesus' personality for the origin and formation of faith in Christ, the basic religious and ethical character of Jesus' teaching and the transformation of his teaching in the earliest Christian congregations with their Christ cult. In my opinion the decisive chief facts can here be ascertained with certainty despite all the questions which remain open.

That is sufficient for properly religious purposes – the acknowledgment of the historical existence of Jesus and the religious interpretation of his teaching. One only needs a basic overall picture. That would not of course be enough if the historical person Jesus were the sole source of Christian faith's knowledge and its power for life. However, this is set in a wide context of historical preparations and effects. He cannot be understood apart from preparation in the prophets and psalms and the effects of his historical existence in Paul's faith in Christ and in the abundance of Christian personalities down to Luther and Schleiermacher. Where the historical existence of Jesus is looked at in its social-psychological significance and not as the only authority and source of power opposed to original sin, there is no objection to seeing it always in this broader historical context. Preparation and effects can be drawn into the interpretation. Preaching and congregational life do not depend upon philological exactitude in the details of the picture of Jesus. One might easily wander from one critic to another here. They depend rather on expounding the picture of Christ in the context of the whole history that precedes and follows it.

But that must be accompanied by a consciousness of being able in all truth and honesty to see Jesus as the centre of this living world. It must not feel or worry that it is composing a myth without object or basis in reality, for embodying an idea into which a thousand sources have flowed. Granted this presupposition it can interpret the picture of Christ in practical proclamation very freely and flexibly, using everything that flowed into him and everything which in the course of thousands of years has been accommodated and loved in him. Neither will it concentrate everything in Jesus. Jesus will not be the only historical fact that is significant for our faith. Other historical personalities too can receive their due and be seen in some sense as visible symbols and guarantees of faith that sustain our strength. There is no need either to stop at the Reformation. Such historical facts can be found right down to the present. The Christian character and so the definiteness of the principle is preserved by everything being constantly related to the rallying-point, the personality of Jesus.

So we must in the academic arguments use the weapons of historical science to secure the factuality and knowability of Jesus, otherwise Christianity will not go on. Despite all the remaining gaps in our knowledge the answer has in all essentials been given by the historical study of early Christianity. Sensational denials will disappear when the matter is studied objectively. The importance of historical research is restricted only by the fact that its results have practical significance for nothing but the main point of Jesus' person and teaching and the emergence of the earliest congregation. It is also limited by this historical fact being strengthened by countless others and not having to bear the weight alone. This mastering and limiting of the problem is only possible from the standpoint already described. Both are naturally meaningless and superfluous for orthodox theology.

4. *The historic Jesus as a necessary symbol of the Christian religion*

It might seem as though this solution is basically very similar to the Schleiermacher-Ritschl-Herrmann school type of mediation described earlier. That is more than just appearance. It really is the case. The results for practical proclamation are somewhat similar. The important idea of religious subjectivity holding on to the still historically perceptible religious greatness and strength of a real personality is also accorded its full significance here. This concurrence is reason for rejoicing. What matters is not that we are perpetually clarifying our disagreements and defining our positions. That is offensive or laughable. In the present confusion we must expressly look for the points of contact between us.

Nevertheless, how we understand and establish our view, and therefore the view itself is quite definitely different. The significance of this difference does not lie in a taste for scholastic subtleties and the opposing systems of the theological schools. It rests in a practical difference of mood and feeling in total religious attitude. The argument I have produced is a matter of social psychology. It applies to Christianity as to any other spiritual and ethical religious faith which is neither tied to the natural divisions of society nor expressed in a magical cult. It is not a matter of original sin making any divine certainty and power outside Christianity impossible. Neither is it Christianity's special position of alone controlling a historical fact which produces certainty. Instead we have a general law at work in all human affairs and applied to religion in particular – especially spiritual and ethical religion. It has nothing to do with original sin and the impossibility of true faith in God outside Christianity, any more than death and suffering, the struggle for existence and the dysteleological character of the natural process are punishment for sin. The old doctrine derived all this from original sin, the dislocation of an originally perfect world by the sin of Adam and Eve or of the demons and the devil. Today we understand it all in terms of the inner and necessary arrangement of nature. So too we understand this social psychological law not as the expression of some primal sin but as a feature of man and the mysterious relationship which obtains between the individual and the community. With the central place it gives to the personality of Jesus Christianity does not have something special which distinguishes it from all other religions and makes redemption possible here alone. Rather, in this it only fulfils in its own particular way what is a general law of man's spiritual life.

The decisive point in evaluating the significance of Jesus is therefore not that redemption outside Christianity is impossible, but the need a religious community has for a support, centre and symbol of its religious life. The marvel is then that the centre and symbol is constituted not in a fixed dogma or an equally fixed moral law but in the picture of a living, many-sided and at the same time elevating and strengthening personality. We can adopt its innermost orientation for life and from it find in full freedom an application which gives shape to our contemporary religious and ethical tasks.

Again, this personality does not stand in isolation. There is a rich extension of historical life which can without hesitation be taken into account with it in determining the Christian idea and filling it with living power. There have always been attempts to transform the person of Jesus into a dogma or make a moral law out of him. But the living basis of an indefinable personal life has always broken through all this and on it rests the capacity of Christianity for ever new simplification and rejuvenation. There have always been those too who isolate Jesus from the whole preceding and succeeding history, wanting to make him the only support and basis for faith. This is present in the latest teaching about Christ too. But the quite unmistakeable links between Jesus' world of ideas and ethos and the quite definite situation of late Judaism make that impossible. The idea of a purely religious prophet who anticipates in his preaching of the kingdom of God a new world and humanity under new conditions determined purely by a religious ideal, and who expects it soon to come to pass, is crude and one-sided.

Against this even the primitive church's faith freed the spirit of Christ from his appearance in history and saw it as a principle capable of development. But this development is found not so much in ideal consequences and systematic conceptions of life as in a broader succession of strong religious personalities which have drawn from him and produced new things from his spirit, just as the spirit of the prophets was at work in Jesus himself producing new growths from this prophetic seed. So it is not the absolute uniqueness of the redeemer which matters but the centre around which all the preparations and effects of the Christian and prophetic type of belief cluster. These receive a unitary interpretation from this centre.

Where all the emphasis is placed upon necessities of social psychology, there is a corresponding stress upon the ideas of community and cult. It was the requirement of community and cult which gave to the personality of Christ its central position. They continue to give it this central position. Where community is dissolved into free and isolated religious convictions of individuals and the cult is transformed into mood and reflexion, there too the link with Jesus is less prominent. Even where it is apparently preserved intact, we have instead of Jesus the inner Christ or the free mystical presence of God in the soul. Where on the other hand this weakness and dispersion is abandoned in favour of a return to community and cult, this brings with it a renewed emphasis upon the significance of Jesus' historical personality. That can be seen quite clearly in Schleiermacher. In his *Speeches* (which it is wrong to regard as presented for the uninitiated)[18] the historical element is quite subordinate whereas it is more strongly emphasised in the sermons written at the same time. Above all, once he participated in the tasks of the church and composed systematic theology for the church, the person of Jesus became the central object

[18] This was O. Ritschl's interpretation in *Schleiermachers Stellung zum Christentum in seinen Reden über die Religion*, 1888.

of his whole conception, viewed as the symbol of Christian faith and the source of its power, and as the focus of preaching and cult. Schleiermacher does not consciously base his conception on social psychology, but this is certainly the motive for the development. His dogmatic argument is based on the weakness of the non-Christian God consciousness and the inauguration of a new era of humanity by the second Adam or bringer of strength to an otherwise feeble consciousness of God. This view harshly contradicts his usual thinking which is based on historical development. It is probably a bit of accommodation to the dominant language of Bible and church.

The social psychology motive is further concealed in the work of Ritschl and Herrmann, where the decisive idea is the redeeming miracle of Christ's authority. But in fact even here the formation of a community and cult is linked with an emphasis upon the historical personality. Few have stressed the significance of faith in Christ for church, cult and kingdom of God as strongly as Ritschl and Herrmann. All we have to do is to show that what is in fact the dominant motive for their reverence of Jesus is also its objective basis and inner necessity. In his *Speeches* Schleiermacher supplies the beginnings of such a justification when he describes the still flexible formation of groups around superior centres. Unfortunately he did not pursue this line of thought but where possible approximated his final justification to the church's forms of expression. But they are all substantially right. To say that, puts us at odds with the favourite religious opinions of today which feel related to the idealism without cult or history characteristic of mysticism and protestant sectarianism, but cannot make anything of community, church, cult and preaching.

It is hard to identify which caused what here. Did the idea of community wither because faith in Christ dissolved, or did the latter evaporate because the former disintegrated? Either way, it will prove impossible to maintain in the sphere of religion an individualism that has had to be overcome in all other realms of life. The effect of individualism is to scatter, evaporate and weaken the powers of religion; and then again the need for community and cult will erupt. Whether this will take place inside or outside of our present churches is a question of its own which only the future can decide. But there will be this kind of reversal, and it will bring with it a better understanding of the significance of Jesus' historical existence. The present chaos and poverty of religion cannot last. Within our cultural sphere it would be impossible and wrong to expect some other religiosity than the Christian one which is the result and the foundation of West Asian, European and American intellectual history. If within our culture religious life is to re-emerge at all, it will in all essentials stream from Christianity and find its symbol in the person of Jesus.

This brings us to our final difference from the mediating type of doctrine already discussed. Not only the meaning and justification but also the consequences are different. And here the difference is particularly clear. If Jesus' central position is based on the miracle of a strength and certainty which overcomes all original sin's weakness and incapacity for faith, then the religion of humanity will always have to remain Christianity; all religious community for all eternity will have to centre on the person of Jesus. Then Christ will be called the Second Adam, as in Schleiermacher, or he and his church will be designated as with Ritschl as the essential divine goal, identical with the goal of the world; either way a bridge will be made to the ancient christology of Nicaea and Chalcedon. If however, Jesus' central position is based on general social-psychological necessities the following consequence must be drawn: For as long as the peculiarly Christian-prophetic religion bearing within itself the Stoa, Platonism and various other elements continues, all possibilities of a community and cult, and so all real power and the extension of belief, will be tied to the central position of Christ for faith. It is, however, another question whether Christianity itself will remain for ever the religion of humanity unto the end, or whether overseas mission will make it that for all eternity. That is of course a question which cannot be answered for certain. But even to raise it has important implications for how we understand our whole religious character.

For as long as our culture which has in essence arisen around the Mediterranean lasts it is highly improbable that a new religion will emerge which will compare with Christianity in versatility, profundity and grandeur. Our religious life has probably gained for all time its base and driving force from here. The modern substitutes for Christianity, and the religions of science are strong in criticism but extremely weak in constructive religious power. They often confuse religion with science, art or morality. But whether this culture itself will last for ever and extend to the whole world is a question which no one can answer. It is therefore impossible either to affirm or to deny that Christianity will last for ever and community and cult remain bound to the historical personality of Jesus.

Anyone who considers the possibilities of several hundred thousand years of the future of man will be unwilling to say anything about the connexion of the future to the present. But this does not devalue the present. What here is true and is life will be preserved or will recur. It will not be made untrue by anything yet to come. We can only maintain and develop the religious powers of the present, certain of doing what is required by the present and of standing within the stream of divine life. Whatever is true, great and profound in our faith today will still be so two hundred thousand years hence, even if perhaps in a quite different form. Since we possess these religious powers of the present only in association with the present and reverenced person of Christ, we gather around him unconcerned whether in a hundred thousand years religion will still be nourished on Jesus or will have some other centre. Indefinite future possibilities do not reduce the value of what the present contains in experienced strength and truth. This haunting anxiety of a relativism that plays with big numbers must be driven from our heads. We have resolutely to grasp the divine as it presents itself to us in our time. In our time it presents itself in history and in the connexion of the individual's subjectivity with the substance of an overarching totality of historical life. This in turn receives its most important strength and certainty from the historical person of Jesus. For us 'God in Christ' can only mean that in Jesus we reverence the highest revelation of God accessible to us and that we make the picture of Jesus the rallying-point of all God's testimonies to himself found in our sphere of life. And we had best abandon altogether reading this meaning into the christological dogmas of Nicaea and Chalcedon (however elastic they may be). There is no need to bring that page of thought into the foreground. There is nothing in it for preaching, devotion and catechism; academic training in theology can also place it in the background. But where the principal idea has to be made clear one cannot keep silent about it. On the other side it would be good in practical work not to emphasise too much the eternal dependence of millions yet unborn upon the person of Jesus, and instead to bring alive in a practical way how one is oneself bound to him in the present. People who can be happy in their own faith only when they tie all the future millions of years to it know nothing of the real freedom and grandeur of faith.

That is decisive and must determine religious work in the present. It too has therefore an interest in the historical existence of Jesus. If it could not presuppose this, it would have to pioneer totally new paths at least in everything concerning community and cult. But that would mean total dissolution. Thus there is a great deal at stake in the whole question. Only rigorous historical science can in fact bring about a decision. But there is in fact no doubt that this discipline gives us a kernel of facts on which we can base our common interpretation and valuation of Jesus as the embodiment of faith. More than this we do not need if what is at stake is not the church's dogma about Christ but the redeeming truth of the Christian knowledge of God and the gathering of a congregation by which this truth can be carried on and rendered effective.

Troeltsch and Christian Theology
Robert Morgan

1

No theologian from before the First World War has featured so prominently in the footnotes of learned journals in recent years as Ernst Troeltsch. Discussions about historical method(s) frequently begin with his classical statement of the principles of analogy, correlation and criticism.[1] The great awakening to sociological questions inevitably directs renewed attention to this pioneer in the field.[2] And above all, contributors to the modern debate about 'Theologie als Wissenschaft' rightly reflect upon the man who made some of his most important contributions in this area.[3]

This renewal of interest presents a striking contrast to the premature burial of Troeltsch in the theology of the 1920s. He died in 1923, and after the obituaries had subsided was not very much discussed in Germany.[4] He had admirers in England[5] and America,[6] but his influence was restricted by the lack of English translations of

[1] E.g. W. Pannenberg, *Basic Questions in Theology*, (Eng.tr. SCM Press, London, 1970), pp.40-50. P. Stuhlmacher, *Schriftauslegung*, Göttingen, 1975, pp.14f, 82f. James Luther Adams, 'Why the Troeltsch Revival?' *The Unitarian Universalist Christian*, 29, 1974, pp.4-15, emphasises this aspect of his work.

[2] See U. Mann (ed.) *Theologie und Religionswissenschaft*, Darmstadt, 1973, pp.210, 400, and various articles by G. Theissen on NT studies.

[3] See especially G. Sauter (ed.) *Theologie als Wissenschaft*, Munich, 1971. W. Pannenberg, *Wissenschaftstheorie und Theologie*, Frankfurt, 1973.

[4] The most important exceptions are the monographs of Paul Spiess (1927) H. Benckert (1932) and the biography of W. Köhler (1941). The bibliography published by H-H. Schrey, *ThR NF* 12, 1940, pp.130ff is quite substantial, but does not compare with the flood of literature on Troeltsch around 1910.

[5] Especially von Hügel who edited his *Christian Thought*, London, 1923. R.S. Sleigh, *The Sufficiency of Christianity*, London, 1923 is a Scottish Ph.D. thesis begun before the war, in 1914.

[6] E.g. H. Richard Niebuhr (see *The Meaning of Religion*, p.x, *Christ and Culture*, p.x); also W. Pauck (see *Harnack and Troeltsch*, New York, 1968) and James Luther Adams. See also R.H. Bainton, 'Ernst Troeltsch Thirty Years Later', *Theology Today*, 8, 1951, pp. 70-96.

most of his important works, apart from the *Social Teachings*.[7] Like the history-of-religions school with which he was associated,[8] Troeltsch was in part a victim of the iron curtain between English and German theology which fell around August 1914 and despite important exceptions lasted almost fifty years.[9]

Troeltsch's lack of impact upon the German theological scene after the First World War had several causes. The passionate involvement of those who have described the dramatic break with liberal protestantism has oversimplified what is a rather complex picture.[10] It is natural, in view of the subsequent development, to concentrate upon the reaction within the 'dialectical theology'. But even that was more differentiated than is usually realised, and there were other factors too. The dialectical theologians were not the only people appealing to Luther in the 1920s. This was the period of the 'Luther renaissance' led by Karl Holl.[11] It had been partly inspired decades earlier by Ritschl, given a foundation in the Weimar Auflage (from 1883), and a glorious impulse by the rediscovery of the *Lectures on Romans*.[12] Veneration for Luther was a feature of liberal protestantism as well as of Lutheran orthodoxy, and both continued to contribute significantly to Luther research.[13]

Largely in justified reaction against the modernisation of Luther by Ritschl and Herrmann, Troeltsch emphasised the medieval elements in his thought at the expense of the modern.[14] He identified as the watershed between the religious world of antiquity and the Middle Ages, and the modern, secular world, not the Reformation but the

---

[7] A.O. Dyson, *History in the Philosophy and Theology of Ernst Troeltsch*, (Diss. Oxford, 1968, p.2).

[8] See above, pp.3-5, and 'The Dogmatics of the "religionsgeschichtliche Schule",' *AJT*, 17, 1913, pp.1-21.

[9] *Mysterium Christi*, ed. G.K.A. Bell and A. Deissmann, London, 1930 is a monument to a renewal of contact by the older generation. The dialectical theology was better received in Scotland than in England, where E.C. Hoskyns was a solitary figure, admired more by his students than his colleagues. Among NT scholars R.H. Lightfoot was exceptional in his sympathy for form criticism; J.M. Creed admired Wellhausen, and A.E.J. Rawlinson treated Wrede fairly. W. Sanday, who knew the German scene intimately, died in 1920. His junior partner A.C. Headlam read German critical scholars – but disliked most of what he read and exercised considerable influence.

[10] E.g. H.R. Mackintosh, *Types of Modern Theology*, London, 1937.

[11] 1866-1926. The first volume of his collected works, *Luther* (1921), contains essays from 1903 onwards. Vol. 3 (1928) contains further contributions.

[12] Ed. J. Ficker (1908).

[13] E.g. W. Elert and P. Althaus, on the orthodox side.

[14] See above, p.6 and cf. H. Fischer, 'Luther und seine Reformation in der Sicht Ernst Troeltschs', *NZST*, V, 1963, pp.132-72.

Enlightenment of the eighteenth century. It was here that the Renaissance came to fulfilment, not in the Reformation – which was followed by protestant scholasticism.[15] Despite the lack of specialist knowledge on Luther which made him at certain points an easy target for Holl,[16] Troeltsch's position was a valuable corrective. But to make what could be construed as an attack upon Luther, by associating him with the Middle Ages and catholicism, was not the way to make friends and influence people in Germany.[17]

Luther's Pauline interpretation was rediscovered around 1920 as a power for the present. In terms of Horst Stephan's contrast between 'extensive' theologies which are open to the world and relate themselves to natural knowledge, and 'intensive' ones which concentrate upon the purity, seriousness and completeness of the inherited faith,[18] the near collapse of Western civilisation meant that the latter type was more likely to find a hearing in the 1920s. The cultured religion of Troeltsch's generation had proved unable to give sufficient constructive support to sustain the old civilisation. Now it was the turn of a theology which could call to repentance and judgment.

Troeltsch's offence in failing to subscribe to any of the preferred Luthers of the day[19] was compounded by the reservations he had about Lutheranism on account of its social conservatism. He evidently admired the social efficacy of Calvinism and protestant sectarianism most obvious in English and American puritanism. And he recognised both the place of the sects within the mystical tradition, and their relationship to his own spirituality which derived from German idealism.[20]

Both his personal preference for an individualistic, mystical type of

[15] This periodisation of history is emphasised throughout his writings from 1891 onwards.

[16] Holl criticised especially Troeltsch's reading Melanchthon's view of natural law into Luther. He also thought Troeltsch was led astray by his theoretical approach through fixed concepts, such as church and sect. But Holl admitted that his own personal and political outlook caused some of the antipathy he felt. He accused Troeltsch of 'tastelessness' in bracketing Luther with Machiavelli, and thought that what he wrote about Luther and the peasants' revolt 'should not be written in a scientific work'.

[17] Subsequent Luther research, especially that of G. Ebeling and H. Oberman and their pupils, has investigated the links between Luther and late medieval thought more thoroughly, both vindicating and correcting Troeltsch.

[18] *Geschichte der Deutschen Evangelischen Theologie*, Berlin, 1960,[2] pp.3f.

[19] The controversy between Gogarten and Holl indicates the range of interpretations. The Luther enthusiasts found their own (differing) theologies reflected in this particularly authoritative part of the tradition, no less than in the NT.

[20] *Social Teachings*, II, ch.3 § 4, especially p.985.

religion, and also his sense of the intellectual's responsibility for society alienated Troeltsch from the narrower 'churchly' concerns of the theological faculties.[21] The older liberals who, like Troeltsch (though sometimes less critically), had seen in the war a struggle for German culture were, after the war and German revolution, generally less open to 'Western Europe' and the task of social reconstruction than he was.[22] The younger generation were more emphatically working as 'Church theologians' and wished to concentrate (or reduce) the Christian religion to theology.[23] It has taken half a century for a new appreciation to emerge of Troeltsch's significance for theological work.[24]

The essays translated in this volume stem from Troeltsch's most influential period as a professor of Christian theology. By 1913 he was faced with the charge 'that I have become basically more interested in the general analysis of culture and religion than in specifically Christian theological issues'. His sharp comment provides the key to the still disputed topic of 'Troeltsch as theologian': 'the question of course is what we take theology and its task to be' (*G.S.* II, 227).

In 1915 he moved to Berlin for the sake of serving the needs of the hour. Barth's interpretation of his 'giving up his chair in theology for one in philosophy'[25] reflects his own, rather than Troeltsch's, understanding of the matter. Again, it depends on 'what we take theology and its task to be'. The astonishing fact that some people today would even deny Troeltsch the name of theologian shows how effectively the dialectical theology expelled Troeltsch posthumously from the charmed circle. But anyone who accepts that theology has more than one task and that there is room for both 'intensive' and 'extensive' types of faith and theology will remain open to Troeltsch's contribution even if it appears less fruitful for the immediate needs of a confessing Church than was Barth's biblical interpretation and church dogmatics.

If 'God' is the reality that determines everything, then however permanent the need of the Church for an 'intensive' confessional theology in the service of its evangelistic task, it will always be necessary, too, for Christian intellectuals to develop the 'extensive'

---

[21] He claimed to have rather outgrown these. *G.S.* IV, p.12.

[22] See 'The Ideas of Natural Law and Humanity in World Politics' (1925), Eng. tr. in O. Gierke, *Natural Law and the Theory of Society 1500-1800*, Cambridge, 1934; Beacon Press, 1957.

[23] Cf. T. Rendtorff, *Kirche und Theologie*, Gütersloher Verlagshaus, Gerd Mohn, 1966, pp.179 ff.

[24] See, for example, A.O. Dyson, *The Immortality of the Past*, London, 1974.

[25] *The Humanity of God*, London, 1967, p.12.

type of theology represented by Troeltsch. The Berlin philosophers who did not want Troeltsch in their faculty because he was a theologian, were, in a narrow-minded way, more perceptive than the churchmen who, against the wishes of some of the theologians, blocked his entry into the theological faculty.

The melancholy image of Troeltsch as a theologian who lost his faith[26] helped discredit his work. This was reinforced in the 1920s by the story of his general gloom and despondency towards the end of his life. It is remarkable how self-evidently his opponents speak of his 'failure',[27] and claim that the road he took *could* only end in failure. One purpose of this republication of some of Troeltsch's work is to provoke discussion about the possibility of a 'historical theology' in the sense of an appreciation and interpretation of the Christian tradition which is true to contemporary experience and rationality as this is reflected by historical science, but which also remains faithful to the tradition by being true to its theological subject-matter and avoiding reductionism. Troeltsch's place in that enterprise which has its roots in Hegel and Schleiermacher, its first flower in F.C. Baur, and its finest contemporary spokesman in W. Pannenberg, makes talk of his 'failure' trite. Whatever the flaws in his position (and they are serious), one who integrated philosophy and history so effectively within the theological task must command respect today.

The early 1920s were hardly a time for German rejoicing, and Troeltsch may well have felt depressed as he surveyed both church and society. But the rumour and innuendo by which this was used as an argument against his work is contradicted by the combination of optimism and realism no less evident at the end of *Der Historismus und seine Probleme* (1922) than in his earlier ebullience. He writes of the 'creative act and venture of those who believe in the future ... believing, courageous men, not sceptics and mystics, rationalistic fanatics and historical know-alls'. These men, among whom he included himself, will work 'first in the quiet of their own personality and then in wider circles', and 'from such circles there will come new life'.[28] Until such time as new symbols are given, the work must go on, and never more urgently than in the present. Troeltsch's attempt to create, as the goal of his philosophy of history, a cultural synthesis for the present, was interrupted by a premature death. But his strenuous

---

[26] Gertrud von Le Fort's picture of Troeltsch in her novel, *Der Kranz der Engel*, and especially the phrase 'the sunset of Christianity' which 'still glows' has been influential. See W. Pauck (*op. cit.*), p.92.

[27] Most recently W. Bodenstein, *Neige des Historismus*, Gütersloher Verlagshaus, Gerd Mohn, 1959 and B. Reist, *Towards a Theology of Involvement*, London, 1966.

[28] *G.S.* III, p.771. This part of *Der Historismus* first appeared in 1920.

efforts to prepare the platform for this by developing various lines of thought, are not the products of gloom and pessimism. The repudiation of Troeltsch in the dialectical theology of the 1920s is better explained and therefore excused, by its own positive impulses, than justified by appeal by any inherent impossibility in advancing along Troeltsch's lines.

2

As Rade's editorial assistant on the *Christliche Welt*, Barth was in 1908-9 familiar with Troeltsch's general position.[29] But even as he sowed his wild liberal protestant oats there were strict limits to how far he would go in support of the then dominant theology, and Troeltsch was very definitely outside them.[30] Barth's hostility marks him as a loyal pupil of Wilhelm Herrmann. The relationship between the two giants of systematic theology in the first decade of the century is well-known: 'Especially from Herrmann's side it was on occasion made quite unmistakeable what a great gulf he saw between his own work and the methods and scientific aims of Troeltsch.'[31]

The hostility has proved extremely significant for the subsequent history of protestant theology in Germany, because the two most influential figures of the century, Barth and Bultmann, as decided pupils of Herrmann, were particularly blind to all for which Troeltsch stood. It was not simply that he was the ripest fruit of the century-long movement which the new theology wished to repudiate. He was indeed, and a reaction was necessary if the Christian tradition was not to be entirely dissipated. But if that were the heart of the matter the dialectical theologians would have argued with Troeltsch as they argued with Schleiermacher. With the exception of Gogarten they did not. They ignored him and so ignored the points at which he may now be judged to have been right.

It is scarcely an exaggeration to say that of the alternatives posed for Christian theology at the beginning of the century it was in essence

[29] His 'name stood at that time at the centre of our discussions'. From the 'Autobiographical Sketch' given in the *Gesamtausgabe*, V, 1 (*Karl Barth-Rudolf Bultmann Briefwechsel*, 1922-1966), Zürich, 1971, p.305. In 1910 he heard with 'dark foreboding' the lecture on 'The Significance of the Historical Existence of Jesus for Faith'. See *Theology and Church*, London, 1962, p.60f.

[30] That name 'designated the limits *this* side of which I thought I must refuse to follow the then dominant theology.' *Ibid.*

[31] H. Diehl in *ZThK* XVIII, 1908, p.473. See also Barth, *Theology and Church*, pp.261, 258.

Herrmann's development of Ritschl which lived on in the dialectical and existentialist theologies of the early Barth and consistent Bultmann.[32] The reaction against liberalism did not exclude several of its strands being maintained,[33] and these strands were derived from the particular stables in which the dialectical theologians were variously trained. Since it was the Marburg systematics stable which achieved the leadership, it has taken a further fifty years and the unwilling surrender of neo-reformation theology to a new era, for Troeltsch's insights, worked out in criticism of Ritschl and opposition to Herrmann, to receive due attention. The points at which Bultmann's theology, for example, is least satisfactory are all points where he is the insufficiently critical heir to the Ritschl-Herrmann tradition. In each case Troeltsch had explored genuine alternatives which are now being taken seriously, though often without reference to Troeltsch.[34] In summary: In his concern for metaphysics, for social ethics, for the real course of history (including its social as well as its intellectual aspects), and for a pluralism of real living religions, Troeltsch forced Christian theology to take seriously the reality of the world – a world which includes nature as well as history, society as well as ideas, other religions as well as Christianity. He opposed at all these points the loss of worldly reality involved in the way the Ritschlians were using Kant.

This serious accusation against the dialectical theology is necessary if Troeltsch's re-emergence in the contemporary debate is to be justified. The charge that it ignored a man who had so much to teach it requires some expansion in view of the great variety within the movement. The conclusion and prescription which emerge were given as early as 1923 by Bornhausen in an obituary notice: 'Anyone beginning the study of protestant theology in Germany at the start of the twentieth century would, in the course of his study inevitably be led to two theological positions that it seemed *both necessary and impossible to unite*. Wilhelm Herrmann and Ernst Troeltsch often and without success exchanged statement and reply in their lifetime. They even almost took umbrage at any of their pupils trying to synthesise their views.'[35] Bornhausen's dream remains unrealised, and a

---

[32] Witness their hostility, derived from Ritschl and Herrmann, towards mysticism, metaphysics and natural theology.

[33] This is sometimes concealed by a change in terminology. The dialectical theology's polemic against 'religion', for example, does not touch Herrmann, since what he called religion was close to what they called revelation.

[34] A.O. Dyson, *Immortality* (*op.cit.*), provides just such a comparison and finds Troeltsch more satisfactory than Bultmann.

[35] *ZThK NF* 4, 1923-24, p.196. Italics mine.

'synthesis' between Troeltsch and the dialectical theology does not sound particularly attractive. But it is surely necessary to ask how far the insights of Troeltsch can be made fruitful for the present situation without abandoning the legitimate concerns of the dialectical theology and all that sprung from that very fruitful seed-bed.

Apart from an extended footnote on the *Glaubenslehre* in *Church Dogmatics* IV, 1, pp.383-7, Barth never considered Troeltsch worthy of the serious attention he gave to Schleiermacher. His occasional minimising comments[36] so far hindered the reception of Troeltsch, that even today it is sometimes impossible for orthodox 'Barthians' to take an unjaundiced view of him. He never reached the projected chapter on Troeltsch in his *Protestant Theology in the Nineteenth Century*, allegedly (p.11) because the end of semester intervened. Instead, he undertook a massive counter-achievement to the way of neo-protestant theology from Schleiermacher to Troeltsch. Its grandeur is indisputable, and it may be that this was the best possible answer to liberal protestantism. Barth remains the one great theologian of the century who understood the reasons for the neo-Protestant option and nevertheless rejected it in favour of a classical form of dogmatics. Nevertheless, his system remains vulnerable to attack from the sides where Troeltsch is strongest, and it still 'seems both necessary and impossible to unite' the insights of both geniuses.[37]

Of the lesser men in the movement, Thurneysen knew and respected his former teacher, but never fulfilled his 'obligation to argue with your friend Troeltsch'.[38] Brunner's incautious remarks on Troeltsch reflect a negative aspect of the youthful *élan* and propaganda which contributed to the new movement.[39]

The one real pupil of Troeltsch in the new movement was Gogarten. He argued with his former *Doktorvater*[40] and continued the debate for a short time after Troeltsch's death. But the promising lines of advance opened up in this discussion were not pursued. Gogarten's

[36] It is unfortunately obvious which 'feeble epigone and eulogist' Barth has in mind at *CD* II, 1, 1940, Eng. tr. Edinburgh 1957, p.73. For other references, see my essay in J.P. Clayton (ed.), *Ernst Troeltsch and the Future of Theology*, London, 1976: 'Ernst Troeltsch and the Dialectical Theology,' p.53, n.92.
[37] H. Richard Niebuhr attempted this (see n.6) but unsuccessfully.
[38] The sardonic phrase is Barth's. *Gesamtausgabe* V, 3. (*Karl Barth-Eduard Thurneysen Briefwechsel*, Band 1, 1913-1921) Zürich, 1973, p.144.
[39] The details are provided in 'Ernst Troeltsch and the Dialectical Theology', *op. cit.*, pp.49-51.
[40] See especially 'Against Romantic Theology' (1922) and 'Historicism' (1924) in *The Beginnings of Dialectical Theology*, ed. J.M. Robinson, Richmond, 1969, pp.317-27, 343-58. Other references in 'Ernst Troeltsch and the Dialectical Theology' *op. cit.*, pp.42-7.

interests moved (unfortunately) with the times and his break with Barth deprived him of the influence his brilliance merited. Thus one line through which Troeltsch's insights might have been channelled into the new situation was effectively blocked until Gerhard Ebeling took up elements of the Troeltsch-Gogarten heritage after the Second World War[41] and combined them with Herrmann's and Bultmann's insights, though not Barth's.

Gogarten opposed Troeltsch's allegedly 'contemplative view' of history with a more existential emphasis.[42] A similar move was adopted by Bultmann – but without reference to Troeltsch. He was stimulated rather by the publication of Dilthey's posthumous manuscripts, another factor contributing to the shift of interest away from Troeltsch.[43] Although he expected everyone to have read the *Social Teachings*[44] Bultmann had little interest in the great *Aporetiker* of liberal theology, and his one attempt to use Troeltsch as a target in his critique of liberalism was a failure.[45] It appears that Bultmann was unaware of Troeltsch's careful distancing himself from the 'bad historicism' which led to relativistic scepticism and which applied to history the aims and methods of natural science.[46] Such subtle differentiation did not accord with the style of the dialectical theologians for whom *Historismus*, like *Psychologismus*, was a cudgel with which to beat liberalism rather than a problem to be faced.[47]

Bultmann's alliance with Barth is understandable against the background of his dissatisfaction with the liberal theology in which he had been educated. But it is fairly clear that, unlike Barth who always recognised the gulf which separated them, even while he valued this unexpected support,[48] Bultmann overemphasised the measure of what they had in common,[49] and that he failed to recognise how much he had in common with Troeltsch. He rightly noted at the beginning of their friendly association the difference between his own and Barth's

[41] *Theology and Proclamation* (1962, Eng. tr. 1966) is dedicated to Gogarten. See pp.17, 140 on Troeltsch, and the clear echo in the Ch.2 heading 'Historical and Dogmatic Theology'.

[42] *Beginnings*, p.350. See above, Introduction n.129 for an answer to this.

[43] His fruitful collaboration with Heidegger began a little later, in 1925.

[44] Cf. *Briefwechsel, op.cit.*, p.26. His own criticisms of it are contained in 'Ethische und Mystische Religion im Urchristentum' (1920).

[45] *Faith and Understanding* I (Eng. tr. London, 1969), pp.30-2.

[46] Compare Bultmann, p.32 with Troeltsch *G.S.* III, p.67! Dyson, *Immortality*, p.58 also makes this point against Bultmann.

[47] This is most painfully clear in Brunner's polemics.

[48] See the Preface to the third edition of his *Romans*. This judgment emerges very clearly from the correspondence.

[49] Despite his recognition of the importance of their disagreement about *Sachkritik*.

'educational experience' (*Briefwechsel*, p.9), and was aware of the enormous difference it made. But he seems not to have appreciated sufficiently the conservative elements in Barth's background[50] which emerge very clearly in the private letters to Thurneysen.[51]

Despite the difference in their specialist fields, and their very different evaluations of Luther, and despite the blind spots which Bultmann inherited from Herrmann, Bultmann and Troeltsch are both Christian theologians thoroughly shaped by critical historical work. This, together with their philosophical sensitivity and basically idealist outlook, is sufficient to ensure a similarity of approach to theological questions which far outweighs their particular philosophical differences. The similarity of Bultmann's hermeneutical theology to Troeltsch's method as this reflected in his 'essence of Christianity' essay in this volume deserves consideration.[52] It is also arguable that both Troeltsch's and Bultmann's emphases are necessary in a theologically and philosophically adequate account of history.[53]

In view of the intention of this volume to contribute to the renewal of dialogue with 'the greatest and most modern of modernists'[54] it is necessary in this essay to concentrate upon the virtues of Troeltsch. That should not be understood to mean that the turn of the tide against him in the 1920s was a misfortune, or that Christian theologies of the future will owe more to him than to Barth or Bultmann. It is possible to learn from all three, and since each has strengths where the other two have weaknesses, it will be wise to do so. Barth and Troeltsch in particular are difficult to read without strong feelings of aversion – and gratitude for the other. Troeltsch's reasonableness on the historical questions and his recognition of their significance is very impressive. On the other hand it is difficult for a theologian with strong roots in the classical Christian tradition to read *The Significance of the Historical Existence of Jesus for Faith* without being profoundly thankful for the *Church Dogmatics*. The history of dogma is, as D.F. Strauss observed,[55] at the same time its criticism. The great

[50] See *Faith and Understanding* (London, 1969), p.28, and the high expectations throughout his early letters of reaching understanding and agreement.

[51] E.g. in his attitudes to his liberal teachers, the OT, and Acts.

[52] See above, p.40f. and 161 on the notion of decision. Consider also the discussion of existence and history in *G.S.* II, p.725.

[53] This is the conclusion of H. Ganse Little, *History, Decision and Responsibility: an examination of a problem central to the thought of Ernst Troeltsch and Rudolf Bultmann* (Diss. Harvard, 1965).

[54] Brunner's sarcastic phrase. *The Theology of Crisis*, London and New York, 1930, p.7.

[55] *Die Christliche Glaubenslehre*, reprint Darmstadt, 1973, vol.1, p.71.

strength of liberalism may be found here. But the acids of criticism threaten to dissolve the tradition, and if the creative theological interpretations of the liberals are not strong enough to counter this, then Christian theology must look elsewhere, and perhaps even in the direction of Barth's refined biblicism within the Christian church.[56]

The recovery of the awareness of the close relation between theology and the preaching Church was the greatest achievement of the dialectical theology. Troeltsch in particular had become a Christian intellectual with rather loose links with the established churches. But he himself saw the importance of community and cult more clearly than anyone, and therefore had doubts about the future of his own 'free protestantism'. Despite his personal preference for an individualistic, mystical 'religion of the educated' he was well aware that the new springs of religious life must come from the 'popular religion' which contained so much that a thinking person could not accept. And despite his understandable disillusionment with the churches for their appalling failure to come to grips realistically with their changed position in society he was prepared to work for mutual enrichment between his own free *Religionsphilosophie* and the practical theology of the Church.[57]

The essay 'Half a Century of Theology: a Review' documents Troeltsch's repudiation of theologies of mediation, on account of their unacceptable compromises. But *genuine* mediation between the Christian tradition and the modern world is the theme which dominates his entire life's work, including that of the latter years in which 'Europeanism' occupies the centre of the stage (*G.S.* III, 703-30).

That, in Troeltsch's view, is the task of theology: to mediate between a religious faith and the contemporary world of thought within which it exists. If he failed to achieve a satisfactory synthesis, he is not alone. Neither Schleiermacher nor Barth have done more than make important contributions from which their successors can learn. The same is true of this continuator of the Schleiermacher tradition. Our brief recapitulation of some of the factors which hindered a proper appreciation of his contribution suggests that his efforts should be re-considered.

Two central areas in which the importance of Troeltsch's reflexions

[56] Barth accepts the charge of biblicism, in his own sense. *The Epistle to the Romans* (Eng. tr. London, 1933), pp.10f. The question is whether an adequate Christology can be maintained without according to Scripture a greater authority than can be rationally justified by historical arguments. Here as elsewhere authority is a matter of common consent.

[57] 'Religionsphilosophie' *op. cit.*, pp.132f. and 161f.

has not diminished are, first, the implications of historical study for Christian theology, including the question of the historical Jesus and the broadening of perspective to embrace sociological issues; and, secondly, the question of God, as this is reflected in arguments about the nature and 'scientific' character of theology. Behind both topics stands the wider question of the possibility of doing theology in a way that is true to contemporary experience and rationality as this is reflected in historical science, while at the same time remaining faithful to the tradition by being true to its theological subject-matter and avoiding reductionism. The task of integrating modern philosophy and scientific history within the theological task, attempted each in his own way by Baur and Bultmann, was undertaken by Troeltsch in a way that is no less instructive. And since he can claim as close affinity with those two greatest of *historical* philosophical theologians as he can with Schleiermacher, reconsideration of his work may help to heal a breach which has been a source of weakness in twentieth as in nineteenth-century theology: the breach between historical and systematic theology.

3

In the confrontation of traditional Christian faith and theology with the modern intellectual situation it has been the effect of the new critical attitude towards the past upon Bible and dogma that has made the greatest impact, at least so far as university theology is concerned. The authority of the tradition in which the revelation was located has been radically called in question and protestantism was particularly vulnerable to such critique on account of the way it invested supreme authority in 'scripture alone'.[58]

Some conservative churchmen have still not faced the issues[59] but they were posed in all their sharpness during the nineteenth and at the beginning of the twentieth centuries. Troeltsch gives a sketch of the successive waves of the onslaught (above pp.182f.) and was himself the finest example of a systematic theologian facing them in their most severe form. One reason why Troeltsch speaks to us as a contemporary on this issue is that in Gospel criticism, where the problems posed for faith and theology by historical research are most acute, the shape of the problem has not changed much since

[58] It is not by chance that modern biblical criticism was first explored as a means of anti-protestant polemic (R. Simon). But the church authorities of the time were wise to repudiate such a dangerous weapon.

[59] Cf. the hysterical response to Bishop Hanson's article in *The Times*, 11 May 1974: 'The dangerous gulf between pulpit and pew.'

Troeltsch's day. Intensive research upon the New Testament during the present century has extended our knowledge of its history of religions background and opened up new avenues of theological interpretation, but the shape of the faith-history question has scarcely been affected and it has certainly not been solved. It remains at the centre of the stage where it has stood for two hundred years, and in very much the same form now as seventy years ago.

Troeltsch was intimately acquainted with the work of the original Göttingen group, the 'history-of-religions school', and was therefore fully familiar with the extent to which history of traditions work and the new wave of historical scepticism associated with this, sharpened the problem for Christian theology. Bultmann and Dibelius developed the technical aspects of form critical study of the New Testament after the war by applying some of Gunkel's insights into the Old Testament to the synoptic tradition. But the chief roots of Bultmann's historical scepticism, which was the aspect of form criticism which caused the theological stir, especially in England, where it was not linked with kerygmatic theology,[60] are to be found in the history of traditions research of Wrede and Wellhausen.[61] Troeltsch must be admitted to have adjusted to the new situation caused by Wrede's *Messianic Secret* more readily than his friend the New Testament specialist, Bousset.[62] His general assessment of the historicity of the Gospels, provoked by the 'silly' denials that Jesus ever lived[63] stands in no need of revision. Of the (literally) hundreds of contributions made to the debate about Drews' work, few are so judicious as to have justified reprinting in Germany two generations later, in 1969, and translating into English.

As well as being the father of twentieth-century historical scepticism in gospel criticism, Wrede saw more clearly than anyone the gulf between the historical Jesus and the Christ of Paul. In calling the latter 'the second founder of Christianity'[64] he made Troeltsch aware of the problem of Christianity's 'double gospel' (*G.S.* II, 412 and see above, p.126) first raised by Reimarus and still implicit in modern discussion of the historical Jesus and the Christ of faith. The

---

[60] English theology underwent a perceptible change on this issue during the 1960s. A flood of German gospel criticism appeared in translation.

[61] See Bultmann's recognition of this in *Existence and Faith* (London, 1964), pp.41-3.

[62] See Bousset's uneasy discussion of the work in *ThR* 5 (1902), pp.307-16, 347-62.

[63] See above, p.182. This essay was written in the context of the 'Christ myth' debate provoked by Drews' book. The scale of the debate owed more to the theological questions raised by Drews' hypothesis than to its historical merits. See B.A. Gerrish (*op. cit.*). Troeltsch would have been equally brusque about the historical merits of J.M. Allegro's theories.

[64] *Paul* (London, 1907), p.179.

rediscoverer of eschatology in the message of Jesus, Johannes Weiss,[65] was also associated with the history-of-religions school, and Troeltsch was possibly the first systematic theologian to face this issue.[66] But that in turn was only one aspect of the much wider question posed by the new awareness of the 'late' Jewish background to the New Testament, and by parallels to it from the history of religions generally. Further work in this area, especially on the rabbis, was done in the 1920s[67] and our knowledge has been enriched by the finds at Qumran and Nag Hammadi, which have forced hypotheses about hellenistic and direct Iranian influences to yield to a more diversified account of the Jewish background.[68] But the issue for Christian theology has not been substantially altered by these later developments, and Troeltsch was the first to draw the consequences for theology of the new trends in historical study which were already apparent about the beginning of the century.

The details are less important than the basic recognition that the absolute dichotomy between Christianity and other religions, in which one is simply true and the others simply false, is incredible when once the links between Christianity and the surrounding world of religions are acknowledged. Ritschl's compromise between ecclesiastical supernaturalism and scientific history was not a possibility for anyone who had learned to place Jesus and Christianity back into the stream of history. Within that stream the attempt to seal it off from its neighbours is doomed to failure. The appeal to miracle, already abandoned by F.C. Baur, was no longer possible; Christian origins are open to historical study in exactly the same way as are the origins of any other historical movement.

The surrender of the apologetic notion of miracle undermined traditional ideas of the absoluteness of Christianity. Naive absoluteness might still be asserted in the freshness of religious faith,

---

[65] See *Jesus' Proclamation of the Kingdom of God* (1892, 1900²) Eng. tr. of 1st ed., Philadelphia and London, 1971.

[66] At first he rejected Weiss' apocalyptic interpretation of the concept 'kingdom of God' in Jesus' teaching (*ZThK* VI, 1896, p.198), as Bousset did, and interpreted it in Kantian terms as 'true righteousness and true good'. But in the *Social Teachings* he has a clear grasp of its eschatological character. E.g. vol. I, p.174. Admittedly this did not prevent him from speaking of Jesus' 'religious and ethical teaching of the value of the soul and God's kingdom of brotherly love' (*Glaubenslehre*, p.102). His religious interpretation of Jesus' personality did not cater for a Schweitzerian Jesus – but we have no reason to believe that Schweitzer's account of Jesus' eschatology was correct. See also *Absoluteness*, p.145.

[67] Strack-Billerbeck was first published in 1922-8, and Kittel's *TWNT* began to appear in 1933.

[68] See M. Hengel, *Judaism and Hellenism*, Eng. tr. London, 1974.

but it could not be rationally defended and was therefore to be excluded from scientific theology.[69] Instead, Christian theologians must argue rationally for the superiority of their own tradition to other options available in a pluralist world. This Troeltsch did throughout his life, despite a waning confidence in how much he could achieve by such comparisons. He was scrupulous enough to recognise the ambiguity of any appeal to historical Christianity. In every generation this is the result of a 'compromise' with the social conditions of the time. Determining the essence of Christianity involves a projection into the future as well as historical abstraction (see above, p.156). 'Christianity' for a believer, cannot be simply identified with its historical manifestations. But Troeltsch saw the importance of Christian apologetics remaining firmly based upon the realities of history, and this is his great strength.

Christianity is a religion among others, a very complex religious tradition containing meanings and values which can be rationally discussed. To abstract from its rich and varied history little more than the personal decision required by the Kantian imperative would be to engage in a massive reduction. Yet this was the tendency of Herrmann's concentration upon what he considered essential, and it has lived on impressively in Reformation and existentialist terminology in Bultmann's theology. Troeltsch's alternative, which was to follow Schleiermacher and attempt to develop a doctrine of worldly 'goods' or material values in his ethics (*G.S.* II, pp.616-72) is surely more helpful in a world which may well have something to learn from the resources of the Christian tradition.

The same contrast between Bultmann's purely formal call to decision and Troeltsch's readiness to articulate what the hearer is invited to take seriously is clear in their attitudes to the question of the historical Jesus. The reaction of Barth and Bultmann against liberalism at this point contained a necessary and important emphasis, but their position cannot be sustained in the crude form of saying that the historical Jesus, as well as being historically inaccessible, is also theologically irrelevant for Christianity. Troeltsch was prepared to accept the consequences of insisting upon the importance for Christianity of the picture of Jesus mediated by historical research. There could be no side-stepping of rigorous

[69] The suggestion made in 'Die Selbständigkeit der Religion' that the claim to absoluteness was a distinguishing mark of Christianity (*ZThK* VI, 1896, pp.213-18) was soon abandoned. Even in this essay Troeltsch realised that to relate other religions to Christianity as seeking to finding was arbitrary, and could be equally done by advocates of other religions (*ZThK* V, 1895, p.375). See also *Absoluteness*, pp.131-63.

historical research, and since this is a specialist exercise it does imply, in Kähler's emotionally loaded phrase, a certain dependence upon (perish the thought) professors (see above, p.199). Troeltsch immediately and properly defuses the emotion by adding, 'better, a dependence upon the general feeling of historical reliability produced by the impression of scientific research'. In his misplaced sarcasm about this, Bultmann fails to distinguish between his own proper insistence that 'historical research can never lead to any result which could serve as a basis for faith, for *all its results have only relative validity*' (*Faith and Understanding*, p.30), and the further assumption that constructive historical work is *irrelevant* for faith. His argument holds good against the Life of Jesus theology, but not against Troeltsch, who saw correctly that historical work could have a *negative* significance for faith. Christian theology, therefore, dare not be indifferent to it, but must seek to establish at least enough to be able to counter the attacks which may be made upon Christianity by attempting to discredit its historical basis. Beyond this, Troeltsch's account of the *positive* significance of gospel criticism for christology in *Glaubenslehre* § 8 is very subtly nuanced and deserves more attention than it has yet received. His insistence that the religious interpretation of Jesus be distinguished but not separated from scientific historical research is relevant to the current debate about the relationship of history and kerygma in presentations of Jesus of Nazareth.[70]

The not-so-new quest[71] of the historical Jesus was provoked by a variety of sometimes conflicting motives. Its most powerful representative, Ernst Käsemann, was driven by a concern for the primacy of christology which he saw to be lost in Bultmann's theological position. The early dialectical theology had made good the idealist theologians' loss of the biblical emphasis upon God's transcendence. But their loss of an adequate christology was surely more serious, and this was not countered by the new theologians until Barth's later work. The hostility of Barth and Bultmann to the liberals' quest for the historical Jesus therefore led to a lack of emphasis upon, and a sense of unreality about, the Lordship of Christ. Käsemann's recovery of this owes something to Barth, and nothing to Troeltsch, although the latter did not ignore this motif in his christology (*Glaubenslehre*, p.104). But his unease about the unreality and abstraction of some contemporary existentialist theology provides

---

[70] E.g. Leander Keck, 'Bornkamm's *Jesus of Nazareth* revisited', *JR* XLIX, 1969, pp.1-17, and Bornkamm's response in the new edition (1975) of his book.

[71] In 'How new is the "New Quest of the Historical Jesus"?' in *The Historical Jesus and the Kerygmatic Christ*, ed. C. Braaten and R. Harrisville, Nashville, 1964, pp.197-242, Van Harvey and S. Ogden show its similarities to the old liberal one.

an unexpected point of contact with Troeltsch for whom it was self-evident that Christian faith finds its chief symbol in this historical figure. Whether Troeltsch and the new questers are right to place so much theological weight on the so-called historical Jesus remains, of course, a burning question.[72] But the activity of studying the gospels historically will retain some religious significance even if the details of its conclusions are agreed to be theologically irrelevant.

The same awareness that Christianity is a fact of history and that the Gospel proves its reality and power within the historical sphere, not as a bloodless abstraction, has brought the successors of the dialectical theologians closer to Troeltsch in other respects too. The new sense of political activism and social responsibility within theology, reflected in different ways by Moltmann and Sölle, for example, is in accord with his concern for political, economic and social realities. There is, however, an unresolved tension in Troeltsch's thought between his metaphysical idealism and the robust realism with which he investigated history. His idealism continues to alienate him theologically from his successors, even as they learn from his 'sociologically oriented history of Protestantism' (above, p.44). It is responsible for some misplaced accents in his picture of the historical Jesus as well as the more serious defects in his christology, and it is reflected in his pessimism about the capacity of contemporary religion to make a relevant contribution to social ethics. Subsequent theology has been right to break with Troeltsch at this point, even if it has failed to solve his problems.

The failure of German idealism to overcome the gulf which the Enlightenment had fixed between history and the idea haunts Troeltsch's systematic theology, and is especially apparent in his christology. The natural implication of Troeltsch's position is, as Gerrish argues (above, p.39), to deny the necessity of the historical Jesus for Christian faith. Unlike Strauss and Bousset, Troeltsch would not take this step. Like Baur and Bultmann, he realised that the necessity of Jesus of Nazareth is axiomatic for traditional Christianity, and may not be lightly abandoned, however ill it accords with a basically idealist frame of reference. If he cannot ground this philosophically, he will at least justify it in practical terms, as a social and psychological necessity. But it remains a question whether that is enough to sustain for long a living Christian faith. Anyone who doubts this will be forced, perhaps uneasily, back to orthodoxy, and will have to ask whether it is not intellectually possible to assert in language which makes sense today the traditional belief in the divinity of Jesus

---

[72] B.A. Gerrish (*op.cit.*) thinks that they are wrong to do so and argues that the community's experience of Jesus is sufficient for Troeltsch's requirements.

Christ. Troeltsch saw that it was this christology and the idea of the church which made 'the religion of the people' more potent than his own 'religion of the educated'. He saw the perpetual need of the latter for blood transfusions from the former. But he saw no way of combining the two and producing a version of Christianity which is both intellectually viable and religiously effective in the modern world. That, and not the defects of his series of attempts to build a new natural theology, is his weakness as a constructive theologian. After Schleiermacher's failure to combine the historical and the 'ideal' in Christ, Troeltsch did not even try. Barth certainly tried, but failed to achieve a satisfactory integration of historical critical work in his dogmatic theology. The problem of maintaining a christology which is true to the Christian tradition within a historically conscious theology, remains outstanding. It is the problem of combining the insights of a Troeltsch and a Barth, the Enlightenment and the Reformation, the modern world and the classical Christian tradition.

The *critical* interpretation of the tradition, which Troeltsch defined so memorably as one aspect of the theological task (see above, p.141), must be complemented by the *constructive* aspect of this theological interpretation (see above, p.162). That will involve more than scientific historical work – as Troeltsch acknowledged. But it will also involve more than a philosophy of history can encompass. If God is the reality which determines everything, then a historically responsible theological interpretation of the Christian tradition cannot be confined within the limits of a purely historical world-view. There are more things in heaven and earth than are dreamt of in Troeltsch's philosophy of history. This does not legitimate a direct flight back to revelation, but it does suggest that Christian theology's interpretative lens should be redesigned to disclose the clue to all reality in the particular patch of history in which Christians locate the event of revelation. Whether or not this is possible is the question which divides Troeltsch from orthodoxy.

4

Critical historical method was the point at which modern rationality made its most dramatic impact upon Christian thought. But this was only a part of the larger intellectual revolution in the West which came to a head in the seventeenth and eighteenth centuries and introduced the transition from a religious to an autonomous, secular culture. It transformed the intellectual situation of Christianity, destroying the older ways of mediation between religion and reason, revelation and natural knowledge. Troeltsch's life was spent looking for new links between faith and knowledge following the destruction by Kant of the old natural theology. He explored psychological and epistemological justifications of religious belief, and his later attempts to create a philosophy of culture, in which he expected the philosophy of religion to occupy the key position (see above, p.50) were directed to the same end.

Troeltsch's philosophical reflexions have dated, as his contributions to the question of faith and history have not. The rise of analytic philosophy, the widespread distrust of metaphysics and the eclipse of idealism have relegated him to the generation of our grandfathers. But appearances are partly deceptive. The whole question of contemporary theology's relation to the German idealist tradition remains open, as the rediscovery of Schleiermacher is making plain. Empiricist philosophy may despise metaphysics, but it is difficult to see how Christian theology can afford to do so. And the need for something to take the place of the older natural theology is seen to be an urgent necessity by the majority of modern theologians.

Troeltsch decisively rejected the way the Ritschlians evaded the problems posed to Christian theology by the new intellectual situation (see above, pp.6-14). He saw that Christian theology must confront the problems facing it by engaging in metaphysics and defending the superiority of a religious, which for him meant an idealist (broadly defined), view of the world over materialism and positivism. Without this the possibility of religion being taken seriously was surrendered. He did not think that he could demonstrate the existence of God, but he did think that he could defend both the independence and cognitive import of religion in general, and the supremacy of Christianity in particular – at least for Western civilisation. In view of the failure of his theory of the religious *a priori* to win assent, and his own admission that the history of religions gave less support to Christianity than he had hoped, it is not surprising that Troeltsch's opponents and successors struck out on other paths (see above, pp.213f.). But it was one thing to judge that the idealist apologetic, based upon the notion of religion, had failed; it was quite another to say that it had been wrong in principle. It is also one thing to argue that Christian theology ought not to proceed by way of apologetics, and quite another to claim that the whole enterprise of tying knots between faith and knowledge is misguided. It is also one thing to question the relevance of a science of religion to Christian theology and quite another to assert that such a science is actually impossible.

In the controversy surrounding Troeltsch's work these questions were insufficiently distinguished, and the resulting confusions have lasted seventy years. Herrmann and his pupils were probably right that if Christian revelational claims are to be maintained, it is a misguided apologetics to surrender them at the outset and then hope to recover them by means of philosophical reflexion upon the history of religion. But this good point was supported by a bad argument: The only way that we possess what we consider the true idea of religion is in the form of a view which has grown out of our own religious life. We cannot communicate this to anybody else in the way that we ourselves possess it. It therefore follows that a science of religion is impossible.[73] Herrmann's claim that the 'non-objectifiability' of religion precludes a science of religion is, as it stands, clearly false. Whether or not Troeltsch was able to do justice to the reality of religion in his descriptions, the phenomenology of religion has meanwhile had some success. Herrmann's real concern becomes clear in his assertion that only Christianity qualifies as genuine religion. What he misleadingly calls 'religion' would be better called revelation in order to make clear that what is at issue here is the believer's natural and legitimate claim that the truth about his religion exceeds the limits of the phenomenologist's descriptive account.

This position reappears in a less vulnerable form in the dialectical theology where the possibility of a science of religion is conceded, but its relevance for Christian theology disputed on the grounds that this is based on revelation and proceeds from faith. It is true that Christian theologising proceeds on the assumption of the truth of Christianity. Troeltsch describes this 'presentation of religious ideas as truth'[74] very positively, and insists upon its necessity. It must follow on from the task to which Troeltsch's own main efforts were devoted: the laying a foundation upon which its claim to truth could stand. It is therefore misleading to pose theology and the science of religion as alternatives, as though Troeltsch's work were inimical to the Church's doctrinal theology. What is in dispute is how Christian belief is related to ordinary knowledge and experience. It is natural to see in the human phenomenon of religion a link or middle term, even if this will not serve as an apologetic step towards 'the justification of Christianity' (see above, pp.4,21). If Christian claims are to be rooted in human experience, religion is the most natural soil to consider. The scientist of religion may be compared to a gardener who does not tend plants which will yield Christian theological fruits but who prepares the soil in which the seeds of a historical religion can be sown by proclamation. They are more likely to take root if the stony ground of

[73] See Herrmann, *op.cit.*, Teil 1, pp.282-6, Teil 2, pp.1-6, 32-42, 282-9.
[74] Art, 'Religionsphilosophie' in W. Windelband (ed.) *Die Philosophie im Beginn des 20 Jahrhunderts*, 1904, 1907². Cited according to the first edition, pp.104-62.

positivism has been broken up and the rich depths of human experience brought to the surface and made ready for the interpretation which a religion or ideology provides. The way the ground is prepared might affect which seed takes root, but will not of itself produce much fruit – as Troeltsch himself experienced in his reflexions on 'the religion of the educated'.[75] (See also above, pp.88f.)

The alternative to this sort of model is to assert boldly that revelational claims do not need defending by reference to general truth and knowledge. Rather, this must be understood in the light of revelation. But in a world that is rightly suspicious of claims to revelation that is to risk isolating Christian theology from the world it claims to interpret, and rendering it incredible. By excluding natural theology in principle, Barth took this option. The other dialectical theologians, who around 1930 re-opened the question of anthroplogy, saw the need to ground the question of God in their view of man. That was in principle to side with Troeltsch, as Barth insisted (*Briefwechsel*, pp.100f.), even though they defined the relevant sphere of human reality rather differently.

The 'anthropological turn' in theology has vindicated itself. Human experience as such, including social experience, is indeed the field in which talk of God as the reality which determines everything, must be shown to be meaningful. But human experience in all its breadth and depth is only available to theology as mediated by interpretations, and surely none is more important than the interpretations of existence offered by the great religions of the world. Troeltsch's attention to these took full account of the new historical and anthropological knowledge of his day. Equally important, he anticipated the phenomenologists' principle that 'the believer is always right' by taking seriously *within* his descriptive account of religion, the theological categories of revelation, inspiration and miracle. The perceptiveness with which he did this can be measured by seeing how accurately his account of these categories in his article 'Religionsphilosophie' reflects the actual procedures of the dialectical theologians, in particular their relation to scripture[76] and their view of

[75] Troeltsch's account of the relationship between his science of religion and Christian theology is admittedly rather imprecise and varies a little. See also 'The Dogmatics of the "religionsgeschichtliche Schule"', *op.cit.*

[76] 'There always goes with revelation some kind of document of revelation, out of which it can be known in a classical and normative way. This may take the catholic form of Bible plus tradition authorised by the church, or the protestant form of a living Bible that is to be interpreted out of itself. Despite all possible freedom in its interpretation and the development of its implications, this document nevertheless remains the authority which the religion cannot dispense with. It needs it both for the education of the community and for the conviction that its idea is true. The

faith as response to proclamation.[77]

Troeltsch saw the importance of doing justice to the 'irrationality of every concept of God, the incomprehensible mystery of divine communication to the soul in living religions' ('Religionsphilosophie', p.129). He could not subscribe to the 'exclusive supranaturalism' by which this had in the past been defended, but neither would he settle for the reductionism of a 'rationalism which would strip religion of its mystery' (p.134). Against this, sympathetic historical study of religion and philosophy of history disclosed the possibility of doing justice to the supranatural elements of religion in a modern way by what Troeltsch called 'inclusive supranaturalism'.

The combination of psychological, epistemological and historical (including anthropological) investigations in Troeltsch's science of religion was intended to vindicate religion in general and Christianity (the highest religion) in particular and so give to the theological 'task of presenting religious truth for the community' a rational basis. He rejected the Ritschlian (and Barthian) revival of 'exclusive supranaturalism' in which 'this miracle (of faith), like revelation, is only acknowledged for one's own religion, (and) the miracles of other religious groups, formerly attributed to demons, are today surrounded to rationalist criticism' (pp.128f.). It could all too easily be turned against Christianity. He was surely right to insist upon a rational defence of Christian belief, and he was not so foolish as to suppose that an element of rational knowledge in religion would necessarily displace faith. But his 'inclusive supranaturalism' depended upon a metaphysics of the Absolute and fell victim to the twentieth-century reaction against idealism.[78] When the prevailing religious interpretation of history fell into disrepute, it was easy to assume that

---

recognition and interpretation of such a document as document and bearer of revelation is therefore the first basic concept of theology' ('Religionsphilsophie', p.128). See also above, p.85.

[77] 'The miracle of religious feeling and religious conviction itself ... the miracle of conversion, illumination, rebirth, removal of sin, satisfaction of the soul – takes place again and again through contact with the revelation, i.e. contact with the church, or the Bible, or persons who are filled with the spirit of revelation ... It makes one certain of the divine powers which proceed from these bearers ... only this gives clear satisfaction and the decisive means of proof to the need for a truth of whose validity we can be sure' (*ibid.*, pp.128f.).

[78] What T. Ogletree wrote about Troeltsch's later theology of history is even more applicable to this less secularised form of it: 'At the present stage of historical development, an idea of universal history can probably be made intelligible only within a dogmatic perspective, that is, a perspective which does not claim to be derived from empirical fact but which comes to empirical fact with the assumption that its own legitimacy is already given' (*Christian Faith and History: A critical comparison of Ernst Troeltsch and Karl Barth*, Nashville, 1965, p.163).

the whole approach to religion in terms of a theory of values in human history, as begun by Schleiermacher and developed by Troeltsch, was discredited. Because Troeltsch saw the problem of relativism so clearly and wrestled with it so honestly, it was easy to label him an 'advocate of an almost boundless historical relativism' with whom neo-protestantism 'began to sink into a sea of relativistic scepticism'.[79]

In this climate it was possible to evade Troeltsch's difficulties by abandoning the justification of religious belief and concentrating on the inner-churchly task of proclamation. If Barth's subsequent attempt to re-establish the rationality of Christian belief on a dogmatic basis lacks cogency, and the attempts of hermeneutical theology to broaden the base of kerygmatic theology by reflexion upon 'the linguistic character of reality' lack clarity, there is good reason to ask whether Troeltsch's attempts to relate Christian belief to the knowledge of his day may not contain elements which survive the collapse of idealism.

The historical realism which stands in some tension to Troeltsch's metaphysical idealism provides possible lines of advance. The social reality of religion and the pluralism of religions can no longer be disregarded by theology. The most natural way for them to be integrated into the theological task is through the scientific study of religion. The relationship between this and the church's theological task of expressing Christian faith can still be seen in Troeltschian terms. A science of religion and university departments of 'Religious Studies' are necessary, in which an interest in the truth content of religion supplies the integrating factor. Instead of luke-warm departments in which interest is restricted to the purely descriptive, phenomenological task, the passion for truth which motivated Troeltsch's philosophy of religion could become the driving force. It would be free of all party interests and yet be of more than merely academic interest.

The truth and value of religion cannot today be discussed along the lines pursued in Troeltsch's dated philosophical proposals. It belongs within a discussion about truth in the social sciences, which is where Troeltsch located it when he came to grips with Rickert's investigation of the methodology of the historical sciences. But the contemporary debate stands in no direct relationship to Rickert.[80] It is therefore the form and context of Troeltsch's contribution, rather than its content, which is instructive.

For Troeltsch the questions about the truth of theories of religion

---

[79] E. Brunner, *The Theology of Crisis*, New York, 1929, p.7.

[80] It owes much to Max Weber who himself had learned from Rickert. But Troeltsch rejected Weber's ideal of a value-free social science.

could not be isolated from the question of their fruitfulness. A science of religion which merely bred boredom and cynicism about its subject-matter, and finally destroyed it with relativistic scepticism, would not be worth much. That was an option which Troeltsch simply refused to take. His science of religion presupposes something of its truth and value. There is no escaping personal decisions of a philosophical nature at the outset. That means that (despite Ritschl and his successors – see above, pp.82f.) elementary metaphysics remains a prerequisite for the student of religion – even after Troeltsch's particular metaphysical constructions have followed Baur's into oblivion.

The student of religion's commitment to his subject-matter, defended by Troeltsch, does not make him a church theologian, attempting to show that the tradition he has inherited is, in essence, true. If he were to set about defining the essence of Christianity he would have changed hats and become a theologian, mediating between the tradition and modern knowledge, between the living faith of the church and the scientifically instructed position of the Christian intellectual. That was a legitimate and necessary task, and indeed one of his duties in the Heidelberg *theological* faculty.[81] But it was not his science of religion. This is an academic task which can defend its right to exist in a fully secular university. The engaged, but non-apologetic, character of the scientist of religion may be clarified by an analogy with the science of politics. A political scientist might not himself be a politician (except in his spare time) but may nevertheless hope that his analyses have some significance for the future of politics. The 'truth' that the human activity of politics has meaning and value is a matter of prior philosophical commitment without which only a knave would engage in the discipline. But this prior decision does not prevent the study of politics from being 'open'. The student must immerse himself without reservations in the study of history and draw from it ethical resources which can guide his evaluations, while at the

---

[81] 'It aims to serve a religious community and to develop the religious idea and power for this community. Its basic presupposition is therefore a conviction of the validity of the religious idea of its own religious group. Its most essential aim is to articulate this idea further as a normative truth which can assert its own special truth in the face of all other kinds of knowledge. This need not be merely flat apologetics or the justification of what exists. In its sense for the task of constantly reshaping and deepening, it can be a continually advancing process of accommodation and immersion into the substance of one's own thought. But the meaning of theology always remains the drive towards what is normative in religion, to personal conviction and the combination of this conviction with the community's tradition, because this is generally and in principle regarded or recognised as containing truth and validity' ('Religionsphilosophie', pp.126f.).

same time allowing his ethical impulses to be tested and confirmed or modified in confrontation with historical reality.

This fundamental 'openness' of Troeltsch's science of religion contrasts sharply with the authority-bound procedures of traditional theological method – what Troeltsch called the 'dogmatic method' of supernaturalism. It respects the phenomenon of religion and provides a solution to the dilemma faced by university faculties of theology which want to maintain their traditional concern with normative religious truth in a secular and pluralist climate in which confessional faculties, such as survive in Germany and Scotland, are arguably anachronistic. It avoids both that confessional Scylla and the unconfessional Charybdis of a purely historical 'Christian Studies' or purely descriptive comparative study of religions, which exclude or bracket the question of truth, and therefore fail to provide any justification for their existence outside historical, classical or oriental faculties. Troeltsch's multidisciplinary and polymethodic approach to the study of religion and religions, in which their truth-claims are considered philosophically alongside the necessary descriptive studies, provides the appropriate model for Religious Studies in a secular university. Within it, Christian theology might well receive more emphatic recognition than it did in non-confessional departments of historical theology or Biblical studies, because it is important data for the student of religion ('Religionsphilosophie', p.128). Troeltsch saw that nineteenth-century protestant thought would require especially close attention because it was here that a great religious tradition learned painfully to re-express itself in confrontation with the intellectual revolution of the modern era. By the same token Troeltsch himself is now a key figure in the study of modern religious thought within departments of religion.

The most important question is whether this Troeltschian style of Religious Studies will lead into more truth than the old-fashioned dogmatics of the confessional faculties. Troeltsch's own solutions will not suffice, but his method can be developed. Instead of narrowing theology to a 'science of Christianity', which is the option taken by most modern theology since Schleiermacher, it might be right to broaden it to embrace (in principle) all reality. That would correspond to the Christian view of God as the reality that determines everything and is advocated in Pannenberg's account of theology as the 'science of God'.[82]

Those who follow the Schleiermacherian rather than the Hegelian strand in Troeltsch's thought, and prefer to concentrate upon religion

---

[82] *Wissenschaftstheorie und Theologie, op.cit.*, pp.299ff.

as an autonomous field of enquiry, will find his suggestions for a comparative historical study of religions fruitful. They provide a basis for the kind of discussion between competing religious traditions which today is clearly needed. It is not necessary to abandon the fundamentally missionary stance of Christianity (or Buddhism) to recognise that this must today proceed on a basis of mutual respect and understanding. Syncretism is inevitable, and it may well be as enriching today as it was in the early period of Christianity.[83] But in this situation, a criterion of what is distinctively Christian is more necessary than ever, and it is difficult to find this anywhere except in christology. With all due appreciation of Troeltsch's achievement, and gratitude for the continuing validity of his insights, it is therefore necessary to end these comments on Troeltsch and Christian theology by repeating the note of criticism which has already been sounded. Approval may be expressed through a quotation from Kant which Troeltsch took more seriously than most of his successors: 'A religion which rashly declares war on reason will not be able to hold out in the long run against it.'[84] In criticism one may strike a note of personal confession, in the form of a Luther quotation.[85] Since 'the cross is the basis and test of christology' (Kähler), the limits of one editor's agreement with Troeltsch may be summed up thus: *crux sola est nostra theologia.*

[83] The concept has had an unhappy history in Christian theology, ever since Gunkel called Christianity a syncretistic religion (1903). But see M. Pye 'Syncretism and Ambiguity', *Numen* XXVIII, 1971, pp.83-93 for a positive evaluation. The possibilities of mutual enrichment are well exemplified by J.S. Donne, *The Way of all the Earth*, Sheldon Press, London, 1974.

[84] *Religion within the Limits of Reason Alone*, New York, 1960, p.9.

[85] *WA* 5, 176, 32f.

Troeltsch and the Science of Religion
Michael Pye

The importance of Troeltsch's thought for the study of religion is greater than is sometimes realised. Those who have laboured on his substantial corpus of writings have tended to approach problems defined either in theological terms or in sociological terms. Major theses have concentrated for example on the implications of his historicist theorising for the truth of Christianity or for the validity of permanent religious values.[1] On the sociological side Troeltsch's classification of church, sect and mystical religion has been so influential that he can no longer be subtracted from the admittedly erratic story of attempts to categorise religious groups.[2] His relationship to Weber and his gradually emergent position with respect to Marxist theory have also been taken up in an interesting way.[3]

The 'science of religion', however, is neither just theology nor just sociology. In Troeltsch's writings we see it emerging as an independent third force and indeed as something of a pivotal centre between theology and sociology. Its importance and its strength lies in the fact that it sets out a two-branched presupposition which theology and sociology ignore at their peril. First, theology has to reckon at every turn with a range of religious data which are relevant to itself yet firmly set in the varied cultural and social contexts of human history. Secondly, sociology, unless it is hopelessly to prejudge questions which lie far beyond its competence as an empirical discipline, has to reckon with the fact that religious data are phenomena which require

[1] Walter Bodenstein, *Neige des Historismus. Ernst Troeltschs Entwicklungsgang*, Gütersloh, 1959; Eckhard Lessing, *Die Geschichtsphilosophie Ernst Troeltschs*, Hamburg-Bergstedt, 1965; A.O. Dyson, *History in the Philosophy and Theology of Ernst Troeltsch*, Diss. Oxford Univ., 1968; and J. Klapwijk, *Tussen Historisme en Relativisme*, Amsterdam, 1970.

[2] The matter is summarised and the difficulties made apparent in James Allen Dator's account of a Japanese religious movement, *Soka Gakkai; Builders of the Third Civilization: American and Buddhist Members*, Seattle, 1969.

[3] See Hans Bosse's *Marx, Weber, Troeltsch*, München and Mainz, 1970. On Bosse's account of Troeltsch's view of Marx, however, see further below.

to be explored in their own right, and, at least in the first instance, in their own terms. The 'science of religion' is therefore aligned at one and the same time with a thorough-going historicism and with an 'idealist' non-reductionism. This uneasy yet unavoidable balancing act reflects indeed the central problem of Troeltsch's philosophy of history. Precisely the rejection of any easy foreclosure of this problem by the introduction of neo-orthodox religious or anti-religious 'positivist' presuppositions is the typically modern and critical feature of his approach. Because of it there emerges a middle ground for the modern scientific study of religion which takes the data of its own research seriously and attempts to provide a satisfactory başis of knowledge and understanding for the consideration of various more broadly ranging questions. Troeltsch's writing furthermore reflects particularly broadly the emergence of the science of religion from the nurseries of philosophy, theology and history.[4] For this reason, and because of the presuppositions already mentioned, he represents a nodal point in the clarification of the status of the study of religion as a discipline in its own right. In this respect he deserves to be accorded a position at least comparable to the early figures of the so-called 'phenomenological' school in the study of religion. Indeed, as the most theoretically reflective representative of the 'history-of-religions school' in late nineteenth and early twentieth century theology, it is surprising that Troeltsch has not been considered much more widely by later writers in this field.

Two of the essays translated in the present volume are particularly interesting in this regard. The first of course is 'Religion and the Science of Religion'. This essay is of great historical interest in that it shows how a leading thinker in this field conceived of the inter-relationships between the various areas of investigation and reflection which today in the English-speaking world are often collectively referred to as 'Religious Studies'. Diverse judgments on various aspects of this will no doubt be maintained by many, but Troeltsch's main point of emphasis, which will be discussed further below, remains quite relevant to contemporary work. The second essay of interest here is 'What Does"Essence of Christianity"Mean?'. It is obvious from the title as it is from the argument that Troeltsch did not himself explicitly conceive of this essay as being about the 'science of religion' as such. Nevertheless its presuppositions are uniform with his understanding of the latter and it is strikingly relevant not only to the understanding of Christianity, but to the understanding of any major, coherent and

---

[4] See also for example his essay: 'Theologie und Religionswissenschaft des 19 Jahrhunderts'.

cumulative tradition. This has implications for a set of problems in the general study of religion which have not hitherto come sufficiently to the fore. What follows below is mainly based on these two essays, and is an attempt to bring out, in all brevity, some principles evident in Troeltsch's writing which remain of importance for the scientific study of religion today.

1. *The science of religion*

Troeltsch was anything but one of those narrow and cautious academics who try to keep a private little patch of thought all to themselves, where strangers are strictly discouraged and whence they themselves never venture to emerge. On the contrary it is evident that Troeltsch was attracted precisely by the complexity of things and by the way in which one set of questions leads on to another. Thus while speaking of 'the science of religion' in a limited sense, in the essay on the subject translated above, he could not forbear to set his ideas in the whole historical context of European thought, nor to show how the study of religion as a datum may be linked to much wider questions about its truth and value. However, in spite of the breadth of his perspective, the reader should not overlook his central assertion. This is that within the welter of problems which arise in the general interpretation of religion there is an initial study of it which neither rejects the potential truth of religion out of hand as an illusion, nor in itself is affirmative or prescriptive of particular religious values.

In the very first part of his argument there is a fine statement of the need to maintain the internal integrity of the data before developing comprehensive explanations or appraisals. 'The way must be held open for religion to be fully apprehended. It must be possible to analyse it in its own terms. It must be examined at least provisionally as a completely independent phenomenon, which it claims itself after all to be. It must not be made subject from the start to general theories which prescribe in a prejudicial way what in religion is justifiable and what is not.'[5] The reader should not be confused by his characterisation of the alternatives in this context as 'critical idealism', which he prefers, and 'positivism' which he rejects. He stresses that 'idealism' is intended to bear here a most limited meaning: 'It by no means entails an interpretation of religion determined in advance or the unfair insertion of philosophical postulates of a metaphysical kind into the religious ideas.'[6] What has emerged as important is 'the examination of religious phenomena as

[5] ET, p.85.
[6] ET, p.86.

these are available in the realm of historical, psychological reality', or an 'independent enquiry into the factual world of the religious consciousness'.[7] It is on the basis of such an equiry that more comprehensive questions arise, questions for the philosophy of religion or for theology.

The fact that Troeltsch himself, at this other level of discussion, did arrive at positive conclusions about religion should not be allowed to obscure his scrupulous concern to demarcate these judgments in his mind from the enquiry into the way in which religion exists as a historical, social and psychological phenomenon. The opening sentence of the second part of the essay is quite clear: 'The science of religion therefore does not produce religion or give birth to true religion, but it analyses and appraises religiosity as a datum.'[8] In other words, the science of religion as such is not theologically creative, but it observes and characterises religion as it historically exists. It may be a prolegomenon for theology, or it may not. Admittedly there are various contexts in Troeltsch's writing where the characterisation of the nature of religion took the place formerly held by natural theology, that is, where it turns out to be a value which seeks confirmation and completion in revelation. Indeed the closing sentences of the essay under discussion reflect this too. However, he saw the science of religion as being, in principle, 'an independent field of work'.[9] The further possibilities about the meaning of religion arise from the phenomenon itself, and Troeltsch was certainly desirous of letting them arise, not as what was originally to be demonstrated all along, but as problems to be taken up at a further philosophical or theological level.

The 'idealist' presupposition is pressed into service to maintain precisely the integrity of the datum spoken of above, and it may be argued indeed that Troeltsch was aiming at the effect more generally associated in recent times with the 'phenomenology of religion' school. Indeed, although Troeltsch is also sometimes to be described, quite correctly, as 'a theologian', he was often clearer in his distinctions between 'the science of religion' and theology than were some of the 'phenomenologists of religion' who attempted self-consciously to distance themselves from theology. Or one had perhaps better say that Troeltsch as a thinker could not be entirely described with just any one of these available disciplinary labels, for he moved from history to philosophy and from science to theology, with full knowledge of what he was about. At the same time it might seem

[7] ET, p.86.
[8] ET, p.88.
[9] ET, p.88.

today that his account of the frontiers with which he was familiar is more heavily laden with philosophical allegiance than is strictly necessary. Is it not possible to share his recognition of a non-prejudicial science of religion which allows the various important questions of interpretation to arise out of the existence of the datum before us, but which does not necessarily require a neo-Kantian or Schleiermacherian view of the religious *a priori*?

This point needs a little more attention. Given the four possible major theories of religion which Troeltsch set out in competition with each other,[10] it may indeed be that the neo-Kantian stance is to be preferred. However, one may argue that in adopting this position[11] Troeltsch was taking a distinct further step beyond the definitions immediately available to the scientific study of religion. He was in fact going on to relate what is scientifically knowable about religion to the major problems of human thought in general. It would be a pity if these further endeavours led the reader to lose sight again of what earlier had been won for the integrity of the science of religion as an independent field of activity based on 'the *possibility* of seeing in religion a qualitatively individual and creative power of spiritual life'.[12] If his writing is taken carefully, as a whole, what we observe is the emergence of an initial non-partisan study of religion followed by wider excursions into questions of a necessarily more controversial nature. When he writes that 'the following sketch of what, in the opinion of the present writer, the science of religion should be, cannot be a neutral one',[13] this refers apparently to the initial selection of the presupposition that the data of religion, as cultural facts, should be treated unprejudicially with respect to their coherent integrity and possible general validity. It is on such a basis that Troeltsch conceived of a broadening out of the enquiry into other areas which he specified as epistemology, philosophy of history and the philosophical treatment of the idea of God.

It is perhaps unfortunate that Troeltsch spoke rather loosely of all these, too, as part of 'the science of religion' in what must be taken as a broader sense. In fact the problems which he refers to under these three heads all pertain to questions of truth and value, and of course they are problems which the existence of the data, considered unprejudicially, challenge us to face. Sometimes he puts it more clearly. 'However much the modern development of the science of religion has led to the aim of understanding religion in the first

---

[10] ET, pp.102-110.
[11] ET, p.110.
[12] ET, p.86, italics added.
[13] ET, p.110.

instance in its own terms, this is always a matter of "in the first instance". In the last analysis there quite rightly persist the questions ... about the validation of religious ideas or about the way in which they are related to knowledge as a whole."[14] In sum 'the science of religion' in the narrower sense is really a distinct and necessary phase in the overall articulation of our thought about religion. The question of an overall interpretation of religion, whether neo-Kantian, Marxist, neo-Orthodox, Buddhist, or anything else, is one which goes much further, but for the solution of which the distinct, unprejudicial, reliably ordered phase of 'the science of religion' is in any case an indispensable prerequisite.

2. *The nature of religion*

According to Troeltsch the modern science of religion is correctly described as 'an enquiry into the *essence of religion*' provided that the expression 'is intended to imply a methodological shift from the attempt at a metaphysical determination of the religious objects or of the idea of God to an enquiry into religion as a phenomenon of consciousness'.[15] Here again we observe the shift of stance so often associated with the 'phenomenological' school in the study of religion, a shift away from philosophical or theological reflection upon God himself, or his equivalents, and towards the religious system, or the religious powers, as something present to the believer or the participant.

The phrase 'nature of religion' translates the German *Wesen der Religion*, which is an embarrassment to any translator. *Wesen* must surely sometimes be rendered with the more high-flown 'essence' as indeed it was in the title and text of the third essay presented in this volume. The title of the essay now under consideration was more difficult and it seemed better to speak here of 'the nature of religion'.[16] In the main text the term 'essence' has been preferred with reference to religion as a phenomenon in order to bring out the suggestion of 'true nature' or 'essential character' which the word *Wesen* tends to bear. It has been argued elsewhere that this idea of 'the essence of religion' in some ways led Troeltsch astray,[17] but it will be noticed

[14] ET, p.112, cf. ET, p.86.

[15] ET, p.111.

[16] This was partly demanded because the second half of the title 'Wesen der Religion und der Religionsgeschichte' reads 'and of the science of religion', and with respect to this latter the term 'essence' is less appropriate than 'nature'.

[17] 'The End of the Problem About "Other" Religions', among papers from the University of Lancaster Colloquium of January 1974, edited by John Powell Clayton under the title *Ernst Troeltsch and the Future of Theology*, London, 1976.

that he himself warns in this essay about the confusions which it can easily engender. All in all, 'it gives the impression that it might be possible to answer the various problems tied up in it all by one and the same enquiry, at a stroke'.[18] Whatever we may think of the usefulness of the expression 'essence of religion', Troeltsch was surely right to distinguish at this point[19] between the enquiry into religion as an object of consciousness, that is, as historical and cultural, sociological and psychological fact, and all those further questions about the meaning and validity of religion to which the brute fact gives rise.

A striking feature of the notion *Wesen der Religion*, however it is translated, is that it is above all a *reflective* notion. As an idea, it belongs firmly in that area of reflection about religion which has gradually crystallised into 'the science of religion', a process which Troeltsch took considerable pains to characterise. The object of reflection itself, however, lies on the side of what Troeltsch called 'naive' religion. To speak of 'naive' religion is not to speak disparagingly, but to distinguish quite appropriately between spontaneous, unaffected religion, and religion influenced by the developing rational and scientific consciousness of man. The distinction is perhaps rather similar to that drawn by Schiller between 'naive' and 'sentimental' poetry (*naive und sentimentale Dichtung*), in which the latter is more expressly conceived, even contrived, than the former, while nevertheless being dependent upon the unreflective naive form for its understanding of what poetry really is to begin with. In the case of religion the distinction gives rise to a major and unavoidable tension, the importance of which is signalised by the lengthy passages on the scientific treatment of religion in Troeltsch's essay. Along with these are to be found his suggestions on how, indirectly, it is still possible now in this extremely self-conscious age to approach 'naive' religion. He argues for one thing, as others have done, that help in this direction may be sought in the observation of primitive societies still relatively unaffected by science. Other methods are to observe outstanding religious personalities, one-sided or extreme religious groups, and the most distinctly religious moments in the experience of the observer himself. Of course there are difficulties with all of these, but it is along such paths, says Troeltsch, that 'one is likely to grasp the characteristic and essential features of this sphere of culture'.[20]

For all this Troeltsch does not hold up naive religion as something for which we should have a romantic yearning. It may 'indicate for us

---

[18] ET, p.111.
[19] ET, pp.111f.
[20] ET, p.92.

the essential characteristics of the phenomenon'[21] but it also 'requires everywhere the correctives of scientific education and discipline, quietness and harmony, objective knowledge of the world ... '[22]. In this respect the science of religion may have a distinctive role to play, and indeed Troeltsch becomes perhaps a little too enthusiastic about the positive necessity for scientific work on religion to influence religion itself.[23] At that point he is of course speaking from an evaluatory position as a surveyor of the role of science in civilisation as a whole. He is not speaking with regard to the more limited question of the identity and integrity of the study of religion as a specific area of enquiry.

Another route along which Troeltsch travelled in his attempt to indicate the distinctive nature or essential characteristics of religion was in his discussion of religious sensibility as an *a priori* in a neo-Kantian sense. This is an extremely vexed and confusing subject and it cannot be pursued in detail here.[24] However it should be pointed out at least that Troeltsch's use of Kantian terms in this respect was quite different from that of Rudolf Otto in his well-known book *The Idea of the Holy* (*Das Heilige*).[25] Otto attempted to argue, in a most un-Kantian way, that the sense of the numinous is an *irrational a priori*. For Troeltsch, by contrast, there is 'an *a priori* law of the formulation of religious ideas existing in the nature of reason, and standing in an organic relationship to the other *a priori* principles of reason'.[26] Troeltsch did not believe that epistemological considerations along these lines constituted in any sense a proof of the existence of that which in the religious consciousness is believed to be known. However he did find that religion held a place analogous to that of other important areas of reason, namely the philosophical, historical, ethical and aesthetic.[27] His discussion of this matter, it should again be stressed, really begins to go beyond the science of religion in the narrower sense referred to earlier. It is possible to share many of Troeltsch's methodological distinctions without necessarily sharing the view that it is in terms of such an *a priori* that the validity or truth of religion is to be established.

A third characteristic of Troeltsch's approach towards the nature, or the essence, of religion, is his stress on 'the psychology of religion'

[21] ET, p.92.
[22] ET, p.92.
[23] Cf. ET, p.93f.
[24] The details of his argument with Paul Spiess can be pursued in the article 'Zur Frage des religiösen Apriori', reprinted in *G.S.* II.
[25] Rudolf Otto, *The Idea of the Holy*, Harmondsworth, 1923, 1959.
[26] ET, p.115.
[27] Cf. ET, p.116.

as the basic prerequisite for further reflections.[28] This expression comes into play for two reasons. One simple reason is that he is looking ahead to the discussion about 'epistemology' for which the 'psychology' is the prolegomenon. The other reason is that Troeltsch half shares a general assumption that it is inward religious experience which really counts. This general assumption is widely found in studies of religion today because of the influence of Otto's work referred to above and of later writers such as Joachim Wach.[29] The latter's stress on religious feeling as that which is distinctively essential to religion has already been criticised by the present writer, in favour of the view that religion begins and ends as an interrelated complex including social form as well as affective states.[30] But Troeltsch's specific use of the term 'psychology' perhaps needs more sympathetic attention, if only to avoid anachronism. He is clearly using it in a very much broader sense than we should expect it to bear today. The reader should therefore not take too seriously the phrase 'psychology of religion' itself, but examine the way in which Troeltsch elaborates his theme.

He uses the phrase to include, oddly enough, such varied items as 'faith in a presence of the divine', 'the ethical and social elements of religion', and 'the forms taken by ritual and by mythical thought'.[31] Troeltsch even speaks in this connection of 'a morphology of religious thought', as well as investigating psychological states of affairs in religion. The whole importance of this very general enquiry for him is that 'the phenomenon has to be seen in its factuality and in its objective individuality before we can ask about its validity'.[32] It seems indeed to be more or less equivalent to the initial science of religion already discussed. It is perhaps a justifiable gloss on Troeltsch's argument to say that there are social, ritual, conceptual and affective aspects to the phenomenon, none of which should be subtracted from the whole or arbitrarily subordinated to the other aspects. That is, there should be no methodological favouritism in this respect. There may indeed turn out to be a case of religion in which the particular data themselves include the attachment of particular importance to some one of these, for example to inward mystical experience rather than to social or conceptual aspects. This however would have to be the conclusion of particular studies which proceed without an initial presupposition that inward experience is necessarily always the most

---

[28] ET, pp.114ff.
[29] Joachim Wach, *The Comparative Study of Religions*, New York, 1958.
[30] Michael Pye, *Comparative Religion*, Newton Abbot, 1972, pp.26f.
[31] ET, pp.114f.
[32] ET, p.114.

important aspect. It is to be regretted that Troeltsch somewhat obscured the variety of the data of religion at this point (though he could scarcely help but betray it again) by subsuming everything under the phrase 'psychology of religion'. His real underlying interests call for an articulated yet phenomenological approach to what in every case is a complex set of data, presenting conceptual, behavioural, psychological and social aspects in continuous interaction.

3. *Correlations and criticisms*

If Troeltsch breathed Kantian air he also breathed Hegelian. The partial stress on the inwardness of religion noticed above has to be counter-balanced by the way in which Troeltsch viewed it as one of the major forces of social and intellectual history. He saw these matters on the same scale as Hegel, but it is important to notice that he rejected Hegelian metaphysics. This is made clear not only in the essay translated above[33] but also in the section on Hegel in *Der Historismus und seine Probleme*, where he emphasised the need for an empirical rather than a metaphysical basis for historical understanding.[34] Hegel, he characterised, saw history as Mind understanding itself and its own emergence, and this Spinoza-like identity theory, he argued, meant that for Hegel things changed in form but not in reality. This in turn meant that Hegel's history, when all is said and done, turned into a set of schemes illustrating an idea. Troeltsch himself therefore was not a Hegelian in any precise sense.

At the same time he could be described as post-Hegelian, as in different ways were also Marx, and Weber. These three all thought of history as being to do with the development and interaction of social and cultural forces. They all took history to be about, not dynasties and battles, but broadly based social, economic and ideological trends and conflicts. They all thought it was possible on the basis of detailed empirical studies to speak in more general terms about matters of far-ranging importance. Each one in his own way contrived to develop specialised abstractions which were meant to have a wide application as a means to this end.

At a personal level Troeltsch was attracted to Weber's work in Heidelberg and by this route he developed further, if rather late, his appraisal of Marxist theory. In one important respect Troeltsch had what one might call a purely professional respect for Marx which

---

[33] ET, pp.104-6.
[34] *G.S.* III, pp.243-77.

finds expression in *Der Historismus und seine Probleme*.[35] By contrast with Hegel's interest in nation-states Marx's achievement was to bring out a whole new range of complexes in history, namely economically defined social classes which cut across and beyond the rise and fall of nation-states. Troeltsch seems to have admired this perspective quite theoretically as a skilful new departure in our way of looking at the past. In this judgment he left on one side the issue of the materialist world-view and indeed he left on the other side questions about practical socialism. He stressed that Marx's dialectic of history was not inextricably linked to materialist metaphysics. As to practical socialism, he seemed to think of this as a quite separate matter, just as practical Church questions were rather left on one side in his theoretical reflections on theology.

It is odd that Troeltsch's respect for Marx as an innovator and a creator of useful new abstractions for dealing with historical data seems to have been rather ignored in Bosse's *Marx, Weber, Troeltsch*. Perhaps the main reason for this is that Troeltsch is there being cast in the role of 'idealist' over against the Marxist world-view. Bosse stresses Troeltsch's attachment to 'idealist' metaphysics quite strongly, emphasises the deep gulf between this and the thought of Marx, and repeats Gollwitzer's warning that Christian theology should not necessarily be attached to such metaphysics.[56] Bosse seems to be using Troeltsch here as an example of what one should not do from the Christian point of view in the context of the Christian-Marxist dialogue of today. It is indeed appropriate, one may concur, to point out that Christian faith is not inevitably tied to specifically idealist metaphysics. It is also fair to follow Troeltsch in differentiating between different aspects of Marx's thought, namely metaphysics, history and practical prescription. It is a matter of present-day importance to point out, as is done by some Polish Catholics, that socialism as a practical programme ('ideology') is not inevitably tied to a materialist and atheist world-view ('*Weltanschauung*').[37]

In spite of the exigencies of contemporary debate, however, care should be taken over the treatment of Troeltsch's relationship to Marxism. Admittedly Troeltsch was in a sense a 'critical idealist', namely in the sense that he disciplined himself with the limitations imposed on all thinking about truth and values since Kant. The starting point for any knowledge of truth or of values must be located

[35] Especially *G.S.* III, pp.315-17.

[36] Bosse, *Marx, Weber, Troeltsch*, p.99, n.50.

[37] See e.g. Jozef Wojcik, 'Christianity, Socialism and Peace', in *Catholic Life in Poland*, 4 (99), Warsaw, 1974.

in the mind of man and not elsewhere within or without the universe. He could also be described loosely as an idealist in that he shared with Weber the belief that ideas are a potent initiatory factor in history. To go further, however, Troeltsch was quite strikingly other than Kantian in his stress on the social and cultural conditioning of all ideas. Indeed it is remarkable that, in spite of some neo-Kantian passages, that which became the major problem for Troeltsch was exactly the problem about how, *taking account of historical change*, it is possible to locate normative values in any finally secure position at all. This is the central problem of his investigations into the philosophy of history. It is ironic that Marxists have generally had a much more naive view of the way in which normative values may be linked to or perceived in historical movements.

As far as religion in particular is concerned, Troeltsch to some extent shared Marx's criticism of the values promulgated by Christian institutions. This point is admitted by Bosse who wrote, perhaps again reflecting present-day fashions: 'Troeltsch does not want to lag behind Marx in the criticism of hypocritical religious forms.'[38] However Troeltsch remained convinced that there is also positive value in religious ideas, as well as mere potency, and that there is a particular value in Christian ideas. Insofar as such value is denied in Marx's thought, Troeltsch's assessment was bound to include a negative note as well as a positive one, as when he wrote: 'Nowhere was Marx so *diabolically perceptive* as in the disclosure of these interconnexions (*sc.* between class conflicts and ideologies) and in the tracing back of all political, ethical and religious pathos to material class interests.'[39] The give-away phrase certainly reflects Troeltsch's loyalty to the Christian theological tradition, and to that extent he cannot escape responsibility for all that is justified in Marxist criticism. However, it is also quite necessary to recognise that Troeltsch viewed this tradition from a modern viewpoint and in a critical manner, and for this reason the patronising comment that 'supported by idealist metaphysics he can confidently assert the independence of religion'[40] is too simple. It has already been seen that Troeltsch's overall response to the Marxist view and to the problem of history is more complex than this. Indeed Troeltsch's reflections on historical method must make uncomfortable reading equally for the naive Marxist and for the naive idealist.

A further complication lies in the fact that Weber's critique of the

[38] Bosse, *Marx, Weber, Troeltsch*, p.97.
[39] *G.S.* III, p.352. The italics were quite fairly introduced by Bosse who also quotes this passage.
[40] Bosse, *Marx, Weber, Troeltsch*, p.97.

unicausality of Marxist theory, a critique of which Troeltsch approved, has not been refuted, and indeed it is not easy to see how the problem ever will be resolved. This important matter is not a question of a mere confrontation between 'materialism' and 'idealism'. It remains a problem for all empirical, historical and sociological investigation, that is for the kind of investigation which all three writers took to be the real basis of their work with abstractions, ideal types, historical periodisations, and so on. Methodological affinities and differences are more interesting than a mere division into materialists and idealists.

With respect to religion the interests of the three can perhaps be described briefly as follows. Marx and Weber both attempted correlations between socio-economic factors and religious factors, but stressed the causal priority of the one or the other set respectively. Weber and Troeltsch both stressed the importance of the religious idea (whatever it may be in a particular case) in the form in which the believer or the participant himself took it to be important. However, Troeltsch and Marx also have something very important in common which lies at the heart of their method. They both assumed that socio-historical data are not just raw material for historical and comparative study, but also provide the area within which our grasp of values and goals for humanity is to be fashioned. In this sense they are both not only historians and social theorists but, in a manner, prophets too. Marx, one might say, worked in a manner analogous to the later historicist theologian, and it is a pity that his followers have so often lapsed into the sort of obscurantist piety which also besets Christianity. The truly modern Marxist, and the modern theologian, are above all critical in their appraisal and restatement of tradition.

These various points of contact, methodologically speaking, between the three writers, can be expressed diagrammatically as below. The triangular form may help to correct impressions given by the linear series 'Marx, Weber, Troeltsch'.

Explanatory correlations between religious
and socio-economic factors

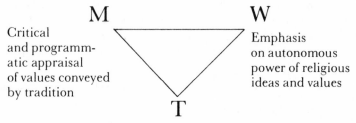

M   W

Critical   Emphasis
and programm-   on autonomous
atic appraisal   power of religious
of values conveyed   ideas and values
by tradition

T

Of course, qualifications are immediately called for with respect to such a simple diagram. For example, Troeltsch certainly also recognised the appropriateness of the search for explanatory correlations between religious and socio-economic factors, though this did not become a major preoccupation for him as it was for Weber. Moreover, the methodological analogies must of course not be confused with the varying intentions and substantial conclusions of the three writers.

These reflections have taken us beyond 'the science of religion' in the narrower sense referred to earlier, and quite rightly so. The very existence of the data of religion in history poses *first* a task of characterisation and structured appraisal, but then leads the observer on to major questions such as whether religious ideas have an independent validity of their own, or not. Troeltsch was quite aware that this was *an issue*, and hence spent time on it. As an issue however it must be seen to lie beyond the initial task of the science of religion. It is 'in the first instance' that the phenomena are to be treated in their own terms. Thereafter 'idealist metaphysics' are certainly put to the test just as any other overall theory of religion has to be, and the fact that some religious forms are themselves historically 'idealist' is neither here nor there. The perspectives envisaged by Troeltsch lead us on from the initial characterisation of religion to much wider issues in the philosophy of religion, in the sociological interpretation of religion and in critical theology, in short to the whole field of what we nowadays call, in English, religious studies.

4. *Interpreting religious traditions*

There is one remaining aspect of Troeltsch's thought which needs to be drawn into the picture here, namely his view of what it means to interpret a religious tradition in its total historical perspective. His understanding of this was better than that of the sociologists, which is understandable though regrettable, better than that of 'the phenomenological school' in the study of religion, who have unfortunately rather ignored the matter, and better also than that of many theologians who have worked since, which is quite inexcusable. The classical statement of what it means to interpret a religious tradition on the basis of an uncompromisingly modern historical perspective is found in the essay 'What does "essence of Christianity" mean?' translated above.

The essay is really an analysis of theological method and was not intended specifically to be a contribution to the scientific study of religion. Nevertheless it so happens that since it is about theological method based upon the presuppositions of modern history it deals with problems which arise in the attempt to discuss or define any major religious tradition approached on the same basis. Although the essay no doubt remains relevant to contemporary theology, the following brief characterisation of his approach, and remarks thereon, are directed not towards theology as such but towards the relevance of Troeltsch's perspective to the general study of religious traditions. A related but different argument, including a brief summary of the essay, was published some time ago.[41]

In Troeltsch's experience the work of a Christian theologian emerges as that of critically attending to the tradition which bears to him that with which he is concerned, recognising the full breadth and intricacy of all the competing formulations which have come into being through the centuries, testing and distilling and then creatively expressing the central meaning in the context of modern knowledge. The 'essence' of the tradition is elaborated and chiselled in a process of historical abstraction, in a manner analogous indeed to the way in which the 'spirit' of any great historical movement has to be discerned. At the same time that which is conveyed to us through the tradition has the possibility of communicating itself as an overwhelming value which by its sheer power finds its way on through the lives of its living mediators. 'To define the essence is to shape it afresh'[42] is one of Troeltsch's shortest sentences, and one of his best. This refers neither to some antiquarian interest in the past, nor to some arbitrary theology plucked from the skies. He is speaking rather of a creative joining of historical reflection, which is open to all the discipline of science, and theological affirmation in a new form, meeting the exigencies of the present time.

Theology is more than history because of the creative opening to the future. At the same time theology for Troeltsch emerged intimately from the previous historical forms of the Christian religion among which of course the time of Christian origins has a quite special place. There is no source for Christian theology which is not historically and socially conditioned and mediated, and indeed it is for this reason that there is no absolute touch-stone and no final definition of the essence of Christianity. On the other hand even general historical work of the most modest kind soon has to begin to use abstracted concepts such as Christianity, Stoicism, Islam, Renaissance, and so on, and this means that any historical perspective which goes beyond the most circumscribed field of research is gradually drawn to a stage where

[41] 'Comparative Hermeneutics in Religion', in M. Pye and R. Morgan (eds.), *The Cardinal Meaning*, The Hague, 1973.

[42] ET, p.162.

stances are adopted, judgements are made and values formed.

In this sense, however, *any* religious tradition which has a more or less coherent history must as a series of data give rise to questions about its value or meaning. Such questions can perhaps be suppressed or set aside in some kinds of historical work which are not directly concerned with religious traditions. However if the subject of study is nothing less than a religious tradition itself, and if this is to be understood according to 'the science of religion', and at least 'in the first instance' in its own terms, the question of the essential meaning of the tradition inevitably arises with great force. Moreover, the question is answered again and again by every successive exponent of the tradition who stands within it, and this means that the historian of the tradition has to know at each point how and where the matter is being taken, and at what point he himself either retires from offering definitions of any kind or else himself becomes a participant theologian or the equivalent of such. To begin to give an answer to the question about the essential meaning is really to go on beyond the history, just as theology goes beyond history in Troeltsch's essay. But to pretend that the question does not arise at all, or that it cannot be answered in any way, is to court disaster at a fairly elementary stage in the study of religion. To be aware of this subtle boundary is one of the chief responsibilities of anyone who strives to understand religion in terms of 'the science of religion' or 'the phenomenological study of religion'.

Troeltsch himself did not extend the analogies given in the essay on the essence of Christianity to the problems of interpreting *any* religion, except by incidental suggestion.[43] Such an extension of the argument is justifiable because, as Troeltsch himself rightly held, all the religious traditions are fundamentally analogous systems of human culture, even though they may by no means be of equal value or significance. The important fact for the present time is that the varied religious traditions which have any claim to diachronic coherence all stand in an analogous position to each other for the historian of religion. If the historian of religion takes the coherence of these traditions as seriously as the believers or participants do, and he must in the first instance do this insofar as he is studying just those believers or participants, then he finds himself on the verge of diverse possibilities of meaning and interpretation. At this point he has to recognise that the science of religion may be left behind, though it is still to be presupposed, and that the shaping afresh of that which is

---

[43] ET, p.130. The present writer has attempted both to take this step and to urge the possible value of a comparative approach to such questions (see note 41 above).

before him cannot help but begin. At such a point he can either withdraw, return to the history, and perhaps just fall short of grasping the inner heartbeat of the religion in question, or he can allow himself to be impelled forward and assume responsibility for a critically refined affirmation or rejection of some specific meaning or value. What begins to happen at this threshold goes beyond the science of religion in the narrow sense, and it jostles in with all those further questions raised in the philosophy of religion or in the attempts to create an overall sociological explanation or critique of religion, etc. Religion is at this point certainly open to diverse modes of interpretation, but at least one of the possible ones is the theological mode, or whatever in each case is the equivalent of the theological, namely that which critically searches the tradition in question in its own terms, and seeks to convey the net meaning in a contemporary affirmation of value.

Even from the start, however, the science of religion must itself be sensitive to this matter of changing, developing tradition, for otherwise the main point of meaning in a given instance of religion may well be missed. Unfortunately even at the level of initial characterisation the matter is not at all simple in that the modern observer, like Troeltsch, cannot just accept some arbitrary miraculous or dogmatic indication of what the tradition is. He is required to take 'a broad view over the totality of all the manifestations which are related to this idea'.[44] At the same time he will see in the dogmatic norms of tradition signposts to the location of the religious meaning which is being sought out.

For the believers themselves these signposts are discerned first of all in retrospect, the canon is formed from among a great number of available possibilities precisely with the intention of excluding some of them, later definitions take on their own importance in determining what it is that the canon is supposed to be about, competing lines of patriarchal or priestly authority are invented, conflated, redesigned, and so on. At any one point the future destiny of a religious tradition is not known, but what is clear is that its character up till then has continually been re-decided, even if the changes are almost imperceptible for long periods. In fact one may say that religious tradition is created retrospectively from out of each successive present, and with a view to the future. It is not really created authoritatively from the beginning of the religion, as most people naively conceive of it, and then simply unrolled towards them as the centuries pass. Rather it is continually recreated, so to say, backwards, and this is a

[44] ET, p.10.

process in which the believers share, more or less naively or purposefully.

The *shape* of the tradition is problematic at the outset, and it retains this problematic quality through decades and centuries. This is not in the least surprising, once it is perceived, for every new statement of what the tradition is about is a statement for its own time and place, and introduces a new style or a new way of linking ideas together. Such change is even a precondition of long-term loyalty, for history as a whole is always changing and a completely rigid idea begins to have a different meaning from before when it is given in a new context. Thus there is no rest from the question about the essence of a religious tradition either for believers or for observers. At the same time the tradition can never be completely shapeless or arbitrary without dissolving altogether. It is the shape given to it which locates the values or the meanings which are important for the believers or the participants.

Such matters, and the approach to them, discussed by Troeltsch with respect to Christianity, really arise in the discussion of any complex religious tradition. It is hopeless for the observer to imagine that he can capture a religion in a frozen state and ignore the diverse lines of interpretation which it almost certainly bears within itself. He must recognise the complexities involved in defining what it is that is being interpreted, and the varying possibilities have to be taken into account in any appraisal of the religious meanings or values. To some extent it is possible for the observer's characterisation of the meaning to shelter behind a precise definition of the group of believers or participants for whom it can be shown historically to have been valid. But this is only possible in initial small-scale studies. Any wider appraisal is bound to involve a certain venturing out beyond what is immediately controllable in this way.

5. *Conclusions*

Modern reflection upon the way in which religious traditions work and what sort of things it is necessary to enquire about with respect to them is still in a more or less adolescent stage. Troeltsch's general approach to the matter in the two essays mainly commented on above still reflects the struggle against pre-critical and pre-historical modes of thinking, and it is for this reason that it is in some ways too Kantian and in others too Hegelian for the comfort of many today. At the same time, quite apart from the many incidental matters of value in his writings, we shall do well if we remark particularly the following summary points which can be drawn from his work.

Religious meanings are located in the historical experience of mankind and the traditions which bear them are analogous to each other. Religions should be understood first of all in their own terms, without being prejudged as true or illusory. However, the phenomena themselves give rise to many questions of criticism and evaluation. They lead into major problems about human experience and knowledge and in broad terms they are open to diverse modes of explanation and interpretation. This means that there is a science of religion which in an immediate sense is entirely controlled by the data of the enquiry, but which is also the prolegomenon to a variety of more widely ranging questions. Furthermore, religions considered as coherent traditions with a historical dimension give rise to a special set of questions about their interpretation which the initial science of religion can neither ignore nor in itself finally answer.

Appendix
Troeltsch in English Translation

Works are listed in chronological order with date of original publication in German given in brackets. Where applicable, references are given to *Gesammelte Schriften II*, *Zur religiösen Lage*, *Religionsphilosophie und Ethik*, Tübingen, 1913 and 1922, and reprint Aalen, 1962. German titles may be found in Baron's almost complete bibliography at the end of *Gesammelte Schriften IV*, 1925, rp. 1966. This list includes in brackets several articles already translated but awaiting publication under the editorship of Professors James Luther Adams and Walter Bense. Further projects for the translation of *Der Historismus und Seine Probleme* (*G.S.* III, 1922) and *Vorlesungen über 'Glaubenslehre'* (1925) are not listed.

1. ('Historical and Dogmatic Method in Theology' (1898) – forthcoming. *G.S.* II, 729-753.)

2. *The Absoluteness of Christianity and the History of Religions* (1902). Eng.tr. David Reid, Virginia, 1971; London, 1972.

3. 'The Formal Autonomous Ethic of Conviction and the Objective Teleological Ethic of Value' (1902), from *Grundprobleme der Ethik*, *G.S.* II, 618-35, in Warren F. Groff and Donald E. Miller (eds.), *The Shaping of Modern Christian Thought*, Cleveland and New York, 1968.

4. 'The Ethic of Jesus' (1902), from *Grundprobleme der Ethik*, *G.S.* II, 629-39, in *The Unitarian Universalist Christian*, XXIX, no. 1-2 (Spring-Summer, 1974), 38-45.

5. 'What Does "Essence of Christianity" Mean?' (1903): see above, pp.124f. *G.S.* II, 386-451.

6. ('Modern Philosophy of History' (1904) – forthcoming. *G.S.* II, 673-728).

7. (*Political Ethics and Christianity* (1904) – forthcoming.)

8. 'Religion and the Science of Religion' (1906). See above pp.82f. *G.S.* II, 452-99.

9. ('The Essence of the Modern Spirit' (1907) – forthcoming. *G.S.* IV, 297-338.)

10. 'Half a Century of Theology: a Review' (1908). See above, pp.53f. *G.S.* II, 193-226.

11. ('The Dispositional Ethic' (1908) – forthcoming. From 'Luther und die moderne Welt', *G.S.* IV, 221-4, 226-7).

12. Articles in the *New Schaff-Herzog Encyclopedia of Religion* (1908-14) Deism (III, 391-7), Enlightenment (IV, 141-7), Idealism, German (V, 438-42), Moralists, British (VII, 496-502).

13. ('On the Question of the Religious *A Priori*: a reply to the observations of Paul Spiess' (1909) – forthcoming. *G.S.* II 754-68.) (See above, pp.20-32, for quotations from this essay.)

14. 'Calvin and Calvinism', *Hibbert Journal*, VIII (1909), 102-21.

15. 'On the Possibility of a Free Christianity' (An address at the Fifth International Congress for Free Christianity and Religious Progress, Berlin, 1910). *G.S.* II, 837-62. In *The Unitarian Universalist Christian*, XXIX, 1-2 (1974), 27-45. Excerpts also ed. C.W. Wendte.

16. (Articles in *Religion in Geschichte und Gegenwart*, 1st ed. (1910-1913). Eschatology, IV dogmatic (II, 622-32); Faith, III dogmatic (II, 1437-47); Faith and History, IV (II, 1447-56); Natural Law, Christian (IV, 697-704); Principle, Religious (IV, 1842-6) – see no. 42 below; Redemption, II dogmatic (II, 481-8) – forthcoming).

17. *The Significance of the Historical Existence of Jesus for Faith* (1911). See above, pp.182f.

18. ('Stoic-Christian Natural Law and Modern Secular Natural Law' (1911) – forthcoming. *G.S.* IV, 166-91.)

19. ('The Church in the Life of the Present' (1911) – forthcoming. *G.S.* II, 91-108.)

20. *Protestantism and Progress*, (1912). Beacon Press paperback, 1958. (Altered form of a lecture published in 1906 and enlarged 1911.))

21. *The Social Teachings of the Christian Churches* (*G.S.* I, 1912) Eng.tr. Olive Wyon, 1931; New York, 1960.

22. 'Empiricism and Platonism in the Philosophy of Religion' (To the Memory of William James) *Harvard Theological Review*, V 1912, 401-22. *G.S.* II, 364-85.

23. 'Religion, Economics, and Society' (1913) – forthcoming. *G.S.* IV, 21-33. Published also in Norman Birnbaum and Gertrude Lenzer (eds.), *Sociology and Religion*. Englewood Cliffs, N.J., 1969.

24. 'Renaissance and Reformation' (1913) – forthcoming. *G.S.* IV, 261-96. Published already in *History; Selected Readings*, vol. II, Eng.tr. Henry A. Finch, Chicago, 1948. Published also (in part) in a new translation by Lewis W. Spitz (ed.), *Problems in European Civilization: The Reformation: Material or Spiritual?* Boston, 1962.

25. ('Logos and Mythos in Theology and Philosophy of Religion' (1913) – forthcoming. *G.S.* II, 805-36.)

26. (*Christian Natural Law* (1913) – forthcoming. *G.S.* IV, 156-66.)

27. 'The Dogmatics of the "religionsgeschichtliche Schule",' *The American Journal of Theology*, XVII (1913). *G.S.* II, 500-24.

28. ('Ideological and Sociological Methods in Historical Research' (1913) review of Köhler, *Idee und Persönlichkeit in der Kirchengeschichte* – forthcoming. *G.S.* IV, 721-4.)

29. Articles in Hastings' *ERE* (1911-1915). Contingency (IV, 87-89), Free Thought (VI, 120-4), Historiography (VI, 716-23, reprinted in J. Macquarrie (ed.) *Contemporary Religious Thinkers*, London, 1968, pp.76-97), Idealism (VII, 89-95), Kant (VII, 653-9).

30. 'Motley of German War Ideas,' *New York Times*, 13 August 1915.

31. ('The Concept and Method of Sociology,' (1916). Review of Paul Barth, *Geschichtsphilosophie als Soziologie* – forthcoming. *G.S.* IV, 705-20).

32. ('Rival Methods for the Study of Religion,' first section of essay entitled 'Glaube und Ethos der hebräischen Propheten,' (1916) – forthcoming. *G.S.* IV, 34-8.)

33. 'The German Idea of Freedom' (1916), excerpt in W. Ebenstein, *Modern Political Thought* (New York, 1954), 315-16.

34. *Spectator Letters* (1919) excerpts in B.W. Wishy (ed.) *The Western World in the Twentieth Century* (Columbia, 1961), 151-6.

35. ('Max Weber' (1920) – forthcoming. From *Deutscher Geist und Westeuropa*, 1925.)

36. 'Adolf von Harnack and Ferdinand Christian von Baur' (1921) in W. Pauck, *Harnack and Troeltsch*, New York, 1968.

37. (*The Social Philosophy of Christianity* (1922) – forthcoming. Published originally as a brochure.)

38. ('My Books' (1922) – forthcoming. *G.S.* IV, 3-18.) See above, pp.44-50, for excerpts.

39. *Christian Thought: Its History and Application*, ed., F. von Hügel, London, 1923, rp. Meridian Books, Inc., 1957.

40. 'Public Opinion in Germany: Before, During and After the War.' *Contemporary Review* (London), May, 1923, pp.578-83.

41. 'The Ideas of Natural Law and Humanity in World Politics' (1925) Appendix in O. Gierke, *Natural Law and the Theory of Society, 1500-1800*, Cambridge, 1934. Rp. Beacon Press, 1957.

42. 'The Religious Principle' RGG², (1930) in J. Pelikan (ed.), *Twentieth Century Theology in the Making*, vol. II, New York and London, 1970, pp. 334-41.

Index of Names